Bernhard Tauchnitz

The select poetical works of William Wordsworth

Bernhard Tauchnitz

The select poetical works of William Wordsworth

ISBN/EAN: 9783742837219

Manufactured in Europe, USA, Canada, Australia, Japa

Cover: Foto ©Andreas Hilbeck / pixelio.de

Manufactured and distributed by brebook publishing software
(www.brebook.com)

Bernhard Tauchnitz

The select poetical works of William Wordsworth

THE SELECT
POETICAL WORKS

OF

WILLIAM WORDSWORTH.

COPYRIGHT EDITION.

IN TWO VOLUMES.

VOL. I.

LEIPZIG

BERNHARD TAUCHNITZ

1864.

CONTENTS

OF VOLUME I.

POEMS WRITTEN IN YOUTH.

	Page
Extract from the Conclusion of a Poem, composed in anticipation of leaving School	3
Written in very early Youth	3
An Evening Walk. Addressed to a Young Lady	4
Lines written while sailing in a Boat at Evening	15
Remembrance of Collins, composed upon the Thames near Richmond	16
Guilt and Sorrow; or, Incidents upon Salisbury Plain	17

POEMS REFERRING TO THE PERIOD OF CHILDHOOD.

My heart leaps up when I behold	40
To a Butterfly	40
The Sparrow's Nest	41
Characteristics of a Child three Years old	42
Alice Fell; or, Poverty	42
Lucy Gray; or, Solitude	44
We are seven	47
The Idle Shepherd-boys; or, Dungeon-Ghyll Force. A Pastoral	49
Anecdote for Fathers	52
Rural Architecture	54
The Pet-lamb. A Pastoral	55
To H. C. Six Years Old	58
Influence of Natural Objects in calling forth and strengthening the imagination in Boyhood and early Youth	59
The Norman Boy	61
The Poet's Dream. Sequel to the Norman Boy	62
The Westmoreland Girl. — Part I.	66
" " " Part II.	67

POEMS FOUNDED ON THE AFFECTIONS.

	Page
The Brothers	70
Artegal and Elidure	83
A Farewell	90
Stanzas written in my Pocket-copy of Thomson's Castle of Indolence	92
Louisa. After accompanying her on a Mountain Excursion	94
Strange fits of passion have I known	95
She dwelt among the untrodden ways	96
I travelled among unknown men	96
Ere with cold beads of midnight dew	97
To —	97
The Forsaken	98
'Tis said, that some have died for love	99
A Complaint	100
To —	101
Yes! thou art fair, yet be not moved	101
How rich that forehead's calm expanse	102
What heavenly smiles! O Lady mine	102
To —	103
Lament of Mary Queen of Scots, on the Eve of a New Year	103
The Complaint of a Forsaken Indian Woman	106
The Last of the Flock	109
Repentance. A Pastoral Ballad	112
The Affliction of Margaret ——	113
Maternal Grief	116
The Sailor's Mother	118
The Childless Father	120
The Emigrant Mother	120
Vaudracour and Julia	124
The Idiot Boy	133
Michael. A Pastoral Poem	146
The Widow on Windermere Side	159
Farewell Lines	161
The Redbreast. Suggested in a Westmoreland Cottage	162
Her Eyes are Wild	164

CONTENTS OF VOLUME I.

POEMS OF THE FANCY.

	Page
A whirl-blast from behind the hill	168
The Waterfall and the Eglantine	169
The Oak and the Broom. A Pastoral	171
To a sexton	174
To the Daisy	176
The Green Linnet	179
To a Sky-lark	180
To the Small Celandine	181
To the same Flower	183
The seven Sisters; or, the Solitude of Binnorie	185
Who fancied what a pretty sight	187
Song for the Spinning Wheel. Founded upon a Belief prevalent among the Pastoral Vales of Westmoreland	188
Hint from the Mountains for certain Political Pretenders	188
On seeing a Needlecase in the Form of a Harp	189
Glad sight wherever new with old	191
The Danish Boy. A Fragment	191
Song for the Wandering Jew	193
Stray Pleasures	194
The Pilgrim's Dream; or, the Star and the Glow-worm	195
A Wren's Nest	198
Love lies Bleeding	200
Companion to the foregoing	201
Rural Illusions	202
The Kitten and Falling Leaves	203
THE WAGGONER. — Canto I.	207
,, ,, Canto II.	215
,, ,, Canto III.	220
,, ,, Canto IV.	224

POEMS OF THE IMAGINATION.

There was a Boy	233
To the Cuckoo	234
A Night-piece	235
Yew-trees	236
Nutting	237
She was a Phantom of delight	238
O Nightingale! thou surely art	239
Three years she grew in sun and shower	240

CONTENTS OF VOLUME I.

	Page
A slumber did my spirit seal	241
I wandered lonely as a cloud	242
The Reverie of Poor Susan	242
Power of Music	243
Star-gazers	245
Written in March, while resting on the Bridge at the foot of Brother's Water	246
Beggars	247
Sequel to the Foregoing, composed many Years after	248
Gipsies	250
Ruth	251
Resolution and Independence	259
The Thorn	264
Hart-leap Well. — Part I.	271
" " " Part II.	274
Song at the Feast of Brougham Castle, upon the Restoration of Lord Clifford, the Shepherd, to the Estates and Honours of his Ancestors	277
It is no Spirit who from heaven hath flown	282
Yes, it was the mountain Echo	282
To a Sky-lark	283
Laodamia	284
Dion	289
The Pass of Kirkstone	293
To Enterprise	295
To a Young Lady, who had been reproached for taking long Walks in the Country	300
Water-fowl	301
View from the top of Black Comb	302
The Haunted Tree. To ——	303
The Primrose of the Rock	304
Presentiments	306
To the Clouds	309
A Jewish Family	312
PETER BELL. — A Tale. — Prologue	314
" " Part I.	320
" " Part II.	330
" " Part III.	336

MISCELLANEOUS SONNETS. — Part I.

	Page
Dedication. To ——	349
Nuns fret not at their Convent's narrow room	349
Admonition	350
"Beloved Vale!" I said, "when I shall con"	350
At Applethwaite, near Keswick	351
Pelion and Ossa flourish side by side	351
There is a little unpretending Rill	352
Her only pilot the soft breeze, the boat	352
The fairest, brightest, hues of ether fade	352
Upon the sight of a Beautiful Picture	353
"Why, Minstrel, these untuneful murmurings"	353
Aerial Rock — whose solitary brow	354
To Sleep	354
To Sleep	355
To Sleep	355
The Wild Duck's Nest	356
Written upon a Blank Leaf in "The Complete Angler"	356
To the Poet, John Dyer	357
On the Detraction which followed the Publication of a Certain Poem	357
Grief, thou hast lost an ever ready friend	358
To S. H.	358
Composed in one of the Valleys of Westmoreland, on Easter Sunday	359
Decay of Piety	359
Composed on the Eve of the Marriage of a Friend in the Vale of Grasmere, 1812	360
From the Italian of Michael Angelo	360
From the Same	361
From the Same. To the Supreme Being	361
Surprised by joy — impatient as the Wind	362
Methought I saw the footsteps of a throne	362
Even so for me a Vision sanctified	363
It is a beauteous Evening, calm and free	363
Where lies the Land to which yon Ship must go?	364
With Ships the sea was sprinkled far and nigh	364
The world is too much with us; late and soon	365
A volant Tribe of Bards on earth are found	365
'Weak is the will of Man, his judgment blind'	365
To the Memory of Raisley Calvert	366

PART II.

	Page
Scorn not the Sonnet; Critic, you have frowned	367
How sweet it is, when mother Fancy rocks	367
To B. R. Haydon	368
From the dark chambers of dejection freed	368
Fair Prime of life! were it enough to gild	368
I watch, and long have watched, with calm regret	369
I heard (alas! 'twas only in a dream)	369
Retirement	370
Not Love, not War, nor the tumultuous swell	370
Mark the concentred hazels that enclose	371
Composed after a Journey across the Hambleton Hills, Yorkshire	371
Those words were uttered as in pensive mood	372
While not a leaf seems faded; while the fields	372
How clear, how keen, how marvellously bright	373
Composed during a Storm	373
To a Snow-drop	374
To the Lady Mary Lowther	374
To Lady Beaumont	375
There is a pleasure in poetic pains	375
The Shepherd, looking eastward, softly said	376
When haughty expectations prostrate lie	376
Hail, Twilight, sovereign of one peaceful hour	377
With how sad steps, O Moon, thou climb'st the sky!	377
Even as a dragon's eye that feels the stress	377
The stars are mansions built by Nature's hand	378
Desponding Father! mark this altered bough	378
Captivity. — Mary Queen of Scots	379
St. Catherine of Ledbury	379
Though narrow be that old Man's cares, and near	380
Four fiery steeds impatient of the rein	380
Brook! whose society the Poet seeks	381
Composed on the Banks of a Rocky Stream	381
Pure element of waters! wheresoe'er	382
Malham Cove	382
Gordale	383
Composed upon Westminster Bridge, Sept. 3, 1802	383
Conclusion. To ——	384

Part III.

	Page
Though the bold wings of Poesy affect	385
Ye sacred Nurseries of blooming Youth!	385
Shame on his faithless heart! that could allow	386
Recollection of the Portrait of King Henry Eighth, Trinity Lodge, Cambridge	386
On the death of His Majesty (George the Third)	387
Fame tells of groves — from England far away —	387
A Parsonage in Oxfordshire	388
Composed among the Ruins of a Castle in North Wales	388
To the Lady E. B. and the Hon. Miss P.	389
To the Torrent at the Devil's Bridge, North Wales, 1824	389
In the Woods of Rydal	390
When Philoctetes in the Lemnian isle	390
While Anna's peers and early playmates tread	391
To the Cuckoo	391
To ——	392
The Infant M— M—	392
To ——, in her seventieth year	393
To Rotha Q——	393
A Grave-stone upon the Floor in the Cloisters of Worcester Cathedral	394
Roman Antiquities discovered at Bishopstone, Herefordshire	394
Chatsworth! thy stately mansion, and the pride	395
A Tradition of Oker Hill in Darley Dale, Derbyshire	395
Filial Piety	396
To the Author's Portrait	396
Why art thou silent! Is thy love a plant	397
To B. R. Haydon, on seeing his Picture of Napoleon Buonaparte on the Island of St. Helena	397
A Poet! — He hath put his heart to school	398
The most alluring clouds that mount the sky	398
On a Portrait of the Duke of Wellington upon the Field of Waterloo, by Haydon	399
Composed on a May Morning, 1838	399
Lo! where she stands fixed in a saint-like trance	400
To a Painter	400
On the same Subject	401
Hark! 'tis the Thrush, undaunted, undeprest	401
'Tis He whose yester-evening's high disdain	402

CONTENTS OF VOLUME I.

	Page
Oh what a Wreck! how changed in mien and speech!	402
Intent on gathering wool from hedge and brake	403
A Plea for Authors, May, 1838	403
Valedictory Sonnet	404
To the Rev. Christopher Wordsworth, D. D., Master of Harrow School	404
To the Planet Venus	405
Wansfell! this Household has a favoured lot	405
While beams of orient light shoot wide and high	406
In my mind's eye a Temple like a cloud	406
On the projected Kendal and Windermere Railway	407
Proud were ye, Mountains, when, in times of old	407
At Furness Abbey	408
At Furness Abbey	408
Notes	410

If thou indeed derive thy light from Heaven,
Then, to the measure of that heaven-born light,
Shine, Poet! in thy place, and be content: —
The stars pre-eminent in magnitude,
And they that from the zenith dart their beams,
(Visible though they be to half the earth,
Though half a sphere be conscious of their brightness)
Are yet of no diviner origin,
No purer essence, than the one that burns,
Like an untended watch-fire, on the ridge
Of some dark mountain; or than those which seem
Humbly to hang, like twinkling winter lamps,
Among the branches of the leafless trees!
All are the undying offspring of one Sire:
Then, to the measure of the light vouchsafed,
Shine, Poet! in thy place, and be content.

POEMS WRITTEN IN YOUTH.

I.
EXTRACT.
FROM THE CONCLUSION OF A POEM COMPOSED IN ANTICIPATION OF LEAVING SCHOOL.

Dear native regions, I foretell,
From what I feel at this farewell,
That, wheresoe'er my steps may tend,
And whensoe'er my course shall end,
If in that hour a single tie
Survive of local sympathy,
My soul will cast the backward view,
The longing look alone on you.

Thus, while the Sun sinks down to rest
Far in the regions of the west,
Though to the vale no parting beam
Be given, not one memorial gleam,
A lingering light he fondly throws
On the dear hills where first he rose.

1786.

II.
WRITTEN IN VERY EARLY YOUTH.

Calm is all nature as a resting wheel.
The kine are couched upon the dewy grass;
The horse alone, seen dimly as I pass,
Is cropping audibly his later meal:

Dark is the ground; a slumber seems to steal
O'er vale, and mountain, and the starless sky.
Now, in this blank of things, a harmony,
Home-felt, and home-created, comes to heal
That grief for which the senses still supply
Fresh food; for only then, when memory
Is hushed, am I at rest. My Friends! restrain
Those busy cares that would allay my pain;
Oh! leave me to myself, nor let me feel
The officious touch that makes me droop again.

III.

AN EVENING WALK.

ADDRESSED TO A YOUNG LADY.

General Sketch of the Lakes — Author's regret of his Youth which was passed amongst them — Short description of Noon — Cascade — Noontide Retreat — Precipice and sloping Lights — Face of Nature as the Sun declines — Mountain-farm, and the Cock — Slate-quarry — Sunset — Superstition of the Country connected with that moment — Swans — Female Beggar — Twilight-sounds — Western Lights — Spirits — Night — Moonlight — Hope — Night-sounds — Conclusion.

FAR from my dearest Friend, 'tis mine to rove
Through bare grey dell, high wood, and pastoral cove;
Where Derwent rests, and listens to the roar
That stuns the tremulous cliffs off high Lodore;
Where peace to Grasmere's lonely island leads,
To willowy hedgerows, and to emerald meads;
Leads to her bridge, rude church, and cottaged grounds,
Her rocky sheepwalks, and her woodland bounds;
Where, undisturbed by winds, Winander sleeps
'Mid clustering isles, and holly-sprinkled steeps;
Where twilight glens endear my Esthwaite's shore,
And memory of departed pleasures, more.

Fair scenes, erewhile I taught, a happy child,
The echoes of your rocks my carols wild:

The spirit sought not then, in cherished sadness,
A cloudy substitute for failing gladness.
In youth's keen eye the livelong day was bright,
The sun at morning, and the stars at night,
Alike, when first the bittern's hollow bill
Was heard, or woodcocks roamed the moonlight hill.

In thoughtless gaiety I coursed the plain,
And hope itself was all I knew of pain;
For then the inexperienced heart would beat
At times, while young Content forsook her seat,
And wild impatience, pointing upward, showed,
Through passes yet unreached, a brighter road.
Alas! the idle tale of man is found
Depicted in the dial's moral round;
Hope with reflection blends her social rays
To gild the total tablet of his days;
Yet still, the sport of some malignant power,
He knows but from its shade the present hour.

But why, ungrateful, dwell on idle pain?
To show what pleasures yet to me remain,
Say, will my Friend, with unreluctant ear,
The history of a poet's evening hear?

When, in the south, the wan noon, brooding still,
Breathed a pale steam around the glaring hill,
And shades of deep-embattled clouds were seen,
Spotting the northern cliffs with lights between;
When crowding cattle, checked by rails that make
A fence far stretched into the shallow lake,
Lashed the cool water with their restless tails,
Or from high points of rock looked out for fanning gales;
When school-boys stretched their length upon the green;
And round the broad-spread oak, a glimmering scene,
In the rough fern-clad park, the herded deer
Shook the still-twinkling tail and glancing ear;

When horses in the sunburnt intake * stood,
And vainly eyed below the tempting flood,
Or tracked the passenger, in mute distress,
With forward neck the closing gate to press —
Then, while I wandered where the huddling rill
Brightens with water-breaks the hollow ghyll **
As by enchantment, an obscure retreat
Opened at once, and stayed my devious feet.
While thick above the rill the branches close,
In rocky basin its wild waves repose,
Inverted shrubs, and moss of gloomy green,
Cling from the rocks, with pale wood-weeds between;
And its own twilight softens the whole scene,
Save were aloft the subtle sunbeams shine
On withered briars that o'er the crags recline;
Save where, with sparkling foam, a small cascade,
Illumines, from within, the leafy shade;
Beyond, along the vista of the brook,
Where antique roots its bustling course o'erlook,
The eye reposes on a secret bridge
Half grey, half shagged with ivy to its ridge;
There, bending o'er the stream, the listless swain
Lingers behind his disappearing wain.
— Did Sabine grace adorn my living line,
Blandusia's praise, wild stream, should yield to thine!
Never shall ruthless minister of death
'Mid thy soft glooms the glittering steel unsheath;
No goblets shall, for thee, be crowned with flowers,
No kid with piteous outcry thrill thy bowers;
The mystic shapes that by thy margin rove,
A more benignant sacrifice approve —
A mind, that, in a calm angelic mood
Of happy wisdom, meditating good,
Beholds, of all from her high powers required,
Much done, and much designed, and more desired, —

* The word *intake* is local, and signifies a mountain-inclosure.
** Ghyll is also, I believe, a term confined to this country: ghyll, and dingle, have the same meaning.

Harmonious thoughts, a soul by truth refined,
Entire affection for all human kind.

  Dear Brook, farewell! To-morrow's noon again
Shall hide me, wooing long thy wildwood strain;
But now the sun has gained his western road,
And eve's mild hour invites my steps abroad.

  While, near the midway cliff, the silvered kite
In many a whistling circle wheels her flight;
Slant watery lights, from parting clouds, apace
Travel along the precipice's base;
Cheering its naked waste of scattered stone,
By lichens grey, and scanty moss, o'ergrown;
Where scarce the foxglove peeps, or thistle's beard;
And restless stone-chat, all day long, is heard.

  How pleasant, as the sun declines, to view
The spacious landscape change in form and hue!
Here vanish, as in mist, before a flood
Of bright obscurity, hill, lawn, and wood;
There objects, by the searching beams betrayed,
Come forth, and here retire in purple shade;
Even the white stems of birch, the cottage white,
Soften their glare before the mellow light;
The skiffs, at anchor where with umbrage wide
Yon chestnuts half the latticed boat-house hide,
Shed from their sides, that face the sun's slant beam,
Strong flakes of radiance on the tremulous stream:
Raised by yon travelling flock, a dusty cloud
Mounts from the road, and spreads its moving shroud;
The shepherd, all involved in wreaths of fire,
Now shows a shadowy speck, and now is lost entire.

  Into a gradual calm the breezes sink,
A blue rim borders all the lake's still brink;
There doth the twinkling aspen's foliage sleep,
And insects clothe, like dust, the glassy deep:

And now, on every side, the surface breaks
Into blue spots, and slowly lengthening streaks;
Here, plots of sparkling water tremble bright
With thousand thousand twinkling points of light;
There, waves that, hardly weltering, die away,
Tip their smooth ridges with a softer ray;
And now the whole wide lake in deep repose
Is hushed, and like a burnished mirror glows,
Save where, along the shady western marge,
Coasts, with industrious oar, the charcoal barge.

Their panniered train a group of potters goad,
Winding from side to side up the steep road;
The peasant, from yon cliff of fearful edge
Shot, down the headlong path darts with his sledge;
Bright beams the lonely mountain-horse illume,
Feeding 'mid purple heath, "green rings,"* and broom;
While the sharp slope the slackened team confounds,
Downward the ponderous timber-wain resounds;
In foamy breaks the rill, with merry song,
Dashed o'er the rough rock, lightly leaps along;
From lonesome chapel at the mountain's feet,
Three humble bells their rustic chime repeat;
Sounds from the water-side the hammered boat;
And *blasted* quarry thunders, heard remote!

Even here, amid the sweep of endless woods,
Blue pomp of lakes, high cliffs and falling floods,
Not undelightful are the simplest charms,
Found by the grassy door of mountain-farms.

Sweetly ferocious, round his native walks,
Pride of his sister-wives, the monarch stalks;
Spur-clad his nervous feet, and firm his tread;
A crest of purple tops the warrior's head.
Bright sparks his black and rolling eye-ball hurls
Afar, his tail he closes and unfurls;

* "Vivid rings of green." — GREENWOOD'S POEM ON SHOOTING.

AN EVENING WALK.

On tiptoe reared, he strains his clarion throat,
Threatened by faintly-answering farms remote:
Again with his shrill voice the mountain rings,
While, flapped with conscious pride, resound his wings!

  Where, mixed with graceful birch, the sombrous pine
And yew-tree o'er the silver rocks recline;
I love to mark the quarry's moving trains,
Dwarf panniered steeds, and men, and numerous wains:
How busy all the enormous hive within,
While Echo dallies with its various din!
Some (hear you not their chisels' clinking sound?)
Toil, small as pigmies in the gulf profound;
Some, dim between the lofty cliffs descried,
O'erwalk the slender plank from side to side;
These, by the pale-blue rocks that ceaseless ring,
In airy baskets hanging, work and sing.

  Just where a cloud above the mountain rears
An edge all flame, the broadening sun appears;
A long blue bar its ægis orb divides,
And breaks the spreading of its golden tides;
And now that orb has touched the purple steep
Whose softened image penetrates the deep.
'Cross the calm lake's blue shades the cliffs aspire,
With towers and woods, a "prospect all on fire;"
While coves and secret hollows, through a ray
Of fainter gold, a purple gleam betray.
Each slip of lawn the broken rocks between
Shines in the light with more than earthly green:
Deep yellow beams the scattered stems illume,
Far in the level forest's central gloom:
Waving his hat, the shepherd, from the vale,
Directs his winding dog the cliffs to scale, —
The dog, loud barking, 'mid the glittering rocks,
Hunts, where his master points, the intercepted flocks.
Where oaks o'erhang the road the radiance shoots
On tawny earth, wild weeds, and twisted roots;

The druid-stones a brightened ring unfold;
And all the babbling brooks are liquid gold;
Sunk to a curve, the day-star lessens still,
Gives one bright glance, and drops behind the hill.*

In these secluded vales, if village fame,
Confirmed by hoary hairs, belief may claim;
When up the hills, as now, retired the light,
Strange apparitions mocked the shepherd's sight.

The form appears of one that spurs his steed
Midway along the hill with desperate speed;
Unhurt pursues his lengthened flight, while all
Attend, at every stretch, his headlong fall.
Anon, appears a brave, a gorgeous show
Of horsemen-shadows moving to and fro;
At intervals imperial banners stream,
And now the van reflects the solar beam;
The rear through iron brown betrays a sullen gleam.
While silent stands the admiring crowd below,
Silent the visionary warriors go,
Winding in ordered pomp their upward way
Till the last banner of their long array
Has disappeared, and every trace is fled
Of splendour — save the beacon's spiry head
Tipt with eve's latest gleam of burning red.

Now, while the solemn evening shadows sail,
On slowly-waving pinions, down the vale;
And, fronting the bright west, yon oak entwines
Its darkening boughs and leaves, in stronger lines;
'Tis pleasant near the tranquil lake to stray
Where, winding on along some secret bay,
The swan uplifts his chest, and backward flings
His neck, a varying arch, between his towering wings:
The eye that marks the gliding creature sees
How graceful pride can be, and how majestic, ease.

* From Thomson.

While tender cares and mild domestic loves
With furtive watch pursue her as she moves,
The female with a meeker charm succeeds,
And her brown little ones around her leads,
Nibbling the water lilies as they pass,
Or playing wanton with the floating grass.
She, in a mother's care her beauty's pride
Forgetting, calls the wearied to her side;
Alternately they mount her back, and rest
Close by her mantling wings' embraces prest.

Long may they float upon this flood serene;
Theirs be these holms untrodden, still, and green,
Where leafy shades fence off the blustering gale,
And breathes in peace the lily of the vale!
Yon isle, which feels not even the milk-maid's feet,
Yet hears her song, "by distance made more sweet,"
Yon isle conceals their home, their hut-like bower;
Green water-rushes overspread the floor;
Long grass and willows form the woven wall,
And swings above the roof the poplar tall.
Thence issuing often with unwieldy stalk,
They crush with broad black feet their flowery walk;
Or, from the neighbouring water, hear at morn
The hound, the horse's tread, and mellow horn;
Involve their serpent-necks in changeful rings,
Rolled wantonly between their slippery wings,
Or, starting up with noise and rude delight,
Force half upon the wave their cumbrous flight.

Fair Swan! by all a mother's joys caressed,
Haply some wretch has eyed, and called thee blessed;
When with her infants, from some shady seat
By the lake's edge, she rose — to face the noontide heat;
Or taught their limbs along the dusty road
A few short steps to totter with their load.

I see her now, denied to lay her head,
On cold blue nights, in hut or straw-built shed,

Turn to a silent smile their sleepy cry,
By pointing to the gliding moon on high.
— When low-hung clouds each star of summer hide,
And fireless are the valleys far and wide,
Where the brook brawls along the public road
Dark with bat-haunted ashes stretching broad,
Oft has she taught them on her lap to lay
The shining glow-worm; or, in heedless play,
Toss it from hand to hand, disquieted;
While others, not unseen, are free to shed
Green unmolested light upon their mossy bed.

Oh! when the sleety showers her path assail,
And like a torrent roars the headstrong gale;
No more her breath can thaw their fingers cold,
Their frozen arms her neck no more can fold;
Weak roof a cowering form two babes to shield,
And faint the fire a dying heart can yield!
Press the sad kiss, fond mother! vainly fears
Thy flooded cheek to wet them with its tears;
No tears can chill them, and no bosom warms,
Thy breast their death-bed, coffined in thine arms!

Sweet are the sounds that mingle from afar,
Heard by calm lakes, as peeps the folding star,
Where the duck dabbles 'mid the rustling sedge,
And feeding pike starts from the water's edge,
Or the swan stirs the reeds, his neck and bill
Wetting, that drip upon the water still;
And heron, as resounds the trodden shore,
Shoots upward, darting his long neck before.

Now, with religious awe, the farewell light
Blends with the solemn colouring of night;
'Mid groves of clouds that crest the mountain's brow,
And round the west's proud lodge their shadows throw,
Like Una shining on her gloomy way,
The half-seen form of Twilight roams astray;

Shedding, through paly loop-holes mild and small,
Gleams that upon the lake's still bosom fall;
Soft o'er the surface creep those lustres pale
Tracking the motions of the fitful gale.
With restless interchange at once the bright
Wins on the shade, the shade upon the light.
No favoured eye was e'er allowed to gaze
On lovelier spectacle in faery days;
When gentle Spirits urged a sportive chase,
Brushing with lucid wands the water's face;
While music, stealing round the glimmering deeps,
Charmed the tall circle of the enchanted steeps.
— The lights are vanished from the watery plains:
No wreck of all the pageantry remains.
Unheeded night has overcome the vales:
On the dark earth the wearied vision fails;
The latest lingerer of the forest train,
The lone black fir, forsakes the faded plain;
Last evening sight, the cottage smoke no more,
Lost in the thickened darkness, glimmers hoar;
And, towering from the sullen dark-brown mere,
Like a black wall, the mountain-steeps appear.
— Now o'er the soothed accordant heart we feel
A sympathetic twilight slowly steal,
And ever, as we fondly muse, we find
The soft gloom deepening on the tranquil mind.
Stay! pensive, sadly-pleasing visions, stay!
Ah no! as fades the vale, they fade away:
Yet still the tender, vacant gloom remains;
Still the cold cheek its shuddering tear retains.

The bird, who ceased, with fading light, to thread
Silent the hedge or steamy rivulet's bed,
From his grey re-appearing tower shall soon
Salute with gladsome note the rising moon,
While with a hoary light she frosts the ground,
And pours a deeper blue to Æther's bound;

Pleased, as she moves, her pomp of clouds to fold
In robes of azure, fleecy-white, and gold.

Above yon eastern hill, where darkness broods
O'er all its vanished dells, and lawns, and woods;
Where but a mass of shade the sight can trace,
Even now she shows, half-veiled, her lovely face:
Across the gloomy valley flings her light,
Far to the western slopes with hamlets white;
And gives, where woods the chequered upland strew,
To the green corn of summer, autumn's hue.

Thus Hope, first pouring from her blessed horn
Her dawn, far lovelier than the moon's own morn,
'Till higher mounted, strives in vain to cheer
The weary hills, impervious, blackening near;
Yet does she still, undaunted, throw the while
On darling spots remote her tempting smile.

Even now she decks for me a distant scene,
(For dark and broad the gulf of time between)
Gilding that cottage with her fondest ray,
(Sole bourn, sole wish, sole object of my way;
How fair its lawns and sheltering woods appear!
How sweet its streamlet murmurs in mine ear!)
Where we, my Friend, to happy days shall rise,
'Till our small share of hardly-paining sighs
(For sighs will ever trouble human breath)
Creep hushed into the tranquil breast of death.

But now the clear bright moon her zenith gains,
And, rimy without speck, extend the plains:
The deepest cleft the mountain's front displays
Scarce hides a shadow from her searching rays;
From the dark-blue faint silvery threads divide
The hills, while gleams below the azure tide;
Time softly treads; throughout the landscape breathes
A peace enlivened, not disturbed, by wreaths

Of charcoal-smoke, that o'er the fallen wood,
Steal down the hill, and spread along the flood.

The song of mountain-streams, unheard by day,
Now hardly heard, beguiles my homeward way.
Air listens, like the sleeping water, still,
To catch the spiritual music of the hill,
Broke only by the slow clock tolling deep,
Or shout that wakes the ferry-man from sleep,
The echoed hoof nearing the distant shore,
The boat's first motion — made with dashing oar;
Sound of closed gate, across the water borne,
Hurrying the timid hare through rustling corn;
The sportive outcry of the mocking owl;
And at long intervals the mill-dog's howl;
The distant forge's swinging thump profound;
Or yell, in the deep woods, of lonely hound.

1787, 8, & 9.

IV.
LINES
WRITTEN WHILE SAILING IN A BOAT AT EVENING.

How richly glows the water's breast
Before us, tinged with evening hues,
While, facing thus the crimson west,
The boat her silent course pursues!
And see how dark the backward stream!
A little moment past so smiling!
And still, perhaps, with faithless gleam,
Some other loiterers beguiling.

Such views the youthful Bard allure;
But, heedless of the following gloom,
He deems their colours shall endure
Till peace go with him to the tomb.

— And let him nurse his fond deceit,
And what if he must die in sorrow!
Who would not cherish dreams so sweet,
Though grief and pain may come to morrow?

1789.

V.
REMEMBRANCE OF COLLINS,
COMPOSED UPON THE THAMES NEAR RICHMOND.

Glide gently, thus for ever glide,
O Thames! that other bards may see
As lovely visions by thy side
As now, fair river! come to me.
O glide, fair stream! for ever so,
Thy quiet soul on all bestowing,
Till all our minds for ever flow
As thy deep waters now are flowing.

Vain thought! — Yet be as now thou art,
That in thy waters may be seen
The image of a poet's heart,
How bright, how solemn, how serene!
Such as did once the Poet bless,
Who murmuring here a later* ditty,
Could find no refuge from distress
But in the milder grief of pity.

Now let us, as we float along,
For *him* suspend the dashing oar;
And pray that never child of song
May know that Poet's sorrows more.
How calm! how still! the only sound
The dripping of the oar suspended!
— The evening darkness gathers round
By virtue's holiest Powers attended.

1789.

* Collins's Ode on the death of Thomson, the last written, I believe, of the poems which were published during his life-time. This Ode is also alluded to in the next stanza.

VI.

GUILT AND SORROW;
OR,
INCIDENTS UPON SALISBURY PLAIN.

ADVERTISEMENT,

PREFIXED TO THE FIRST EDITION OF THIS POEM, PUBLISHED IN 1842.

Not less than one-third of the following poem, though it has from time to time been altered in the expression, was published so far back as the year 1798, under the title of "The Female Vagrant." The extract is of such length that an apology seems to be required for reprinting it here: but it was necessary to restore it to its original position, or the rest would have been unintelligible. The whole was written before the close of the year 1794, and I will detail, rather as matter of literary biography than for any other reason, the circumstances under which it was produced.

During the latter part of the summer of 1793, having passed a month in the Isle of Wight, in view of the fleet which was then preparing for sea off Portsmouth at the commencement of the war, I left the place with melancholy forebodings. The American war was still fresh in memory. The struggle which was beginning, and which many thought would be brought to a speedy close by the irresistible arms of Great Britain being added to those of the allies, I was assured in my own mind would be of long continuance, and productive of distress and misery beyond all possible calculation. This conviction was pressed upon me by having been a witness, during a long residence in revolutionary France, of the spirit which prevailed in that country. After leaving the Isle of Wight, I spent two days in wandering on foot over Salisbury Plain, which, though cultivation was then widely spread through parts of it, had upon the whole a still more impressive appearance than it now retains.

The monuments and traces of antiquity, scattered in abundance over that region, led me unavoidably to compare what we know or guess of those remote times with certain aspects of modern society, and with calamities, principally those consequent upon war, to which, more than other classes of men, the poor are subject. In those reflections, joined with particular facts that had come to my knowledge, the following stanzas originated.

In conclusion, to obviate some distraction in the minds of those who are well acquainted with Salisbury Plain, it may be proper to say, that of the features described as belonging to it, one or two are taken from other desolate parts of England.

I.

A TRAVELLER on the skirt of Sarum's Plain
Pursued his vagrant way, with feet half bare;
Stooping his gait, but not as if to gain
Help from the staff he bore; for mien and air
Were hardy, though his cheek seemed worn with care
Both of the time to come, and time long fled:
Down fell in straggling locks his thin grey hair;
A coat he wore of military red
But faded, and stuck o'er with many a patch and shred.

II.

While thus he journeyed, step by step led on,
He saw and passed a stately inn, full sure
That welcome in such house for him was none.
No board inscribed the needy to allure
Hung there, no bush proclaimed to old and poor
And desolate, "Here you will find a friend!"
The pendent grapes glittered above the door;—
On he must pace, perchance 'till night descend,
Where'er the dreary roads their bare white lines extend.

III.

The gathering clouds grew red with stormy fire,
In streaks diverging wide and mounting high;
That inn he long had passed; the distant spire,
Which oft as he looked back had fixed his eye,
Was lost, though still he looked, in the blank sky.
Perplexed and comfortless he gazed around,
And scarce could any trace of man descry,
Save cornfields stretched and stretching without bound;
But where the sower dwelt was nowhere to be found.

IV.

No tree was there, no meadow's pleasant green,
No brook to wet his lip or soothe his ear;
Long files of corn-stacks here and there were seen;
But not one dwelling-place his heart to cheer.

Some labourer, thought he, may perchance be near;
And so he sent a feeble shout — in vain;
No voice made answer, he could only hear
Winds rustling over plots of unripe grain,
Or whistling thro' thin grass along the unfurrowed plain.

V.

Long had he fancied each successive slope
Concealed some cottage, whither he might turn
And rest; but now along heaven's darkening cope
The crows rushed by in eddies, homeward borne.
Thus warned he sought some shepherd's spreading thorn
Or hovel from the storm to shield his head,
But sought in vain; for now, all wild, forlorn,
And vacant, a huge waste around him spread;
The wet cold ground, he feared, must be his only bed.

VI.

And be it so — for to the chill night shower
And the sharp wind his head he oft hath bared;
A Sailor he, who many a wretched hour
Hath told; for, landing after labour hard,
Full long endured in hope of just reward,
He to an armèd fleet was forced away
By seamen, who perhaps themselves had shared
Like fate; was hurried off, a helpless prey,
'Gainst all that in *his* heart, or theirs perhaps, said nay.

VII.

For years the work of carnage did not cease,
And death's dire aspect daily he surveyed,
Death's minister; then came his glad release,
And hope returned, and pleasure fondly made
Her dwelling in his dreams. By Fancy's aid
The happy husband flies, his arms to throw
Round his wife's neck; the prize of victory laid
In her full lap, he sees such sweet tears flow
As if thenceforth nor pain nor trouble she could know.

VIII.

Vain hope! for fraud took all that he had earned.
The lion roars and gluts his tawny brood
Even in the desert's heart; but he, returned,
Bears not to those he loves their needful food.
His home approaching, but in such a mood
That from his sight his children might have run,
He met a traveller, robbed him, shed his blood;
And when the miserable work was done
He fled, a vagrant since, the murderer's fate to shun.

IX.

From that day forth no place to him could be
So lonely, but that thence might come a pang
Brought from without to inward misery.
Now, as he plodded on, with sullen clang
A sound of chains along the desert rang;
He looked, and saw upon a gibbet high
A human body that in irons swang,
Uplifted by the tempest whirling by;
And, hovering, round it often did a raven fly.

X.

It was a spectacle which none might view,
In spot so savage, but with shuddering pain;
Nor only did for him at once renew
All he had feared from man, but roused a train
Of the mind's phantoms, horrible as vain.
The stones, as if to cover him from day,
Rolled at his back along the living plain;
He fell, and without sense or motion lay;
But, when the trance was gone, feebly pursued his way.

XI.

As one whose brain habitual frensy fires
Owes to the fit in which his soul hath tossed
Profounder quiet, when the fit retires,
Even so the dire phantasma which had crossed

His sense, in sudden vacancy quite lost,
Left his mind still as a deep evening stream.
Nor, if accosted now, in thought engrossed,
Moody, or inly troubled, would he seem
To traveller who might talk of any casual theme.

XII.

Hurtle the clouds in deeper darkness piled,
Gone is the raven timely rest to seek;
He seemed the only creature in the wild
On whom the elements their rage might wreak;
Save that the bustard, of those regions bleak
Shy tenant, seeing by the uncertain light
A man there wandering, gave a mournful shriek,
And half upon the ground, with strange affright,
Forced hard against the wind a thick unwieldy flight.

XIII.

All, all was cheerless to the horizon's bound;
The weary eye — which, wheresoe'er it strays,
Marks nothing but the red sun's setting round,
Or on the earth strange lines, in former days
Left by gigantic arms — at length surveys
What seems an antique castle spreading wide;
Hoary and naked are its walls, and raise
Their brow sublime: in shelter there to bide
He turned, while rain poured down smoking on every side.

XIV.

Pile of Stone-henge! so proud to hint yet keep
Thy secrets, thou that lov'st to stand and hear
The Plain resounding to the whirlwind's sweep,
Inmate of lonesome Nature's endless year;
Even if thou saw'st the giant wicker rear
For sacrifice its throngs of living men,
Before thy face did ever wretch appear,
Who in his heart had groaned with deadlier pain
Than he who, tempest-driven, thy shelter now would gain.

XV.

Within that fabric of mysterious form,
Winds met in conflict, each by turns supreme;
And, from the perilous ground dislodged, through storm
And rain he wildered on, no moon to stream
From gulf of parting clouds one friendly beam,
Nor any friendly sound his footsteps led;
Once did the lightning's faint disastrous gleam
Disclose a naked guide-post's double head,
Sight which tho' lost at once a gleam of pleasure shed.

XVI.

No swinging sign-board creaked from cottage elm
To stay his steps with faintness overcome;
'Twas dark and void as ocean's watery realm
Roaring with storms beneath night's starless gloom;
No gipsy cower'd o'er fire of furze or broom;
No labourer watched his red kiln glaring bright,
Nor taper glimmered dim from sick man's room;
Along the waste no line of mournful light
From lamp of lonely toll-gate streamed athwart the night.

XVII.

At length, though hid in clouds, the moon arose;
The downs were visible — and now revealed
A structure stands, which two bare slopes enclose.
It was a spot, where, ancient vows fulfilled,
Kind pious hands did to the Virgin build
A lonely Spital, the belated swain
From the night terrors of that waste to shield:
But there no human being could remain,
And now the walls are named the "Dead House" of the plain.

XVIII.

Though he had little cause to love the abode
Of man, or covet sight of mortal face,
Yet when faint beams of light that ruin showed,
How glad he was at length to find some trace

Of human shelter in that dreary place.
Till to his flock the early shepherd goes,
Here shall much-needed sleep his frame embrace.
In a dry nook where fern the floor bestrows
He lays his stiffened limbs, — his eyes begin to close;

XIX.

When hearing a deep sigh, that seemed to come
From one who mourned in sleep, he raised his head,
And saw a woman in the naked room
Outstretched, and turning on a restless bed:
The moon a wan dead light around her shed.
He waked her — spake in tone that would not fail,
He hoped, to calm her mind; but ill he sped,
For of that ruin she had heard a tale
Which now with freezing thoughts did all her powers assail;

XX.

Had heard of one who, forced from storms to shroud,
Felt the loose walls of this decayed Retreat
Rock to incessant neighings shrill and loud,
While his horse pawed the floor with furious heat;
Till on a stone, that sparkled to his feet,
Struck, and still struck again, the troubled horse:
The man half raised the stone with pain and sweat,
Half raised, for well his arm might lose its force
Disclosing the grim head of a late murdered corse.

XXI.

Such tale of this lone mansion she had learned,
And, when that shape, with eyes in sleep half drowned,
By the moon's sullen lamp she first discerned,
Cold stony horror all her senses bound.
Her he addressed in words of cheering sound;
Recovering heart, like answer did she make;
And well it was that, of the corse there found,
In converse that ensued she nothing spake;
She knew not what dire pangs in him such tale could wake.

XXII.

But soon his voice and words of kind intent
Banished that dismal thought; and now the wind
In fainter howlings told its *rage* was spent:
Meanwhile discourse ensued of various kind,
Which by degrees a confidence of mind
And mutual interest failed not to create.
And, to a natural sympathy resigned,
In that forsaken building where they sate
The Woman thus retraced her own untoward fate.

XXIII.

"By Derwent's side my father dwelt — a man
Of virtuous life, by pious parents bred;
And I believe that, soon as I began
To lisp, he made me kneel beside my bed,
And in his hearing there my prayers I said:
And afterwards, by my good father taught,
I read, and loved the books in which I read;
For books in every neighbouring house I sought,
And nothing to my mind a sweeter pleasure brought.

XXIV.

A little croft we owned — a plot of corn,
A garden stored with peas, and mint, and thyme,
And flowers for posies, oft on Sunday morn
Plucked while the church bells rang their earliest chime.
Can I forget our freaks at shearing time!
My hen's rich nest through long grass scarce espied;
The cowslip-gathering in June's dewy prime;
The swans that with white chests upreared in pride
Rushing and racing came to meet me at the waterside!

XXV.

The staff I well remember which upbore
The bending body of my active sire;
His seat beneath the honied sycamore
Where the bees hummed, and chair by winter fire;

When market-morning came, the neat attire
With which, though bent on haste, myself I decked;
Our watchful house-dog, that would tease and tire
The stranger till its barking-fit I checked;
The red-breast, known for years, which at my casement pecked.

XXVI.

The suns of twenty summers danced along, —
Too little marked how fast they rolled away:
But, through severe mischance and cruel wrong,
My father's substance fell into decay:
We toiled and struggled, hoping for a day
When Fortune might put on a kinder look;
But vain were wishes, efforts vain as they;
He from his old hereditary nook
Must part; the summons came; — our final leave we took.

XXVII.

It was indeed a miserable hour
When, from the last hill-top, my sire surveyed,
Peering above the trees, the steeple tower
That on his marriage day sweet music made!
Till then, he hoped his bones might there be laid
Close by my mother in their native bowers:
Bidding me trust in God, he stood and prayed; —
I could not pray: — through tears that fell in showers
Glimmered our dear-loved home, alas! no longer ours!

XXVIII.

There was a Youth whom I had loved so long,
That when I loved him not I cannot say:
'Mid the green mountains many a thoughtless song
We two had sung, like gladsome birds in May;
When we began to tire of childish play,
We seemed still more and more to prize each other;
We talked of marriage and our marriage day;
And I in truth did love him like a brother,
For never could I hope to meet with such another.

XXIX.

Two years were passed since to a distant town
He had repaired to ply a gainful trade:
What tears of bitter grief, till then unknown!
What tender vows our last sad kiss delayed!
To him we turned:— we had no other aid:
Like one revived, upon his neck I wept;
And her whom he had loved in joy, he said,
He well could love in grief; his faith he kept;
And in a quiet home once more my father slept.

XXX.

We lived in peace and comfort; and were blest
With daily bread, by constant toil supplied.
Three lovely babes had lain upon my breast;
And often, viewing their sweet smiles, I sighed,
And knew not why. My happy father died,
When threatened war reduced the children's meal:
Thrice happy! that for him the grave could hide
The empty loom, cold hearth, and silent wheel,
And tears that flowed for ills which patience might not heal.

XXXI.

'Twas a hard change; an evil time was come;
We had no hope, and no relief could gain:
But soon, with proud parade, the noisy drum
Beat round to clear the streets of want and pain.
My husband's arms now only served to strain
Me and his children hungering in his view;
In such dismay my prayers and tears were vain:
To join those miserable men he flew,
And now to the sea-coast, with numbers more, we drew.

XXXII.

There were we long neglected, and we bore
Much sorrow ere the fleet its anchor weighed,
Green fields before us, and our native shore,
We breathed a pestilential air, that made

Ravage for which no knell was heard. We prayed
For our departure; wished and wished — nor knew,
'Mid that long sickness and those hopes delayed,
That happier days we never more must view.
The parting signal streamed — at last the land withdrew.

XXXIII.

But the calm summer season now was past.
On as we drove, the equinoctial deep
Ran mountains high before the howling blast,
And many perished in the whirlwind's sweep.
We gazed with terror on their gloomy sleep,
Untaught that soon such anguish must ensue,
Our hopes such harvest of affliction reap,
That we the mercy of the waves should rue;
We reached the western world, a poor devoted crew.

XXXIV.

The pains and plagues that on our heads came down,
Disease and famine, agony and fear,
In wood or wilderness, in camp or town,
It would unman the firmest heart to hear.
All perished — all in one remorseless year,
Husband and children! one by one, by sword
And ravenous plague, all perished: every tear
Dried up, despairing, desolate, on board
A British ship I waked, as from a trance restored."

XXXV.

Here paused she, of all present thought forlorn,
Nor voice, nor sound, that moment's pain expressed,
Yet Nature, with excess of grief o'erborne,
From her full eyes their watery load released.
He too was mute: and, ere her weeping ceased,
He rose, and to the ruin's portal went,
And saw the dawn opening the silvery east
With rays of promise, north and southward sent;
And soon with crimson fire kindled the firmament.

XXXVI.

"O come," he cried, "come, after weary night
Of such rough storm, this happy change to view."
So forth she came, and eastward looked; the sight
Over her brow like dawn of gladness threw;
Upon her cheek, to which its youthful hue
Seemed to return, dried the last lingering tear,
And from her grateful heart a fresh one drew:
The whilst her comrade to her pensive cheer
Tempered fit words of hope; and the lark warbled near.

XXXVII.

They looked and saw a lengthening road, and wain
That rang down a bare slope not far remote:
The barrows glistered bright with drops of rain,
Whistled the waggoner with merry note,
The cock far off sounded his clarion throat;
But town, or farm, or hamlet, none they viewed,
Only were told there stood a lonely cot
A long mile thence. While thither they pursued
Their way, the Woman thus her mournful tale renewed.

XXXVIII.

"Peaceful as this immeasurable plain
Is now, by beams of dawning light imprest,
In the calm sunshine slept the glittering main;
The very ocean hath its hour of rest.
I too forgot the heavings of my breast.
How quiet 'round me ship and ocean were!
As quiet all within me. I was blest,
And looked, and fed upon the silent air
Until it seemed to bring a joy to my despair.

XXXIX.

Ah! how unlike those late terrific sleeps,
And groans that rage of racking famine spoke;
The unburied dead that lay in festering heaps,
The breathing pestilence that rose like smoke,

The shriek that from the distant battle broke,
The mine's dire earthquake, and the pallid host
Driven by the bomb's incessant thunder-stroke
To loathsome vaults, where heart-sick anguish tossed,
Hope died, and fear itself in agony was lost!

####### XL.

Some mighty gulf of separation passed,
I seemed transported to another world;
A thought resigned with pain, when from the mast
The impatient mariner the sail unfurled,
And, whistling, called the wind that hardly curled
The silent sea. From the sweet thoughts of home
And from all hope I was for ever hurled.
For me — farthest from earthly port to roam
Was best, could I but shun the spot where man might come.

####### XLI.

And oft I thought (my fancy was so strong)
That I, at last, a resting-place had found;
'Here will I dwell,' said I, 'my whole life long,
Roaming the illimitable waters round;
Here will I live, of all but heaven disowned,
And end my days upon the peaceful flood.' —
To break my dream the vessel reached its bound;
And homeless near a thousand homes I stood,
And near a thousand tables pined and wanted food.

####### XLII.

No help I sought; in sorrow turned adrift,
Was hopeless, as if cast on some bare rock;
Nor morsel to my mouth that day did lift,
Nor raised my hand at any door to knock.
I lay where, with his drowsy mates, the cock
From the cross-timber of an out-house hung:
Dismally tolled, that night, the city clock!
At morn my sick heart hunger scarcely stung,
Nor to the beggar's language could I fit my tongue.

XLIII.

So passed a second day; and, when the third
Was come, I tried in vain the crowd's resort.
— In deep despair, by frightful wishes stirred,
Near the sea-side I reached a ruined fort;
There, pains which nature could no more support,
With blindness linked, did on my vitals fall;
And, after many interruptions short
Of hideous sense, I sank, nor step could crawl:
Unsought for was the help that did my life recal.

XLIV.

Borne to a hospital, I lay with brain
Drowsy and weak, and shattered memory;
I heard my neighbours in their beds complain
Of many things which never troubled me —
Of feet still bustling round with busy glee,
Of looks where common kindness had no part,
Of service done with cold formality,
Fretting the fever round the languid heart,
And groans which, as they said, might make a dead man start.

XLV.

These things just served to stir the slumbering sense,
Nor pain nor pity in my bosom raised.
With strength did memory return; and, thence
Dismissed, again on open day I gazed,
At houses, men, and common light, amazed.
The lanes I sought, and, as the sun retired,
Came where beneath the trees a faggot blazed;
The travellers saw me weep, my fate inquired,
And gave me food — and rest, more welcome, more desired.

XLVI.

Rough potters seemed they, trading soberly,
With panniered asses driven from door to door;
But life of happier sort set forth to me,
And other joys my fancy to allure —

The bag-pipe dinning on the midnight moor
In barn uplighted; and companions boon,
Well met from far with revelry secure
Among the forest glades, while jocund June
Rolled fast along the sky his warm and genial moon.

XLVII.

But ill they suited me — those journeys dark
O'er moor and mountain, midnight theft to hatch!
To charm the surly house-dog's faithful bark,
Or hang on tip-toe at the lifted latch.
The gloomy lantern, and the dim blue match,
The black disguise, the warning whistle shrill,
And ear still busy on its nightly watch,
Were not for me, brought up in nothing ill:
Besides, on griefs so fresh my thoughts were brooding still.

XLVIII.

What could I do, unaided and unblest?
My father! gone was every friend of thine:
And kindred of dead husband are at best
Small help; and, after marriage such as mine,
With little kindness would to me incline.
Nor was I then for toil or service fit;
My deep-drawn sighs no effort could confine;
In open air forgetful would I sit
Whole hours, with idle arms in moping sorrow knit.

XLIX.

The roads I paced, I loitered through the fields;
Contentedly, yet sometimes self-accused,
Trusted my life to what chance bounty yields,
Now coldly given, now utterly refused.
The ground I for my bed have often used:
But what afflicts my peace with keenest ruth,
Is that I have my inner self abused,
Forgone the home delight of constant truth,
And clear and open soul, so prized in fearless youth.

L.

Through tears the rising sun I oft have viewed,
Through tears have seen him towards that world descend
Where my poor heart lost all its fortitude:
Three years a wanderer now my course I bend—
Oh! tell me whither — for no earthly friend
Have I." — She ceased, and weeping turned away;
As if because her tale was at an end,
She wept; because she had no more to say
Of that perpetual weight which on her spirit lay.

LI.

True sympathy the Sailor's looks expressed,
His looks—for pondering he was mute the while.
Of social Order's care for wretchedness,
Of Time's sure help to calm and reconcile,
Joy's second spring and Hope's long-treasured smile,
'Twas not for *him* to speak—a man so tried.
Yet, to relieve her heart, in friendly style
Proverbial words of comfort he applied,
And not in vain, while they went pacing side by side.

LII.

Ere long, from heaps of turf, before their sight,
Together smoking in the sun's slant beam,
Rise various wreaths that into one unite
Which high and higher mounts with silver gleam:
Fair spectacle,—but instantly a scream
Thence bursting shrill did all remark prevent;
They paused, and heard a hoarser voice blaspheme,
And female cries. Their course they thither bent,
And met a man who foamed with anger vehement.

LIII.

A woman stood with quivering lips and pale,
And, pointing to a little child that lay
Stretched on the ground, began a piteous tale;
How in a simple freak of thoughtless play

He had provoked his father, who straightway,
As if each blow were deadlier than the last,
Struck the poor innocent.   Pallid with dismay
The soldier's Widow heard and stood aghast;
And stern looks on the man her grey-haired Comrade cast.

LIV.

His voice with indignation rising high
Such further deed in manhood's name forbade;
The peasant, wild in passion, made reply
With bitter insult and revilings sad;
Asked him in scorn what business there he had;
What kind of plunder he was hunting now;
The gallows would one day of him be glad;—
Though inward anguish damped the Sailor's brow,
Yet calm he seemed as thoughts so poignant would allow.

LV.

Softly he stroked the child, who lay outstretched
With face to earth; and, as the boy turned round
His battered head, a groan the Sailor fetched
As if he saw—there and upon that ground—
Strange repetition of the deadly wound
He had himself inflicted.   Through his brain
At once the griding iron passage found;
Deluge of tender thoughts then rushed amain,
Nor could his sunken eyes the starting tear restrain.

LVI.

Within himself he said—What hearts have we!
The blessing this a father gives his child!
Yet happy thou, poor boy! compared with me,
Suffering not doing ill—fate far more mild.
The stranger's looks and tears of wrath beguiled
The father, and relenting thoughts awoke;
He kissed his son—so all was reconciled.
Then, with a voice which inward trouble broke
Ere to his lips it came, the Sailor them bespoke.

LVII.

"Bad is the world, and hard is the world's law
Even for the man who wears the warmest fleece;
Much need have ye that time more closely draw
The bond of nature, all unkindness cease,
And that among so few there still be peace:
Else can ye hope but with such numerous foes
Your pains shall ever with your years increase?"—
While from his heart the appropriate lesson flows,
A correspondent calm stole gently o'er his woes.

LVIII.

Forthwith the pair passed on; and down they look
Into a narrow valley's pleasant scene,
Where wreaths of vapour tracked a winding brook,
That babbled on through groves and meadows green;
A low-roofed house peeped out the trees between;
The dripping groves resound with cheerful lays,
And melancholy lowings intervene
Of scattered herds, that in the meadow graze,
Some amid lingering shade, some touched by the sun's rays.

LIX.

They saw and heard, and, winding with the road
Down a thick wood, they dropt into the vale;
Comfort by prouder mansions unbestowed
Their wearied frames, she hoped, would soon regale.
Ere long they reached that cottage in the dale:
It was a rustic inn;—the board was spread,
The milk-maid followed with her brimming pail,
And lustily the master carved the bread,
Kindly the housewife pressed, and they in comfort fed.

LX.

Their breakfast done, the pair, though loth, must part;
Wanderers whose course no longer now agrees.
She rose and bade farewell! and, while her heart
Struggled with tears nor could its sorrow ease,

She left him there; for, clustering round his knees,
With his oak-staff the cottage children played;
And soon she reached a spot o'erhung with trees
And banks of ragged earth; beneath the shade
Across the pebbly road a little runnel strayed.

LXI.

A cart and horse beside the rivulet stood;
Chequering the canvas roof the sunbeams shone.
She saw the carman bend to scoop the flood
As the wain fronted her,—wherein lay one,
A pale-faced Woman, in disease far gone.
The carman wet her lips as well behoved;
Bed under her lean body there was none,
Though even to die near one she most had loved
She could not of herself those wasted limbs have moved.

LXII.

The Soldier's Widow learned with honest pain
And homefelt force of sympathy sincere,
Why thus that worn-out wretch must there sustain
The jolting road and morning air severe.
The wain pursued its way; and following near
In pure compassion she her steps retraced
Far as the cottage. "A sad sight is here,"
She cried aloud; and forth ran out in haste
The friends whom she had left but a few minutes past.

LXIII.

While to the door with eager speed they ran,
From her bare straw the Woman half upraised
Her bony visage—gaunt and deadly wan;
No pity asking, on the group she gazed
With a dim eye, distracted and amazed;
Then sank upon her straw with feeble moan.
Fervently cried the housewife—"God be praised,
I have a house that I can call my own;
Nor shall she perish there, untended and alone!"

LXIV.

So in they bear her to the chimney seat,
And busily, though yet with fear, untie
Her garments, and, to warm her icy feet
And chafe her temples, careful hands apply.
Nature reviving, with a deep-drawn sigh
She strove, and not in vain, her head to rear;
Then said—"I thank you all; if I must die,
The God in heaven my prayers for you will hear;
Till now I did not think my end had been so near.

LXV.

"Barred every comfort labour could procure,
Suffering what no endurance could assuage,
I was compelled to seek my father's door,
Though loth to be a burthen on his age.
But sickness stopped me in an early stage
Of my sad journey; and within the wain
They placed me—there to end life's pilgrimage,
Unless beneath your roof I may remain:
For I shall never see my father's door again.

LXVI.

"My life, Heaven knows, hath long been burthensome;
But, if I have not meekly suffered, meek
May my end be! Soon will this voice be dumb:
Should child of mine e'er wander hither, speak
Of me, say that the worm is on my cheek.—
Torn from our hut, that stood beside the sea
Near Portland lighthouse in a lonesome creek,
My husband served in sad captivity
On shipboard, bound till peace or death should set him free.

LXVII.

"A sailor's wife, I knew a widow's cares,
Yet two sweet little ones partook my bed;
Hope cheered my dreams, and to my daily prayers
Our heavenly Father granted each day's bread;

Till one was found by stroke of violence dead,
Whose body near our cottage chanced to lie;
A dire suspicion drove us from our shed;
In vain to find a friendly face we try,
Nor could we live together those poor boys and I;

LXVIII.

"For evil tongues made oath how on that day
My husband lurked about the neighbourhood;
Now he had fled, and whither none could say,
And *he* had done the deed in the dark wood—
Near his own home:—but he was mild and good;
Never on earth was gentler creature seen;
He'd not have robbed the raven of its food.
My husband's loving kindness stood between
Me and all worldly harms and wrongs however keen."

LXIX.

Alas! the thing she told with labouring breath
The Sailor knew too well. That wickedness
His hand had wrought; and when, in the hour of death,
He saw his Wife's lips move his name to bless
With her last words, unable to suppress
His anguish, with his heart he ceased to strive;
And, weeping loud in this extreme distress,
He cried—"Do pity me! That thou shouldst live
I neither ask nor wish—forgive me, but forgive!"

LXX.

To tell the change that Voice within her wrought
Nature by sign or sound made no essay;
A sudden joy surprised expiring thought,
And every mortal pang dissolved away.
Borne gently to a bed, in death she lay;
Yet still while over her the husband bent,
A look was in her face which seemed to say,
"Be blest: by sight of thee from heaven was sent
Peace to my parting soul, the fulness of content."

LXXI.

She slept in peace,—his pulses throbbed and stopped,
Breathless he gazed upon her face,—then took
Her hand in his, and raised it, but both dropped,
When on his own he cast a rueful look.
His ears were never silent; sleep forsook
His burning eyelids stretched and stiff as lead;
All night from time to time under him shook
The floor as he lay shuddering on his bed;
And oft he groaned aloud, "O God, that I were dead!"

LXXII.

The Soldier's Widow lingered in the cot;
And, when he rose, he thanked her pious care
Through which his Wife, to that kind shelter brought,
Died in his arms; and with those thanks a prayer
He breathed for her, and for that merciful pair.
The corse interred, not one hour he remained
Beneath their roof, but to the open air
A burthen, now with fortitude sustained,
He bore within a breast where dreadful quiet reigned.

LXXIII.

Confirmed of purpose, fearlessly prepared
For act and suffering, to the city straight
He journeyed, and forthwith his crime declared:
"And from your doom," he added, "now I wait,
Nor let it linger long, the murderer's fate."
Not ineffectual was that piteous claim:
"O welcome sentence which will end though late,"
He said, "the pangs that to my conscience came
Out of that deed. My trust, Saviour! is in thy name!"

LXXIV.

His fate was pitied. Him in iron case
(Reader, forgive the intolerable thought)
They hung not:—no one on *his* form or face
Could gaze, as on a show by idlers sought;

No kindred sufferer, to his death-place brought
By lawless curiosity or chance,
When into storm the evening sky is wrought,
Upon his swinging corse an eye can glance,
And drop, as he once dropped, in miserable trance.

1793-4.

POEMS REFERRING TO THE PERIOD OF CHILDHOOD.

I.

My heart leaps up when I behold
    A rainbow in the sky:
So was it when my life began;
So is it now I am a man;
So be it when I shall grow old,
    Or let me die!
The Child is father of the Man;
And I could wish my days to be
Bound each to each by natural piety.

1804.

II.
TO A BUTTERFLY.

Stay near me — do not take thy flight!
A little longer stay in sight!
Much converse do I find in thee,
Historian of my infancy!
Float near me; do not yet depart!
Dead times revive in thee:
Thou bring'st, gay creature as thou art!
A solemn image to my heart,
My father's family!
Oh! pleasant, pleasant were the days,
The time, when, in our childish plays,
My sister Emmeline and I
Together chased the butterfly!

A very hunter did I rush
Upon the prey: — with leaps and springs
I followed on from brake to bush;
But she, God love her! feared to brush
The dust from of its wings.

1801.

III.
THE SPARROW'S NEST.

BEHOLD, within the leafy shade,
Those bright blue eggs together laid!
On me the chance-discovered sight
Gleamed like a vision of delight.
I started — seeming to espy
The home and sheltered bed,
The sparrow's dwelling, which, hard by
My Father's house, in wet or dry
My sister Emmeline and I
    Together visited.

She looked at it and seemed to fear it;
Dreading, tho' wishing, to be near it:
Such heart was in her, being then
A little Prattler among men.
The Blessing of my later years
Was with me when a boy:
She gave me eyes, she gave me ears;
And humble cares, and delicate fears;
A heart, the fountain of sweet tears;
    And love, and thought, and joy.

1801.

IV.
CHARACTERISTICS OF A CHILD THREE YEARS OLD.

Loving she is, and tractable, though wild;
And Innocence hath privilege in her
To dignify arch looks and laughing eyes;
And feats of cunning; and the pretty round
Of trespasses, affected to provoke
Mock-chastisement and partnership in play.
And, as a faggot sparkles on the hearth,
Not less if unattended and alone
Than when both young and old sit gathered round
And take delight in its activity;
Even so this happy Creature of herself
Is all-sufficient; solitude to her
Is blithe society, who fills the air
With gladness and involuntary songs.
Light are her sallies as the tripping fawn's
Forth-startled from the fern where she lay couched;
Unthought-of, unexpected, as the stir
Of the soft breeze ruffling the meadow-flowers,
Or from before it chasing wantonly
The many-coloured images imprest
Upon the bosom of a placid lake.

1811.

V.
ALICE FELL;
OR,
POVERTY.

The post-boy drove with fierce career,
For threatening clouds the moon had drowned;
When, as we hurried on, my ear
Was smitten with a startling sound.

As if the wind blew many ways,
I heard the sound, — and more and more;
It seemed to follow with the chaise,
And still I heard it as before.

At length I to the boy called out;
He stopped his horses at the word,
But neither cry, nor voice, nor shout,
Nor aught else like it, could be heard.

The boy then smacked his whip, and fast
The horses scampered through the rain;
But, hearing soon upon the blast
The cry, I bade him halt again.

Forthwith alighting on the ground,
"Whence comes," said I, "this piteous moan?"
And there a little Girl I found,
Sitting behind the chaise, alone.

"My cloak!" no other word she spake,
But loud and bitterly she wept,
As if her innocent heart would break;
And down from off her seat she leapt.

"What ails you, child?" — she sobbed "Look here!"
I saw it in the wheel entangled,
A weather-beaten rag as e'er
From any garden scare-crow dangled.

There, twisted between nave and spoke,
It hung, nor could at once be freed;
But our joint pains unloosed the cloak,
A miserable rag indeed!

"And whither are you going, child,
To-night along these lonesome ways?"
"To Durham," answered she, half wild. —
"Then come with me into the chaise."

Insensible to all relief
Sat the poor girl, and forth did send
Sob after sob, as if her grief
Could never, never have an end.

"My child, in Durham do you dwell?"
She checked herself in her distress,
And said, "My name is Alice Fell;
I 'm fatherless and motherless.

And I to Durham, Sir, belong."
Again, as if the thought would choke
Her very heart, her grief grew strong;
And all was for her tattered cloak!

The chaise drove on; our journey's end
Was nigh; and, sitting by my side,
As if she had lost her only friend
She wept, nor would be pacified.

Up to the tavern-door we post;
Of Alice and her grief I told;
And I gave money to the host,
To buy a new cloak for the old.

"And let it be of duffil grey,
As warm a cloak as man can sell!",
Proud creature was she the next day,
The little orphan, Alice Fell!

1801.

VI.
LUCY GRAY;
OR,
SOLITUDE.

Oft I had heard of Lucy Gray:
And, when I crossed the wild,
I chanced to see at break of day
The solitary child.

No mate, no comrade Lucy knew;
She dwelt on a wide moor,
— The sweetest thing that ever grew
Beside a human door!

You yet may spy the fawn at play,
The hare upon the green;
But the sweet face of Lucy Gray
Will never more be seen.

"To night will be a stormy night —
You to the town must go;
And take a lantern, Child, to light
Your mother through the snow."

"That, Father! will I gladly do:
'Tis scarcely afternoon —
The minster-clock has just struck two,
And yonder is the moon!"

At this the Father raised his hook,
And snapped a faggot-band;
He plied his work; — and Lucy took
The lantern in her hand.

Not blither is the mountain roe:
With many a wanton stroke
Her feet disperse the powdery snow,
That rises up like smoke.

The storm came on before its time:
She wandered up and down;
And many a hill did Lucy climb:
But never reached the town.

The wretched parents all that night
Went shouting far and wide;
But there was neither sound nor sight
To serve them for a guide.

At day-break on a hill they stood
That overlooked the moor;
And thence they saw the bridge of wood,
A furlong from their door.

They wept — and, turning homeward, cried,
"In heaven we all shall meet;"
— When in the snow the mother spied
The print of Lucy's feet.

Then downwards from the steep hill's edge
They tracked the footmarks small;
And through the broken hawthorn hedge,
And by the long stonewall;

And then an open field they crossed:
The marks were still the same;
They tracked them on, nor ever lost;
And to the bridge they came.

They followed from the snowy bank
Those footmarks, one by one,
Into the middle of the plank;
And further there were none!

— Yet some maintain that to this day
She is a living child:
That you may see sweet Lucy Gray
Upon the lonesome wild.

O'er rough and smooth she trips along,
And never looks behind;
And sings a solitary song
That whistles in the wind.

1799.

VII.
WE ARE SEVEN.

—— A simple Child,
That lightly draws its breath,
And feels its life in every limb,
What should it know of death?

I met a little cottage Girl:
She was eight years old, she said;
Her hair was thick with many a curl
That clustered round her head.

She had a rustic, woodland air,
And she was wildly clad:
Her eyes were fair, and very fair;
— Her beauty made me glad.

"Sisters and brothers, little Maid,
How many may you be?"
"How many? Seven in all," she said,
And wondering looked at me.

"And where are they? I pray you tell."
She answered, "Seven are we;
And two of us at Conway dwell,
And two are gone to sea.

Two of us in the church-yard lie,
My sister and my brother;
And, in the church-yard cottage, I
Dwell near them with my mother."

"You say that two at Conway dwell,
And two are gone to sea,
Yet ye are seven! I pray you tell,
Sweet Maid, how this may be."

Then did the little Maid reply,
"Seven boys and girls are we;
Two of us in the church-yard lie,
Beneath the church-yard tree."

"You run about, my little Maid,
Your limbs they are alive;
If two are in the church-yard laid,
Then ye are only five."

"Their graves are green, they may be seen,"
The little Maid replied,
"Twelve steps or more from my mother's door,
And they are side by side.

My stockings there I often knit,
My kerchief there I hem;
And there upon the ground I sit,
And sing a song to them.

And often after sun-set, Sir,
When it is light and fair,
I take my little porringer,
And eat my supper there.

The first that died was sister Jane;
In bed she moaning lay,
Till God released her of her pain;
And then she went away.

So in the church-yard she was laid;
And, when the grass was dry,
Together round her grave we played,
My brother John and I.

And when the ground was white with snow,
And I could run and slide,
My brother John was forced to go,
And he lies by her side."

"How many are you, then," said I,
"If they two are in heaven?"
Quick was the little Maid's reply,
"O Master! we are seven."

"But they are dead; those two are dead!
Their spirits are in heaven!"
'Twas throwing words away; for still
The little Maid would have her will,
And said, "Nay, we are seven!"

1798.

VIII.

THE IDLE SHEPHERD-BOYS;

OR,

DUNGEON-GHYLL FORCE.*

A PASTORAL.

The valley rings with mirth and joy;
Among the hills the echoes play
A never never ending song,
To welcome in the May.
The magpie chatters with delight;
The mountain raven's youngling brood
Have left the mother and the nest;
And they go rambling east and west
In search of their own food;
Or through the glittering vapours dart
In very wantonness of heart.

Beneath a rock, upon the grass,
Two boys are sitting in the sun;
Their work, if any work they have,
Is out of mind — or done.

---

* *Ghyll*, in the dialect of Cumberland and Westmoreland, is a short and, for the most part, a steep narrow valley, with a stream running through it. *Force* is the word universally employed in these dialects for waterfall.

On pipes of sycamore they play
The fragments of a Christmas hymn;
Or with that plant which in our dale
We call stag-horn, or fox's tail,
Their rusty hats they trim:
And thus, as happy as the day,
Those Shepherds wear the time away,

Along the river's stony marge
The sand-lark chants a joyous song;
The thrush is busy in the wood,
And carols loud and strong.
A thousand lambs are on the rocks,
All newly born! both earth and sky
Keep jubilee, and more than all,
Those boys with their green coronal;
They never hear the cry,
That plaintive cry! which up the hill
Comes from the depth of Dungeon-Ghyll.

Said Walter, leaping from the ground,
"Down to the stump of yon old yew
We'll for our whistles run a race."
—— Away the shepherds flew;
They leapt — they ran — and when they came
Right opposite to Dungeon-Ghyll,
Seeing that he should lose the prize,
"Stop!" to his comrade Walter cries —
James stopped with no good will:
Said Walter then, exulting; "Here
You'll find a task for half a year.

Cross, if you dare, where I shall cross —
Come on, and tread where I shall tread."
The other took him at his word,
And followed as he led.
It was a spot which you may see
If ever you to Langdale go;

Into a chasm a mighty block
Hath fallen, and made a bridge of rock:
The gulf is deep below;
And, in a basin black and small,
Receives a lofty waterfall.

With staff in hand across the cleft
The challenger pursued his march;
And now, all eyes and feet, hath gained
The middle of the arch.
When list! he hears a piteous moan —
Again! — his heart within him dies —
His pulse is stopped, his breath is lost,
He totters, pallid as a ghost,
And, looking down, espies
A lamb, that in the pool is pent
Within that black and frightful rent.

The lamb had slipped into the stream,
And safe without a bruise or wound
The cataract had borne him down
Into the gulf profound.
His dam had seen him when he fell,
She saw him down the torrent borne;
And, while with all a mother's love
She from the lofty rocks above
Sent forth a cry forlorn,
The lamb, still swimming round and round,
Made answer to that plaintive sound.

When he had learnt what thing it was,
That sent this rueful cry, I ween
The Boy recovered heart, and told
The sight which he had seen.
Both gladly now deferred their task;
Nor was there wanting other aid —
A Poet, one who loves the brooks
Far better than the sages' books,
By chance had thither strayed;

And there the helpless lamb he found
By those huge rocks encompassed round.

He drew it from the troubled pool,
And brought it forth into the light:
The Shepherds met him with his charge,
An unexpected sight!
Into their arms the lamb they took,
Whose life and limbs the flood had spared;
Then up the steep ascent they hied,
And placed him at his mother's side;
And gently did the Bard
Those idle Shepherd-boys upbraid,
And bade them better mind their trade.

1800.

IX.

ANECDOTE FOR FATHERS.

"Retine vim istam, falsa enim dicam, si coges." — EUSEBIUS.

I HAVE a boy of five years old;
His face is fair and fresh to see;
His limbs are cast in beauty's mould,
And dearly he loves me.

One morn we strolled on our dry walk,
Our quiet home all full in view,
And held such intermitted talk
As we are wont to do.

My thoughts on former pleasures ran;
I thought of Kilve's delightful shore,
Our pleasant home when spring began,
A long, long year before.

A day it was when I could bear
Some fond regrets to entertain;
With so much happiness to spare,
I could not feel a pain.

ANECDOTE FOR FATHERS.

The green earth echoed to the feet
Of lambs that bounded through the glade,
From shade to sunshine, and as fleet
From sunshine back to shade.

Birds warbled round me — and each trace
Of inward sadness had its charm;
Kilve, thought I, was a favoured place,
And so is Liswyn farm.

My boy beside me tripped, so slim
And graceful in his rustic dress!
And, as we talked, I questioned him,
In very idleness.

"Now tell me, had you rather be,"
I said, and took him by the arm,
"On Kilve's smooth shore, by the green sea,
Or here at Liswyn farm?"

In careless mood he looked at me,
While still I held him by the arm,
And said, "At Kilve I'd rather be
Than here at Liswyn farm."

"Now, little Edward, say why so:
My little Edward, tell me why." —
"I cannot tell, I do not know." —
"Why, this is strange," said I;

"For, here are woods, hills smooth and warm:
There surely must some reason be
Why you would change sweet Liswyn farm
For Kilve by the green sea."

At this, my boy hung down his head,
He blushed with shame, nor made reply;
And three times to the child I said,
"Why, Edward, tell me why?"

His head he raised — there was in sight,
It caught his eye, he saw it plain —
Upon the house-top, glittering bright,
A broad and gilded vane.

Then did the boy his tongue unlock,
And eased his mind with this reply:
"At Kilve there was no weather-cock;
And that's the reason why."

O dearest, dearest boy! my heart
For better lore would seldom yearn,
Could I but teach the hundredth part
Of what from thee I learn.

1798.

X.

RURAL ARCHITECTURE.

There's George Fisher, Charles Fleming, and Reginald
    Shore,
Three rosy-cheeked school-boys, the highest not more
Than the height of a counsellor's bag;
To the top of Great How* did it please them to climb:
And there they built up, without mortar or lime,
A Man on the peak of the crag.

They built him of stones gathered up as they lay:
They built him and christened him all in one day,
An urchin both vigorous and hale;
And so without scruple they called him Ralph Jones.
Now Ralph is renowned for the length of his bones;
The Magog of Legberthwaite dale.

* Great How is a single and conspicuous hill, which rises towards the foot of Thirlmere, on the western side of the beautiful dale of Legberthwaite, along the high road between Keswick and Ambleside.

Just half a week after, the wind sallied forth,
And, in anger or merriment, out of the north,
Coming on with a terrible pother,
From the peak of the crag blew the giant away.
And what did these school-boys? — The very next day
They went and they built up another.

— Some little I 've seen of blind boisterous works
By Christian disturbers more savage than Turks,
Spirits busy to do and undo:
At remembrance whereof my blood sometimes will flag;
Then, light-hearted Boys, to the top of the crag;
And I'll build up a giant with you.

1801.

XI.
THE PET-LAMB.
A PASTORAL.

The dew was falling fast, the stars began to blink;
I heard a voice; it said, "Drink, pretty creature, drink!"
And, looking o'er the hedge, before me I espied
A snow-white mountain-lamb with a Maiden at its side.

Nor sheep nor kine were near; the lamb was all alone,
And by a slender cord was tethered to a stone;
With one knee on the grass did the little Maiden kneel,
While to that mountain-lamb she gave its evening meal.

The lamb, while from her hand he thus his supper took,
Seemed to feast with head and ears; and his tail with pleasure
      shook.
"Drink, pretty creature, drink," she said in such a tone
That I almost received her heart into my own.

'Twas little Barbara Lewthwaite, a child of beauty rare!
I watched them with delight, they were a lovely pair.

Now with her empty can the Maiden turned away:
But ere ten yards were gone her footsteps did she stay.

Right towards the lamb she looked; and from a shady place
I unobserved could see the workings of her face:
If Nature to her tongue could measured numbers bring,
Thus, thought I, to her lamb that little Maid might sing:

"What ails thee, young One? what? Why pull so at thy cord?
Is it not well with thee? well both for bed and board?
Thy plot of grass is soft, and green as grass can be;
Rest, little young One, rest; what is't that aileth thee?

What is it thou wouldst seek? What is wanting to thy heart?
Thy limbs are they not strong? And beautiful thou art:
This grass is tender grass; these flowers they have no peers;
And that green corn all day is rustling in thy ears!

If the sun be shining hot, do but stretch thy woollen chain,
This beech is standing by, its covert thou canst gain;
For rain and mountain-storms! the like thou need'st not fear,
The rain and storm are things that scarcely can come here.

Rest, little young One, rest; thou hast forgot the day
When my father found thee first in places far away;
Many flocks were on the hills, but thou wert owned by none,
And thy mother from thy side for evermore was gone.

He took thee in his arms, and in pity brought thee home:
A blessed day for thee! then whither wouldst thou roam?
A faithful nurse thou hast; the dam that did thee yean
Upon the mountain tops no kinder could have been.

Thou know'st that twice a day I have brought thee in this can
Fresh water from the brook, as clear as ever ran;
And twice in the day, when the ground is wet with dew,
I bring thee draughts of milk, warm milk it is and new.

Thy limbs will shortly be twice as stout as they are now,
Then I 'll yoke thee to my cart like a pony in the plough;
My playmate thou shalt be; and when the wind is cold
Our hearth shall be thy bed, our house shall be thy fold.

It will not, will not rest! — Poor creature, can it be
That 'tis thy mother's heart which is working so in thee?
Things that I know not of belike to thee are dear,
And dreams of things which thou canst neither see nor hear.

Alas, the mountain-tops that look so green and fair!
I 've heard of fearful winds and darkness that come there;
The little brooks that seem all pastime and all play,
When they are angry, roar like lions for their prey.

Here thou need'st not dread the raven in the sky;
Night and day thou art safe, — our cottage is hard by.
Why bleat so after me? Why pull so at thy chain?
Sleep — and at break of day I will come to thee again!"

— As homeward through the lane I went with lazy feet,
This song to myself did I oftentimes repeat;
And it seemed, as I retraced the ballad line by line,
That but half of it was hers, and one half of it was *mine*.

Again, and once again, did I repeat the song;
"Nay," said I, "more than half to the damsel must belong,
For she looked with such a look, and she spake with such a tone,
That I almost received her heart into my own."

1800.

XII.
TO H. C.
SIX YEARS OLD.

O thou! whose fancies from afar are brought;
Who of thy words dost make a mock apparel,
And fittest to unutterable thought
The breeze-like motion and the self-born carol
Thou faery voyager! that dost float
In such clear water, that thy boat
May rather seem
To brood on air than on an earthly stream;
Suspended in a stream as clear as sky,
Where earth and heaven do make one imagery;
O blessed vision! happy child!
Thou art so exquisitely wild,
I think of thee with many fears
For what may be thy lot in future years.

I thought of times when Pain might be thy guest,
Lord of thy house and hospitality;
And Grief, uneasy lover! never rest
But when she sate within the touch of thee.
O too industrious folly!
O vain and causeless melancholy!
Nature will either end thee quite;
Or, lengthening out thy season of delight,
Preserve for thee, by individual right,
A young lamb's heart among the full-grown flocks.
What hast thou to do with sorrow,
Or the injuries of to-morrow?
Thou art a dew-drop, which the morn brings forth,
Ill fitted to sustain unkindly shocks,
Or to be trailed along the soiling earth;
A gem that glitters while it lives,
And no forewarning gives;
But, at the touch of wrong, without a strife
Slips in a moment out of life.   1802.

XIII.
INFLUENCE OF NATURAL OBJECTS

IN CALLING FORTH AND STRENGTHENING THE IMAGINATION IN BOYHOOD AND EARLY YOUTH.

FROM AN UNPUBLISHED POEM.

[This extract is reprinted from "THE FRIEND."]

Wisdom and Spirit of the universe!
Thou Soul, that art the Eternity of thought!
And giv'st to forms and images a breath
And everlasting motion! not in vain,
By day or star-light, thus from my first dawn
Of childhood didst thou intertwine for me
The passions that build up our human soul;
Not with the mean and vulgar works of Man;
But with high objects, with enduring things,
With life and nature; purifying thus
The elements of feeling and of thought,
And sanctifying by such discipline
Both pain and fear,—until we recognise
A grandeur in the beatings of the heart.

Nor was this fellowship vouchsafed to me
With stinted kindness. In November days,
When vapours rolling down the valleys made
A lonely scene more lonesome; among woods
At noon; and 'mid the calm of summer nights,
When, by the margin of the trembling lake,
Beneath the gloomy hills, homeward I went
In solitude, such intercourse was mine:
Mine was it in the fields both day and night,
And by the waters, all the summer long.
And in the frosty season, when the sun
Was set, and, visible for many a mile,
The cottage-windows through the twilight blazed,
I heeded not the summons: happy time

It was indeed for all of us; for me
It was a time of rapture! Clear and loud
The village-clock tolled six—I wheeled about,
Proud and exulting like an untired horse
That cares not for his home.—All shod with steel
We hissed along the polished ice, in games
Confederate, imitative of the chase
And woodland pleasures,—the resounding horn,
The pack loud-chiming, and the hunted hare.
So through the darkness and the cold we flew,
And not a voice was idle: with the din
Smitten, the precipices rang aloud;
The leafless trees and every icy crag
Tinkled like iron; while far-distant hills
Into the tumult sent an alien sound
Of melancholy, not unnoticed while the stars,
Eastward, were sparkling clear, and in the west
The orange sky of evening died away.

   Not seldom from the uproar I retired
Into a silent bay, or sportively
Glanced sideway, leaving the tumultuous throng,
To cut across the reflex of a star;
Image, that, flying still before me, gleamed
Upon the glassy plain: and oftentimes,
When we had given our bodies to the wind,
And all the shadowy banks on either side
Came sweeping through the darkness, spinning still
The rapid line of motion, then at once
Have I, reclining back upon my heels,
Stopped short; yet still the solitary cliffs
Wheeled by me—even as if the earth had rolled
With visible motion her diurnal round!
Behind me did they stretch in solemn train,
Feebler and feebler, and I stood and watched,
Till all was tranquil as a summer sea.

1799.

XIV.
THE NORMAN BOY.

High on a broad unfertile tract of forest-skirted Down,
Nor kept by Nature for herself, nor made by man his own,
From home and company remote and every playful joy,
Served, tending a few sheep and goats, a ragged Norman
    Boy.

Him never saw I, nor the spot; but from an English Dame,
Stranger to me and yet my friend, a simple notice came,
With suit that I would speak in verse of that sequestered child
Whom, one bleak winter's day, she met upon the dreary
    Wild.

His flock, along the woodland's edge with relics sprinkled o'er
Of last night's snow, beneath a sky threatening the fall of
    more,
Where tufts of herbage tempted each, were busy at their feed,
And the poor Boy was busier still, with work of anxious heed.

There *was* he, where of branches rent and withered and de-
    cayed,
For covert from the keen north wind, his hands a hut had
    made.
A tiny tenement, forsooth, and frail, as needs must be
A thing of such materials framed, by a builder such as he.

The hut stood finished by his pains, nor seemingly lacked
    aught
That skill or means of his could add, but the architect had
    wrought
Some limber twigs into a Cross, well-shaped with fingers nice,
To be engrafted on the top of his small edifice.

That Cross he now was fastening there, as the surest power
    and best
For supplying all deficiencies, all wants of the rude nest

In which, from burning heat, or tempest driving far and wide,
The innocent Boy, else shelterless, his lonely head must hide.

That Cross belike he also raised as a standard for the true
And faithful service of his heart in the worst that might ensue
Of hardship and distressful fear, amid the houseless waste
Where he, in his poor self so weak, by Providence was placed.

— Here, Lady! might I cease; but nay, let *us* before we part
With this dear holy shepherd-boy breathe a prayer of earnest heart,
That unto him, where'er shall lie his life's appointed way,
The Cross, fixed in his soul, may prove an all-sufficing stay.

XV.
THE POET'S DREAM.
SEQUEL TO THE NORMAN BOY.

Just as those final words were penned, the sun broke out in power,
And gladdened all things; but, as chanced, within that very hour,
Air black'ened, thunder growled, fire flashed from clouds that hid the sky,
And, for the Subject of my Verse, I heaved a pensive sigh.

Nor could my heart by second thoughts from heaviness be cleared,
For bodied forth before my eyes the cross-crowned hut appeared;
And, while around it storm as fierce seemed troubling earth and air,
I saw, within, the Norman Boy kneeling alone in prayer.

The Child, as if the thunder's voice spake with articulate call,
Bowed meekly in submissive fear, before the Lord of All;
His lips were moving; and his eyes, upraised to sue for grace,
With soft illumination cheered the dimness of that place.

THE POET'S DREAM.

How beautiful is holiness!—what wonder if the sight,
Almost as vivid as a dream, produced a dream at night?
It came with sleep and showed the Boy, no cherub, not transformed,
But the poor ragged Thing whose ways my human heart had warmed.

Me had the dream equipped with wings, so I took him in my arms,
And lifted from the grassy floor, stilling his faint alarms,
And bore him high through yielding air my debt of love to pay,
By giving him, for both our sakes, an hour of holiday.

I whispered, "Yet a little while, dear Child! thou art my own,
To show thee some delightful thing, in country or in town.
What shall it be? a mirthful throng? or that holy place and calm
St. Denis, filled with royal tombs, or the Church of Notre Dame?

"St. Ouen's golden Shrine? Or choose what else would please thee most
Of any wonder Normandy, or all proud France, can boast!"
"My Mother," said the Boy, "was born near to a blessèd Tree,
The Chapel Oak of Allonville; good Angel, show it me!"

On wings, from broad and stedfast poise let loose by this reply,
For Allonville, o'er down and dale, away then did we fly;
O'er town and tower we flew, and fields in May's fresh verdure drest;
The wings they did not flag; the Child, though grave, was not deprest.

But who shall show, to waking sense, the gleam of light that broke
Forth from his eyes, when first the Boy looked down on that huge oak,

For length of days so much revered, so famous where it stands
For twofold hallowing—Nature's care, and work of human
    hands?

Strong as an Eagle with my charge I glided round and round
The wide-spread boughs, for view of door, window, and stair
    that wound
Gracefully up the gnarled trunk; nor left we unsurveyed
The pointed steeple peering forth from the centre of the shade.

I lighted—opened with soft touch the chapel's iron door,
Past softly, leading in the Boy; and, while from roof to floor
From floor to roof all round his eyes the Child with wonder
    cast,
Pleasure on pleasure crowded in, each livelier than the last.

For, deftly framed within the trunk, the sanctuary showed,
By light of lamp and precious stones, that glimmered here,
    there glowed,
Shrine, Altar, Image, Offerings hung in sign of gratitude;
Sight that inspired accordant thoughts; and speech I thus
    renewed:

"Hither the Afflicted come, as thou hast heard thy Mother say,
And, kneeling, supplication make to our Lady de la Paix;
What mournful sighs have here been heard, and, when the
    voice was stopt
By sudden pangs; what bitter tears have on this pavement
    dropt!

"Poor Shepherd of the naked Down, a favoured lot is thine,
Far happier lot, dear Boy, than brings full many to this
    shrine;
From body pains and pains of soul thou needest no release,
Thy hours as they flow on are spent, if not in joy in peace.

"Then offer up thy heart to God in thankfulness and praise,
Give to Him prayers, and many thoughts, in thy most busy
    days;

And in His sight the fragile Cross, on thy small hut, will be
Holy as that which long hath crowned the Chapel of this Tree;

"Holy as that far seen which crowns the sumptuous Church in Rome
Where thousands meet to worship God under a mighty Dome;
He sees the bending multitude, he hears the choral rites,
Yet not the less, in children's hymns and lonely prayer delights.

"God for his service needeth not proud work of human skill;
They please him best who labour most to do in peace his will:
So let us strive to live, and to our Spirits will be given
Such wings as, when our Saviour calls, shall bear us up to heaven."

The Boy no answer made by words, but, so earnest was his look,
Sleep fled, and with it fled the dream—recorded in this book,
Lest all that passed should melt away in silence from my mind,
As visions still more bright have done, and left no trace behind.

But oh! that Country-man of thine, whose eye, loved Child, can see
A pledge of endless bliss in acts of early piety,
In verse, which to thy ear might come, would treat this simple theme,
Nor leave untold our happy flight in that adventurous dream.

Alas the dream, to thee, poor Boy! to thee from whom it flowed,
Was nothing, scarcely can be aught, yet 'twas bounteously bestowed,
If I may dare to cherish hope that gentle eyes will read
Not loth, and listening Little-ones, heart-touched, their fancies feed.*

* See note.

XVI.
THE WESTMORELAND GIRL.
TO MY GRANDCHILDREN.
PART I.

Seek who will delight in fable
I shall tell you truth. A Lamb
Leapt from this steep bank to follow
'Cross the brook its thoughtless dam.

Far and wide on hill and valley
Rain had fallen, unceasing rain,
And the bleating mother's Young-one
Struggled with the flood in vain:

But, as chanced, a Cottage-maiden
(Ten years scarcely had she told)
Seeing, plunged into the torrent,
Clasped the Lamb and kept her hold.

Whirled adown the rocky channel,
Sinking, rising, on they go,
Peace and rest, as seems, before them
Only in the lake below.

Oh! it was a frightful current
Whose fierce wrath the Girl had braved;
Clap your hands with joy my Hearers,
Shout in triumph, both are saved;

Saved by courage that with danger
Grew, by strength the gift of love,
And belike a guardian angel
Came with succour from above.

PART II.

Now, to a maturer Audience,
Let me speak of this brave Child
Left among her native mountains
With wild Nature to run wild.

So, unwatched by love maternal,
Mother's care no more her guide,
Fared this little bright-eyed Orphan
Even while at her father's side.

Spare your blame,—remembrance makes him
Loth to rule by strict command;
Still upon his cheek are living
Touches of her infant hand,

Dear caresses given in pity,
Sympathy that soothed his grief,
As the dying mother witnessed
To her thankful mind's relief.

Time passed on; the Child was happy,
Like a Spirit of air she moved,
Wayward, yet by all who knew her
For her tender heart beloved.

Scarcely less than sacred passions,
Bred in house, in grove, and field,
Link her with the inferior creatures,
Urge her powers their rights to shield.

Anglers, bent on reckless pastime,
Learn how she can feel alike
Both for tiny harmless minnow
And the fierce and sharp-toothed pike.

Merciful protectress, kindling
Into anger or disdain;
Many a captive hath she rescued,
Others saved from lingering pain.

Listen yet awhile;—with patience
Hear the homely truths I tell,
She in Grasmere's old church-steeple
Tolled this day the passing-bell.

Yes, the wild Girl of the mountains
To their echoes gave the sound,
Notice punctual as the minute,
Warning solemn and profound.

She, fulfilling her sire's office,
Rang alone the far-heard knell,
Tribute, by her hand, in sorrow,
Paid to One who loved her well.

When his spirit was departed
On that service she went forth;
Nor will fail the like to render
When his corse is laid in earth.

What then wants the Child to temper,
In her breast, unruly fire,
To control the froward impulse
And restrain the vague desire?

Easily a pious training
And a stedfast outward power
Would supplant the weeds and cherish,
In their stead, each opening flower.

Thus the fearless Lamb-deliv'rer,
Woman-grown, meek-hearted, sage,
May become a blest example
For her sex, of every age.

Watchful as a wheeling eagle,
Constant as a soaring lark,
Should the country need a heroine,
She might prove our Maid of Arc.

Leave that thought; and here be uttered
Prayer that Grace divine may raise
Her humane courageous spirit
Up to heaven, thro' peaceful ways.

POEMS FOUNDED ON THE AFFECTIONS.

I.
THE BROTHERS.

"These Tourists, heaven preserve us! needs must live
A profitable life: some glance along,
Rapid and gay, as if the earth were air,
And they were butterflies to wheel about
Long as the summer lasted: some, as wise,
Perched on the forehead of a jutting crag,
Pencil in hand and book upon the knee,
Will look and scribble, scribble on and look,
Until a man might travel twelve stout miles,
Or reap an acre of his neighbour's corn.
But, for that moping Son of Idleness,
Why can he tarry *yonder?* — In our church-yard
Is neither epitaph nor monument,
Tombstone nor name—only the turf we tread
And a few natural graves."

                          To Jane, his wife,
Thus spake the homely Priest of Ennerdale.
It was a July evening; and he sate
Upon the long stone-seat beneath the eaves
Of his old cottage, — as it chanced, that day,
Employed in winter's work. Upon the stone
His wife sate near him, teasing matted wool,
While, from the twin cards toothed with glittering wire,
He fed the spindle of his youngest child,
Who, in the open air, with due accord

Of busy hands and back-and-forward steps,
Her large round wheel was turning.   Towards the field
In which the Parish Chapel stood alone,
Girt round with a bare ring of mossy wall,
While half an hour went by, the Priest had sent
Many a long look of wonder: and at last,
Risen from his seat, beside the snow-white ridge
Of carded wool which the old man had piled
He laid his implements with gentle care,
Each in the other locked; and, down the path
That from his cottage to the church-yard led,
He took his way, impatient to accost
The stranger, whom he saw still lingering there.

"Twas one well known to him in former days,
A Shepherd-lad; who ere his sixteenth year
Had left that calling, tempted to entrust
His expectations to the fickle winds
And perilous waters; with the mariners
A fellow-mariner; — and so had fared
Through twenty seasons; but he had been reared
Among the mountains, and he in his heart
Was half a shepherd on the stormy seas.
Oft in the piping shrouds had Leonard heard
The tones of waterfalls, and inland sounds
Of caves and trees:—and, when the regular wind
Between the tropics filled the steady sail,
And blew with the same breath through days and weeks,
Lengthening invisibly its weary line
Along the cloudless Main, he, in those hours
Of tiresome indolence, would often hang
Over the vessel's side, and gaze and gaze;
And, while the broad blue wave and sparkling foam
Flashed round him images and hues that wrought
In union with the employment of his heart,
He, thus by feverish passion overcome,
Even with the organs of his bodily eye,

Below him, in the bosom of the deep,
Saw mountains; saw the forms of sheep that grazed
On verdant hills — with dwellings among trees,
And shepherds clad in the same country grey
Which he himself had worn*.

       And now, at last,
From perils manifold, with some small wealth
Acquired by traffic 'mid the Indian Isles,
To his paternal home he is returned,
With a determined purpose to resume
The life he had lived there; both for the sake
Of many darling pleasures, and the love
Which to an only brother he has borne
In all his hardships, since that happy time
When, whether it blew foul or fair, they two
Were brother-shepherds on their native hills.
—They were the last of all their race: and now,
When Leonard had approached his home, his heart
Failed in him; and, not venturing to enquire
Tidings of one so long and dearly loved,
He to the solitary church-yard turned;
That, as he knew in what particular spot
His family were laid, he thence might learn
If still his Brother lived, or to the file
Another grave was added. — He had found
Another grave, — near which a full half-hour
He had remained; but, as he gazed, there grew
Such a confusion in his memory,
That he began to doubt; and even to hope
That he had seen this heap of turf before, —
That it was not another grave; but one
He had forgotten. He had lost his path,
As up the vale, that afternoon, he walked

---

* This description of the Calenture is sketched from an imperfect recollection of an admirable one in prose, by Mr. Gilbert, author of the Hurricane.

Through fields which once had been well known to him:
And oh what joy this recollection now
Sent to his heart! he lifted up his eyes,
And, looking round, imagined that he saw
Strange alteration wrought on every side
Among the woods and fields, and that the rocks,
And everlasting hills themselves were changed.

 By this the Priest, who down the field had come,
Unseen by Leonard, at the church-yard gate
Stopped short,—and thence, at leisure, limb by limb
Perused him with a gay complacency.
Ay, thought the Vicar, smiling to himself,
'Tis one of those who needs must leave the path
Of the world's business to go wild alone:
His arms have a perpetual holiday;
The happy man will creep about the fields,
Following his fancies by the hour, to bring
Tears down his cheek, or solitary smiles
Into his face, until the setting sun
Write fool upon his forehead. — Planted thus
Beneath a shed that over-arched the gate
Of this rude church-yard, till the stars appeared
The good Man might have communed with himself,
But that the Stranger, who had left the grave,
Approached; he recognised the Priest at once,
And, after greetings interchanged, and given
By Leonard to the Vicar as to one
Unknown to him, this dialogue ensued.
 Leonard. You live, Sir, in these dales, a quiet life:
Your years make up one peaceful family;
And who would grieve and fret, if, welcome come
And welcome gone, they are so like each other,
They cannot be remembered? Scarce a funeral
Comes to this church-yard once in eighteen months;
And yet, some changes must take place among you:
And you, who dwell here, even among these rocks,

Can trace the finger of mortality,
And see, that with our threescore years and ten
We are not all that perish. — — I remember,
(For many years ago I passed this road)
There was a foot-way all along the fields
By the brook-side — 'tis gone — and that dark cleft!
To me it does not seem to wear the face
Which then it had!
  Priest.   Nay, Sir, for aught I know,
That chasm is much the same —
  Leonard.   But, surely, yonder —
 Priest. Ay, there, indeed, your memory is a friend
That does not play you false. — On that tall pike
(It is the loneliest place of all these hills)
There were two springs which bubbled side by side,
As if they had been made that they might be
Companions for each other: the huge crag
Was rent with lightning — one hath disappeared;
The other, left behind, is flowing still.
For accidents and changes such as these,
We want not store of them; — a water-spout
Will bring down half a mountain; what a feast
For folks that wander up and down like you,
To see an acre's breadth of that wide cliff
One roaring cataract! a sharp May-storm
Will come with loads of January snow,
And in one night send twenty score of sheep
To feed the ravens; or a shepherd dies
By some untoward death among the rocks:
The ice breaks up and sweeps away a bridge;
A wood is felled: — and then for our own homes!
A child is born or christened, a field ploughed,
A daughter sent to service, a web spun,
The old house-clock is decked with a new face;
And hence, so far from wanting facts or dates
To chronicle the time, we all have here
A pair of diaries, — one serving, Sir,

For the whole dale, and one for each fire-side—
Yours was a stranger's judgment: for historians,
Commend me to these valleys!
  Leonard.   Yet your church-yard
Seems, if such freedom may be used with you,
To say that you are heedless of the past:
An orphan could not find his mother's grave:
Here's neither head nor foot-stone, plate of brass,
Cross-bones nor skull, — type of our earthly state
Nor emblem of our hopes: the dead man's home
Is but a fellow to that pasture-field.
  Priest. Why, there, Sir, is a thought that's new to me!
The stone-cutters, 'tis true, might beg their bread
If every English church-yard were like ours;
Yet your conclusion wanders from the truth:
We have no need of names and epitaphs;
We talk about the dead by our fire-sides.
And then, for our immòrtal part! *we* want
No symbols, Sir, to tell us that plain tale:
The thought of death sits easy on the man
Who has been born and dies among the mountains.
  Leonard. Your Dalesmen, then, do in each other's thoughts
Possess a kind of second life: no doubt
You, Sir, could help me to the history
Of half these graves?
  Priest.   For eight-score winters past,
With what I've witnessed, and with what I've heard,
Perhaps I might; and, on a winter-evening,
If you were seated at my chimney's nook,
By turning o'er these hillocks one by one,
We two could travel, Sir, through a strange round;
Yet all in the broad highway of the world.
Now there's a grave — your foot is half upon it, —
It looks just like the rest; and yet that man
Died broken-hearted.
  Leonard.   'Tis a common case.
We'll take another: who is he that lies

Beneath yon ridge, the last of those three graves
It touches on that piece of native rock
Left in the church-yard wall.
  Priest.   That's Walter Ewbank.
He had as white a head and fresh a cheek
As ever were produced by youth and age
Engendering in the blood of hale fourscore.
Through five long generations had the heart
Of Walter's forefathers o'erflowed the bounds
Of their inheritance, that single cottage —
You see it yonder! and those few green fields.
They toiled and wrought, and still, from sire to son,
Each struggled, and each yielded as before
A little — yet a little, — and old Walter,
They left to him the family heart, and land
With other burthens than the crop it bore.
Year after year the old man still kept up
A cheerful mind, — and buffeted with bond,
Interest, and mortgages; at last he sank,
And went into his grave before his time.
Poor Walter! whether it was care that spurred him
God only knows, but to the very last
He had the lightest foot in Ennerdale:
His pace was never that of an old man:
I almost see him tripping down the path
With his two grandsons after him:—but you,
Unless our Landlord be your host to-night,
Have far to travel, — and on these rough paths
Even in the longest day of midsummer —
  Leonard. But those two Orphans!
  Priest.   Orphans! — Such they were —
Yet not while Walter lived: — for, though their parents
Lay buried side by side as now they lie,
The old man was a father to the boys,
Two fathers in one father! and if tears,
Shed when he talked of them where they were not,
And hauntings from the infirmity of love,

Are aught of what makes up a mother's heart,
This old Man, in the day of his old age,
Was half a mother to them — If you weep, Sir,
To hear a stranger talking about strangers,
Heaven bless you when you are among your kindred!
Ay — you may turn that way — it is a grave
Which will bear looking at.

   Leonard.   These boys — I hope
They loved this good old Man? —

   Priest.   They did — and truly:
But that was what we almost overlooked,
They were such darlings of each other. Yes,
Though from the cradle they had lived with Walter,
The only kinsman near them, and though he
Inclined to both by reason of his age,
With a more fond, familiar, tenderness;
They, notwithstanding, had much love to spare,
And it all went into each other's hearts.
Leonard, the elder by just eighteen months,
Was two years taller: 'twas a joy to see,
To hear, to meet them! — From their house the school
Is distant three short miles, and in the time
Of storm and thaw, when every water-course
And unbridged stream, such as you may have noticed
Crossing our roads at every hundred steps,
Was swoln into a noisy rivulet,
Would Leonard then, when elder boys remained
At home, go staggering through the slippery fords,
Bearing his brother on his back. I have seen him,
On windy days, in one of those stray brooks,
Ay, more than once I have seen him, mid-leg deep,
Their two books lying both on a dry stone,
Upon the hither side: and once I said,
As I remember, looking round these rocks
And hills on which we all of us were born,
That God who made the great book of the world
Would bless such piety—

  Leonard.   It may be then —
  Priest. Never did worthier lads break English bread;
The very brightest Sunday Autumn saw
With all its mealy clusters of ripe nuts,
Could never keep those boys away from church,
Or tempt them to an hour of sabbath breach.
Leonard and James! I warrant, every corner
Among these rocks, and every hollow place
That venturous foot could reach, to one or both
Was known as well as to the flowers that grow there.
Like roe-bucks they went bounding o'er the hills;
They played like two young ravens on the crags:
Then they could write, ay and speak too, as well
As many of their betters — and for Leonard!
The very night before he went away,
In my own house I put into his hand
A bible, and I'd wager house and field
That, if he be alive, he has it yet.
  Leonard. It seems, these Brothers have not lived to be
A comfort to each other —
  Priest.   That they might
Live to such end is what both old and young
In this our valley all of us have wished,
And what, for my part, I have often prayed:
But Leonard —
  Leonard. Then James still is left among you!
  Priest. 'Tis of the elder brother I am speaking:
They had an uncle; — he was at that time
A thriving man, and trafficked on the seas:
And, but for that same uncle, to this hour
Leonard had never handled rope or shroud:
For the boy loved the life which we lead here;
And though of unripe years, a stripling only,
His soul was knit to this his native soil.
But, as I said, old Walter was too weak
To strive with such a torrent; when he died,
The estate and house were sold; and all their sheep,

A pretty flock, and which, for aught I know,
Had clothed the Ewbanks for a thousand years: —
Well — all was gone, and they were destitute,
And Leonard, chiefly for his Brother's sake,
Resolved to try his fortune on the seas.
Twelve years are past since we had tidings from him.
If there were one among us who had heard
That Leonard Ewbank was come home again,
From the Great Gavel, down by Leeza's banks,
And down the Enna, far as Egremont,
The day would be a joyous festival;
And those two bells of ours, which there you see —
Hanging in the open air — but, O good Sir!
This is sad talk — they'll never sound for him —
Living or dead. — When last we heard of him,
He was in slavery among the Moors
Upon the Barbary coast. — 'Twas not a little
That would bring down his spirit; and no doubt,
Before it ended in his death, the Youth
Was sadly crossed. — Poor Leonard! when we parted,
He took me by the hand, and said to me,
If e'er he should grow rich, he would return,
To live in peace upon his father's land,
And lay his bones among us.
    Leonard.   If that day
Should come, 'twould needs be a glad day for him;
He would himself, no doubt, be happy then
As any that should meet him —
    Priest.   Happy! Sir —
    Leonard. You said his kindred all were in their graves,
And that he had one Brother —
    Priest.   That is but
A fellow-tale of sorrow. From his youth
James, though not sickly, yet was delicate;
And Leonard being always by his side
Had done so many offices about him,
That, though he was not of a timid nature,

Yet still the spirit of a mountain-boy
In him was somewhat checked; and, when his Brother
Was gone to sea, and he was left alone,
The little colour that he had was soon
Stolen from his cheek; he drooped, and pined, and pined —
   Leonard. But these are all the graves of fullgrown men!
   Priest. Ay, Sir, that passed away: we took him to us;
He was the child of all the dale — he lived
Three months with one, and six months with another;
And wanted neither food, nor clothes, nor love:
And many, many happy days were his.
But, whether blithe or sad, 'tis my belief
His absent Brother still was at his heart.
And, when he dwelt beneath our roof, we found
(A practice till this time unknown to him)
That often, rising from his bed at night,
He in his sleep would walk about, and sleeping
He sought his brother Leonard. — You are moved!
Forgive me, Sir: before I spoke to you,
I judged you most unkindly.
   Leonard.   But this Youth,
How did he die at last?
   Priest.   One sweet May-morning,
(It will be twelve years since when Spring returns)
He had gone forth among the new-dropped lambs,
With two or three companions, whom their course
Of occupation led from height to height
Under a cloudless sun — till he, at length,
Through weariness, or, haply, to indulge
The humour of the moment, lagged behind.
You see yon precipice; — it wears the shape
Of a vast building made of many crags;
And in the midst is one particular rock
That rises like a column from the vale,
Whence by our shepherds it is called, THE PILLAR.
Upon its aëry summit crowned with heath,
The loiterer, not unnoticed by his comrades,

Lay stretched at ease; but, passing by the place
On their return, they found that he was gone.
No ill was feared; till one of them by chance
Entering, when evening was far spent, the house
Which at that time was James's home, there learned
That nobody had seen him all that day:
The morning came, and still he was unheard of:
The neighbours were alarmed, and to the brook
Some hastened; some ran to the lake: ere noon
They found him at the foot of that same rock
Dead, and with mangled limbs. The third day after
I buried him, poor Youth, and there he lies!
 Leonard. And that then *is* his grave! — Before his death
You say that he saw many happy years?
 Priest. Ay, that he did —
 Leonard.   And all went well with him? —
 Priest. If he had one, the youth had twenty homes.
 Leonard. And you believe, then, that his mind was easy? —
 Priest. Yes, long before he died, he found that time
Is a true friend to sorrow; and unless
His thoughts were turned on Leonard's luckless fortune,
He talked about him with a cheerful love.
 Leonard. He could not come to an unhallowed end!
 Priest. Nay, God forbid! — You recollect I mentioned
A habit which disquietude and grief
Had brought upon him; and we all conjectured
That, as the day was warm, he had lain down
On the soft heath, — and, waiting for his comrades,
He there had fallen asleep; that in his sleep
He to the margin of the precipice
Had walked, and from the summit had fallen headlong:
And so no doubt he perished. When the Youth
Fell, in his hand he must have grasp'd, we think,
His shepherd's staff; for on that Pillar of rock
It had been caught mid way; and there for years
It hung; — and mouldered there.

                                The Priest here ended —
The stranger would have thanked him, but he felt
A gushing from his heart, that took away
The power of speech.   Both left the spot in silence;
And Leonard, when they reached the church-yard gate,
As the Priest lifted up the latch, turned round, —
And, looking at the grave, he said, "My Brother!"
The Vicar did not hear the words: and now,
He pointed towards his dwelling-place, entreating
That Leonard would partake his homely fare:
The other thanked him with an earnest voice;
But added, that, the evening being calm,
He would pursue his journey.   So they parted.

   It was not long ere Leonard reached a grove
That overhung the road: he there stopped short,
And, sitting down beneath the trees, reviewed
All that the Priest had said; his early years
Were with him: — his long absence, cherished hopes,
And thoughts which had been his an hour before,
All pressed on him with such a weight, that now,
This vale, where he had been so happy, seemed
A place in which he could not bear to live!
So he relinquished all his purposes.
He travelled back to Egremont: and thence,
That night, he wrote a letter to the Priest,
Reminding him of what had passed between them;
And adding, with a hope to be forgiven,
That it was from the weakness of his heart
He had not dared to tell him who he was.
This done, he went on shipboard, and is now
A Seaman, a grey-headed Mariner.
                                        1800.

II.
ARTEGAL AND ELIDURE.

(SEE THE CHRONICLE OF GEOFFREY OF MONMOUTH AND MILTON'S
HISTORY OF ENGLAND.)

Where be the temples which, in Britain's Isle,
For his paternal Gods, the Trojan raised?
Gone like a morning dream, or like a pile
Of clouds that in cerulean ether blazed!
Ere Julius landed on her white-cliffed shore,
    They sank, delivered o'er
To fatal dissolution; and, I ween,
No vestige then was left that such had ever been.

Nathless, a British record (long concealed
In old Armorica, whose secret springs
No Gothic conqueror ever drank) revealed
The marvellous current of forgotten things;
How Brutus came, by oracles impelled,
    And Albion's giants quelled,
A brood whom no civility could melt,
"Who never tasted grace, and goodness ne'er had felt."

By brave Corineus aided, he subdued,
And rooted out the intolerable kind;
And this too-long-polluted land imbued
With goodly arts and usages refined;
Whence golden harvests, cities, warlike towers,
    And pleasure's sumptuous bowers;
Whence all the fixed delights of house and home,
Friendships that will not break, and love that cannot roam.

O, happy Britain! region all too fair
For self-delighting fancy to endure
That silence only should inhabit there,
Wild beasts, or uncouth savages impure!

But, intermingled with the generous seed,
    Grew many a poisonous weed;
Thus fares it still with all that takes its birth
From human care, or grows upon the breast of earth.

Hence, and how soon! that war of vengeance waged
By Guendolen against her faithless lord;
Till she, in jealous fury unassuaged
Had slain his paramour with ruthless sword:
Then, into Severn hideously defiled,
    She flung her blameless child,
Sabrina, — vowing that the stream should bear
That name through every age, her hatred to declare.

So speaks the Chronicle, and tells of Lear
By his ungrateful daughters turned adrift.
Ye lightnings, hear his voice! — they cannot hear,
Nor can the winds restore his simple gift.
But One there is, a Child of nature meek,
    Who comes her Sire to seek;
And he, recovering sense, upon her breast
Leans smilingly, and sinks into a perfect rest.

There too we read of Spenser's fairy themes,
And those that Milton loved in youthful years;
The sage enchanter Merlin's subtle schemes;
The feats of Arthur and his knightly peers;
Of Arthur, — who, to upper light restored,
    With that terrific sword
Which yet he brandishes for future war,
Shall lift his country's fame above the polar star!

What wonder, then, if in such ample field
Of old tradition, one particular flower
Doth seemingly in vain its fragrance yield,
And bloom unnoticed even to this late hour?
Now, gentle Muses, your assistance grant,
    While I this flower transplant

Into a garden stored with Poesy;
Where flowers and herbs unite, and haply some weeds be,
That, wanting not wild grace, are from all mischief free!

 A KING more worthy of respect and love
Than wise Gorbonian ruled not in his day;
And grateful Britain prospered far above
All neighbouring countries through his righteous sway;
He poured rewards and honours on the good;
  The oppressor he withstood;
And while he served the Gods with reverence due,
Fields smiled, and temples rose, and towns and cities grew.

He died, whom Artegal succeeds — his son;
But how unworthy of that sire was he!
A hopeful reign, auspiciously begun,
Was darkened soon by foul iniquity.
From crime to crime he mounted, till at length
  The nobles leagued their strength
With a vexed people, and the tyrant chased;
And, on the vacant throne, his worthier Brother placed.

From realm to realm the humbled Exile went,
Suppliant for aid his kingdom to regain;
In many a court, and many a warrior's tent,
He urged his persevering suit in vain.
Him, in whose wretched heart ambition failed,
  Dire poverty assailed;
And, tired with slights his pride no more could brook,
He towards his native country cast a longing look.

Fair blew the wished-for wind — the voyage sped;
He landed; and, by many dangers scared,
"Poorly provided, poorly followèd,"
To Calaterium's forest he repaired.
How changed from him who, born to highest place,
  Had swayed the royal mace,
Flattered and feared, despised yet deified,
In Troynovant, his seat by silver Thames's side!

From that wild region where the crownless King
Lay in concealment with his scanty train,
Supporting life by water from the spring
And such chance food as outlaws can obtain,
Unto the few whom he esteems his friends
    A messenger he sends;
And from their secret loyalty requires
Shelter and daily bread, — the sum of his desires.

While he the issue waits, at early morn
Wandering by stealth abroad, he chanced to hear
A startling outcry made by hound and horn,
From which the tusky wild boar flies in fear;
And, scouring toward him o'er the grassy plain,
    Behold the hunter train!
He bids his little company advance
With seeming unconcern and steady countenance.

The royal Elidure, who leads the chase,
Hath checked his foaming courser: — can it be!
Methinks that I should recognise that face,
Though much disguised by long adversity!
He gazed rejoicing, and again he gazed,
    Confounded and amazed —
"It is the king, my brother!" and, by sound
Of his own voice confirmed, he leaps upon the ground.

Long, strict, and tender was the embrace he gave,
Feebly returned by daunted Artegal;
Whose natural affection doubts enslave,
And apprehensions dark and criminal.
Loth to restrain the moving interview,
    The attendant lords withdrew;
And, while they stood upon the plain apart,
Thus Elidure, by words, relieved his struggling heart.

"By heavenly Powers conducted, we have met;
— O Brother! to my knowledge lost so long,
But neither lost to love, nor to regret,
Nor to my wishes lost; — forgive the wrong,

(Such it may seem) if I thy crown have borne,
  Thy royal mantle worn:
I was their natural guardian; and 'tis just
That now I should restore what hath been held in trust."

A while the astonished Artegal stood mute,
Then thus exclaimed: "To me, of titles shorn,
And stripped of power! me, feeble, destitute,
To me a kingdom! spare the bitter scorn:
If justice ruled the breast of foreign kings,
  Then, on the wide-spread wings
Of war, had I returned to claim my right;
This will I here avow, not dreading thy despite."

"I do not blame thee," Elidure replied;
"But, if my looks did with my words agree,
I should at once be trusted, not defied,
And thou from all disquietude be free.
May the unsullied Goddess of the chase,
  Who to this blessed place
At this blest moment led me, if I speak
With insincere intent, on me her vengeance wreak!

Were this same spear, which in my hand I grasp,
The British sceptre, here would I to thee
The symbol yield; and would undo this clasp,
If it confined the robe of sovereignty.
Odious to me the pomp of regal court,
  And joyless sylvan sport,
While thou art roving, wretched and forlorn,
Thy couch the dewy earth, thy roof the forest thorn!"

Then Artegal thus spake: "I only sought,
Within this realm a place of safe retreat;
Beware of rousing an ambitious thought;
Beware of kindling hopes, for me unmeet!
Thou art reputed wise, but in my mind
  Art pitiably blind:

Full soon this generous purpose thou may'st rue,
When that which has been done no wishes can undo.

Who, when a crown is fixed upon his head,
Would balance claim with claim, and right with right?
But thou — I know not how inspired, how led —
Wouldst change the course of things in all men's sight!
And this for one who cannot imitate
    Thy virtue, who may hate:
For, if, by such strange sacrifice restored,
He reign, thou still must be his king, and sovereign lord;

Lifted in magnanimity above
Aught that my feeble nature could perform,
Or even conceive; surpassing me in love
Far as in power the eagle doth the worm:
I, Brother! only should be king in name,
    And govern to my shame;
A shadow in a hated land, while all
Of glad or willing service to thy share would fall."

"Believe it not," said Elidure; "respect
Awaits on virtuous life, and ever most
Attends on goodness with dominion decked,
Which stands the universal empire's boast;
This can thy own experience testify:
    Nor shall thy foes deny
That, in the gracious opening of thy reign,
Our father's spirit seemed in thee to breathe again.

And what if o'er that bright unbosoming
Clouds of disgrace and envious fortune past!
Have we not seen the glories of the spring
By veil of noontide darkness overcast?
The frith that glittered like a warrior's shield,
    The sky, the gay green field,
Are vanished; gladness ceases in the groves,
And trepidation strikes the blackened mountain-coves.

ARTEGAL AND ELIDURE.

But is that gloom dissolved? how passing clear
Seems the wide world, far brighter than before!
Even so thy latent worth will re-appear,
Gladdening the people's heart from shore to shore;
For youthful faults ripe virtues shall atone;
    Re-seated on thy throne,
Proof shalt thou furnish that misfortune, pain,
And sorrow, have confirmed thy native right to reign.

But, not to overlook what thou may'st know,
Thy enemies are neither weak nor few;
And circumspect must be our course, and slow,
Or from my purpose ruin may ensue.
Dismiss thy followers; — let them calmly wait
    Such change in thy estate
As I already have in thought devised;
And which, with caution due, may soon be realised."

The Story tells what courses were pursued,
Until king Elidure, with full consent
Of all his peers, before the multitude,
Rose, — and, to consummate this just intent,
Did place upon his brother's head the crown,
    Relinquished by his own;
Then to his people cried, "Receive your lord,
Gorbonian's first-born son, your rightful king restored!"

The people answered with a loud acclaim:
Yet more; — heart-smitten by the heroic deed,
The reinstated Artegal became
Earth's noblest penitent; from bondage freed
Of vice — thenceforth unable to subvert
    Or shake his high desert.
Long did he reign; and, when he died, the tear
Of universal grief bedewed his honoured bier.

Thus was a Brother by a Brother saved;
With whom a crown (temptation that hath set
Discord in hearts of men till they have braved
Their nearest kin with deadly purpose met)

'Gainst duty weighed, and faithful love, did seem
    A thing of no esteem;
And, from this triumph of affection pure,
He bore the lasting name of "pious Elidure!"

1815.

III.
A FAREWELL.

Farewell, thou little Nook of mountain-ground,
Thou rocky corner in the lowest stair
Of that magnificent temple which doth bound
One side of our whole vale with grandeur rare;
Sweet garden-orchard, eminently fair,
The loveliest spot that man hath ever found,
Farewell! — we leave thee to Heaven's peaceful care,
Thee, and the Cottage which thou dost surround.

Our boat is safely anchored by the shore,
And there will safely ride when we are gone;
The flowering shrubs that deck our humble door
Will prosper, though untended and alone:
Fields, goods, and far-off chattels we have none:
These narrow bounds contain our private store
Of things earth makes, and sun doth shine upon;
Here are they in our sight — we have no more.

Sunshine and shower be with you, bud and bell!
For two months now in vain we shall be sought;
We leave you here in solitude to dwell
With these our latest gifts of tender thought;
Thou, like the morning, in thy saffron coat,
Bright gowan, and marsh-marigold, farewell!
Whom from the borders of the Lake we brought,
And placed together near our rocky Well.

We go for One to whom ye will be dear;
And she will prize this Bower, this Indian shed,
Our own contrivance, Building without peer!
— A gentle Maid, whose heart is lowly bred,

A FAREWELL.

Whose pleasures are in wild fields gatherèd,
With joyousness, and with a thoughtful cheer,
Will come to you; to you herself will wed;
And love the blessed life that we lead here.

Dear Spot! which we have watched with tender heed,
Bringing thee chosen plants and blossoms blown
Among the distant mountains, flower and weed,
Which thou hast taken to thee as thy own,
Making all kindness registered and known;
Thou for our sakes, though Nature's child indeed,
Fair in thyself and beautiful alone,
Hast taken gifts which thou dost little need.

And O most constant, yet most fickle Place,
That hast thy wayward moods, as thou dost show
To them who look not daily on thy face;
Who, being loved, in love no bounds dost know,
And say'st, when we forsake thee, "Let them go!"
Thou easy-hearted Thing, with thy wild race
Of weeds and flowers, till we return be slow,
And travel with the year at a soft pace.

Help us to tell Her tales of years gone by,
And this sweet spring, the best beloved and best;
Joy will be flown in its mortality;
Something must stay to tell us of the rest.
Here, thronged with primroses, the steep rock's breast
Glittered at evening like a starry sky;
And in this bush our sparrow built her nest,
Of which I sang one song that will not die.

O happy Garden! whose seclusion deep
Hath been so friendly to industrious hours;
And to soft slumbers, that did gently steep
Our spirits, carrying with them dreams of flowers,
And wild notes warbled among leafy bowers;
Two burning months let summer overleap,
And, coming back with Her who will be ours,
Into thy bosom we again shall creep.

1802.

IV.

STANZAS

WRITTEN IN MY POCKET-COPY OF THOMSON'S CASTLE OF INDOLENCE.

Within our happy Castle there dwelt One
Whom without blame I may not overlook;
For never sun on living creature shone
Who more devout enjoyment with us took:
Here on his hours he hung as on a book,
On his own time here would he float away,
As doth a fly upon a summer brook;
But go to-morrow, or belike to-day,
Seek for him, — he is fled; and whither none can say.

Thus often would he leave our peaceful home,
And find elsewhere his business or delight;
Out of our Valley's limits did he roam:
Full many a time, upon a stormy night,
His voice came to us from the neighbouring height:
Oft could we see him driving full in view
At mid day when the sun was shining bright;
What ill was on him, what he had to do,
A mighty wonder bred among our quiet crew.

Ah! piteous sight it was to see this Man
When he came back to us, a withered flower, —
Or like a sinful creature, pale and wan.
Down would he sit; and without strength or power
Look at the common grass from hour to hour:
And oftentimes, how long I fear to say,
Where apple-trees in blossom made a bower,
Retired in that sunshiny shade he lay;
And, like a naked Indian, slept himself away.

STANZAS.

Great wonder to our gentle tribe it was
Whenever from our Valley he withdrew;
For happier soul no living creature has
Than he had, being here the long day through.
Some thought he was a lover, and did woo:
Some thought far worse of him, and judged him wrong;
But verse was what he had been wedded to;
And his own mind did like a tempest strong
Come to him thus, and drove the weary Wight along.

With him there often walked in friendly guise,
Or lay upon the moss by brook or tree,
A noticeable Man with large grey eyes,
And a pale face that seemed undoubtedly
As if a blooming face it ought to be;
Heavy his low-hung lip did oft appear,
Deprest by weight of musing Phantasy;
Profound his forehead was, though not severe;
Yet some did think that he had little business here:

Sweet heaven forefend! his was a lawful right;
Noisy he was, and gamesome as a boy;
His limbs would toss about him with delight
Like branches when strong winds the trees annoy.
Nor lacked his calmer hours device or toy
To banish listlessness and irksome care;
He would have taught you how you might employ
Yourself; and many did to him repair, —
And certes not in vain; he had inventions rare.

Expedients, too, of simplest sort he tried:
Long blades of grass, plucked round him as he lay,
Made, to his ear attentively applied,
A pipe on which the wind would deftly play;
Glasses he had, that little things display,
The beetle panoplied in gems and gold,
A mailèd angel on a battle-day;
The mysteries that cups of flowers enfold,
And all the gorgeous sights which fairies do behold.

He would entice that other Man to hear
His music, and to view his imagery:
And, sooth, these two were each to the other dear:
No livelier love in such a place could be:
There did they dwell — from earthly labour free,
As happy spirits as were ever seen;
If but a bird, to keep them company,
Or butterfly sate down, they were, I ween,
As pleased as if the same had been a Maiden-queen.
1802.

V.
LOUISA.
AFTER ACCOMPANYING HER ON A MOUNTAIN EXCURSION.

I met Louisa in the shade,
And, having seen that lovely Maid,
Why should I fear to say
That, nymph-like, she is fleet and strong,
And down the rocks can leap along
Like rivulets in May?

She loves her fire, her cottage-home;
Yet o'er the moorland will she roam
In weather rough and bleak;
And, when against the wind she strains,
Oh! might I kiss the mountain rains
That sparkle on her cheek.

Take all that's mine "beneath the moon,"
If I with her but half a noon
May sit beneath the walls
Of some old cave, or mossy nook,
When up she winds along the brook
To hunt the waterfalls.
1805.

VI.

Strange fits of passion have I known:
And I will dare to tell,
But in the Lover's ear alone,
What once to me befel.

When she I loved looked every day
Fresh as a rose in June,
I to her cottage bent my way,
Beneath an evening moon.

Upon the moon I fixed my eye,
All over the wide lea;
With quickening pace my horse drew nigh
Those paths so dear to me.

And now we reached the orchard-plot;
And, as we climbed the hill,
The sinking moon to Lucy's cot
Came near, and nearer still.

In one of those sweet dreams I slept,
Kind Nature's gentlest boon!
And all the while my eyes I kept
On the descending moon.

My horse moved on; hoof after hoof
He raised, and never stopped:
When down behind the cottage roof,
At once, the bright moon dropped.

What fond and wayward thoughts will slide
Into a Lover's head!
"O mercy!" to myself I cried,
"If Lucy should be dead!"

1799.

VII.

She dwelt among the untrodden ways
  Beside the springs of Dove,
A Maid whom there were none to praise
  And very few to love;

A violet by a mossy stone
  Half hidden from the eye!
— Fair as a star, when only one
  Is shining in the sky.

She lived unknown, and few could know
  When Lucy ceased to be;
But she is in her grave, and, oh,
  The difference to me!   1709.

VIII.

I travelled among unknown men,
  In lands beyond the sea;
Nor, England! did I know till then
  What love I bore to thee.

'Tis past, that melancholy dream!
  Nor will I quit thy shore
A second time; for still I seem
  To love thee more and more.

Among thy mountains did I feel
  The joy of my desire;
And she I cherished turned her wheel
  Beside an English fire.

Thy mornings showed, thy nights concealed
  The bowers where Lucy played;
And thine too is the last green field
  That Lucy's eyes surveyed.   1799.

IX.

Ere with cold beads of midnight dew
  Had mingled tears of thine,
I grieved, fond Youth! that thou shouldst sue
  To haughty Geraldine.

Immoveable by generous sighs,
  She glories in a train
Who drag, beneath our native skies,
  An oriental chain.

Pine not like them with arms across,
  Forgetting in thy care
How the fast-rooted trees can toss
  Their branches in mid air.

The humblest rivulet will take
  Its own wild liberties;
And, every day, the imprisoned lake
  Is flowing in the breeze.

Then, crouch no more on suppliant knee,
  But scorn with scorn outbrave;
A Briton, even in love, should be
  A subject, not a slave!

                                1826.

X.
TO ——

Look at the fate of summer flowers,
Which blow at daybreak, droop ere even-song;
And, grieved for their brief date, confess that ours,
Measured by what we are and ought to be,
Measured by all that, trembling, we foresee,
    Is not so long!

If human Life do pass away,
Perishing yet more swiftly than the flower,
If we are creatures of a *winter's* day;
What space hath Virgin's beauty to disclose
Her sweets, and triumph o'er the breathing rose?
  Not even an hour!

The deepest grove whose foliage hid
The happiest lovers Arcady might boast,
Could not the entrance of this thought forbid:
O be thou wise as they, soul-gifted Maid!
Nor rate too high what must so quickly fade,
  So soon be lost.

Then shall love teach some virtuous Youth
"To draw, out of the object of his eyes,"
The while on thee they gaze in simple truth,
Hues more exalted, "a refinèd Form,"
That dreads not age, nor suffers from the worm,
  And never dies.

            1824.

XI.
THE FORSAKEN.

The peace which others seek they find;
The heaviest storms not longest last;
Heaven grants even to the guiltiest mind
An amnesty for what is past;
When will my sentence be reversed?
I only pray to know the worst;
And wish as if my heart would burst.

O weary struggle! silent years
Tell seemingly no doubtful tale;
And yet they leave it short, and fears
And hopes are strong and will prevail.
My calmest faith escapes not pain;
And, feeling that the hope is vain,
I think that he will come again.

XII.

'Tis said, that some have died for love:
And here and there a church-yard grave is found
In the cold north's unhallowed ground,
Because the wretched man himself had slain,
His love was such a grievous pain.
And there is one whom I five years have known;
He dwells alone
Upon Helvellyn's side:
He loved — the pretty Barbara died;
And thus he makes his moan:
Three years had Barbara in her grave been laid
When thus his moan he made:

"Oh, move, thou Cottage, from behind that oak!
Or let the aged tree uprooted lie,
That in some other way yon smoke
May mount into the sky!
The clouds pass on; they from the heavens depart:
I look — the sky is empty space;
I know not what I trace;
But when I cease to look, my hand is on my heart.

O! what a weight is in these shades! Ye leaves,
That murmur once so dear, when will it cease?
Your sound my heart of rest bereaves,
It robs my heart of peace.
Thou Thrush, that singest loud — and loud and free,
Into yon row of willows flit,
Upon that alder sit;
Or sing another song, or choose another tree.

Roll back, sweet Rill! back to thy mountain-bounds,
And there for ever be thy waters chained!
For thou dost haunt the air with sounds
That cannot be sustained;

If still beneath that pine-tree's ragged bough
Headlong yon waterfall must come,
Oh let it then be dumb!
Be anything, sweet Rill, but that which thou art now.

Thou Eglantine, so bright with sunny showers,
Proud as a rainbow spanning half the vale,
Thou one fair shrub, oh! shed thy flowers,
And stir not in the gale.
For thus to see thee nodding in the air,
To see thy arch thus stretch and bend,
Thus rise and thus descend, —
Disturbs me till the sight is more than I can bear."

The Man who makes this feverish complaint
Is one of giant stature, who could dance
Equipped from head to foot in iron mail.
Ah gentle Love! if ever thought was thine
To store up kindred hours for me, thy face
Turn from me, gentle Love! nor let me walk
Within the sound of Emma's voice, nor know
Such happiness as I have known to-day.

1800.

XIII.
A COMPLAINT.

There is a change — and I am poor;
Your love hath been, nor long ago,
A fountain at my fond heart's door,
Whose only business was to flow;
And flow it did; not taking heed
Of its own bounty, or my need.

What happy moments did I count!
Blest was I then all bliss above!
Now, for that consecrated fount
Of murmuring, sparkling, living love,

What have I? shall I dare to tell?
A comfortless and hidden well.

A well of love — it may be deep —
I trust it is, — and never dry:
What matter? if the waters sleep
In silence and obscurity.
— Such change, and at the very door
Of my fond heart, hath made me poor.

1806.

XIV.

To ——

Let other bards of angels sing,
   Bright suns without a spot;
But thou art no such perfect thing:
   Rejoice that thou art not!

Heed not tho' none should call thee fair;
   So, Mary, let it be
If nought in loveliness compare
   With what thou art to me.

True beauty dwells in deep retreats,
   Whose veil is unremoved
Till heart with heart in concord beats,
   And the lover is beloved.

1824.

XV.

Yes! thou art fair, yet be not moved
   To scorn the declaration,
That sometimes I in thee have loved
   My fancy's own creation.

Imagination needs must stir;
   Dear Maid, this truth believe,
Minds that have nothing to confer
   Find little to perceive.

  Be pleased that nature made thee fit
   To feed my heart's devotion,
  By laws to which all Forms submit
   In sky, air, earth, and ocean.

XVI.

How rich that forehead's calm expanse!
How bright that heaven-directed glance!
— Waft her to glory, wingèd Powers,
 Ere sorrow be renewed,
And intercourse with mortal hours
 Bring back a humbler mood!
So looked Cecilia when she drew
 An Angel from his station;
So looked; not ceasing to pursue
 Her tuneful adoration!

But hand and voice alike are still;
No sound *here* sweeps away the will
That gave it birth: in service meek
One upright arm sustains the cheek,
And one across the bosom lies —
That rose, and now forgets to rise,
Subdued by breathless harmonies
Of meditative feeling;
Mute strains from worlds beyond the skies,
Through the pure light of female eyes,
Their sanctity revealing!

          1824.

XVII.

WHAT heavenly smiles! O Lady mine
Through my very heart they shine;
And, if my brow gives back their light,
Do thou look gladly on the sight;

As the clear Moon with modest pride
Beholds her own bright beams
Reflected from the mountain's side
And from the headlong streams.

XVIII.
To ——

O DEARER far than light and life are dear,
Full oft our human foresight I deplore;
Trembling, through my unworthiness, with fear
That friends, by death disjoined, may meet no more!

Misgivings, hard to vanquish or control,
Mix with the day, and cross the hour of rest;
While all the future, for thy purer soul,
With "sober certainties" of love is blest.

That sigh of thine, not meant for human ear,
Tells that these words thy humbleness offend;
Yet bear me up — else faltering in the rear
Of a steep march: support me to the end.

Peace settles where the intellect is meek,
And Love is dutiful in thought and deed;
Through Thee communion with that Love I seek:
The faith Heaven strengthens where *he* moulds the Creed.

1824.

XIX.
LAMENT OF MARY QUEEN OF SCOTS.
ON THE EVE OF A NEW YEAR.

1.

SMILE of the Moon! — for so I name
That silent greeting from above
A gentle flash of light that came
From her whom drooping captives love;
Or art thou of still higher birth?
Thou that didst part the clouds of earth,
My torpor to reprove!

II.

Bright boon of pitying Heaven! — alas,
I may not trust thy placid cheer!
Pondering that Time to-night will pass
The threshold of another year;
For years to me are sad and dull;
My very moments are too full
Of hopelessness and fear.

III.

And yet, the soul-awakening gleam,
That struck perchance the farthest cone
Of Scotland's rocky wilds, did seem
To visit me, and me alone;
Me, unapproached by any friend,
Save those who to my sorrows lend
Tears due unto their own.

IV.

To-night the church-tower bells will ring
Through these wide realms a festive peal;
To the new year a welcoming;
A tuneful offering for the weal
Of happy millions lulled in sleep;
While I am forced to watch and weep,
By wounds that may not heal.

V.

Born all too high, by wedlock raised
Still higher — to be cast thus low!
Would that mine eyes had never gazed
On aught of more ambitious show
Than the sweet flowerets of the fields!
— It is my royal state that yields
This bitterness of woe.

VI.

Yet how? — for I, if there be truth
In the world's voice, was passing fair;
And beauty, for confiding youth,
Those shocks of passion can prepare
That kill the bloom before its time;
And blanch, without the owner's crime,
The most resplendent hair.

VII.

Unblest distinction! showered on me
To bind a lingering life in chains:
All that could quit my grasp, or flee,
Is gone; — but not the subtle stains
Fixed in the spirit; for even here
Can I be proud that jealous fear
Of what I was remains.

VIII.

A woman rules my prison's key;
A sister Queen, against the bent
Of law and holiest sympathy,
Detains me, doubtful of the event;
Great God, who feel'st for my distress,
My thoughts are all that I possess,
O keep them innocent!

IX.

Farewell desire of human aid,
Which abject mortals vainly court!
By friends deceived, by foes betrayed,
Of fears the prey, of hopes the sport;
Nought but the world-redeeming Cross
Is able to supply my loss,
My burthen to support.

X.

Hark! the death-note of the year
Sounded by the castle-clock!
From her sunk eyes a stagnant tear
Stole forth, unsettled by the shock;
But oft the woods renewed their green,
Ere the tired head of Scotland's Queen
Reposed upon the block!

1817.

XX.

THE COMPLAINT

OF A FORSAKEN INDIAN WOMAN.

[When a Northern Indian, from sickness, is unable to continue his journey with his companions, he is left behind, covered over with deer-skins, and is supplied with water, food, and fuel, if the situation of the place will afford it. He is informed of the track which his companions intend to pursue, and if he be unable to follow, or overtake them, he perishes alone in the desert; unless he should have the good fortune to fall in with some other tribes of Indians. The females are equally, or still more, exposed to the same fate. See that very interesting work HEARNE'S JOURNEY from HUDSON'S BAY to the NORTHERN OCEAN. In the high northern latitudes, as the same writer informs us, when the northern lights vary their position in the air, they make a rustling and a crackling noise, as alluded to in the following poem.]

I.

BEFORE I see another day,
Oh let my body die away!
In sleep I heard the northern gleams;
The stars, they were among my dreams;
In rustling conflict through the skies,
I heard, I saw the flashes drive,
And yet they are upon my eyes,
And yet I am alive;
Before I see another day,
Oh let my body die away!

II.

My fire is dead: it knew no pain;
Yet is it dead, and I remain:
All stiff with ice the ashes lie;
And they are dead, and I will die.
When I was well, I wished to live,
For clothes, for warmth, for food, and fire;
But they to me no joy can give,
No pleasure now, and no desire.
Then here contented will I lie!
Alone, I cannot fear to die.

III.

Alas! ye might have dragged me on
Another day, a single one!
Too soon I yielded to despair;
Why did ye listen to my prayer?
When ye were gone my limbs were stronger;
And oh, how grievously I rue,
That, afterwards, a little longer,
My friends, I did not follow you!
For strong and without pain I lay,
Dear friends, when ye were gone away.

IV.

My Child! they gave thee to another,
A woman who was not thy mother.
When from my arms my Babe they took,
On me how strangely did he look!
Through his whole body something ran,
A most strange working did I see;
— As if he strove to be a man,
That he might pull the sledge for me:
And then he stretched his arms, how wild!
Oh mercy! like a helpless child.

V.

My little joy! my little pride!
In two days more I must have died.
Then do not weep and grieve for me;
I feel I must have died with thee.
O wind, that o'er my head art flying
The way my friends their course did bend,
I should not feel the pain of dying,
Could I with thee a message send;
Too soon, my friends, ye went away;
For I had many things to say.

VI.

I'll follow you across the snow;
Ye travel heavily and slow;
In spite of all my weary pain
I'll look upon your tents again.
— My fire is dead, and snowy white
The water which beside it stood:
The wolf has come to me to-night,
And he has stolen away my food.
For ever left alone am I;
Then wherefore should I fear to die?

VII.

Young as I am, my course is run,
I shall not see another sun;
I cannot lift my limbs to know
If they have any life or no.
My poor forsaken Child, if I
For once could have thee close to me,
With happy heart I then would die,
And my last thought would happy be;
But thou, dear Babe, art far away,
Nor shall I see another day.

1798.

XXI.
THE LAST OF THE FLOCK.

I.

In distant countries have I been,
And yet I have not often seen
A healthy man, a man full grown,
Weep in the public roads, alone.
But such a one, on English ground,
And in the broad highway, I met;
Along the broad highway he came,
His cheeks with tears were wet:
Sturdy he seemed, though he was sad;
And in his arms a Lamb he had.

II.

He saw me, and he turned aside,
As if he wished himself to hide:
And with his coat did then essay
To wipe those briny tears away.
I followed him, and said, "My friend,
What ails you? wherefore weep you so?"
—"Shame on me, Sir! this lusty Lamb,
He makes my tears to flow.
To-day I fetched him from the rock:
He is the last of all my flock.

III.

When I was young, a single man,
And after youthful follies ran,
Though little given to care and thought,
Yet, so it was, an ewe I bought;
And other sheep from her I raised,
As healthy sheep as you might see;
And then I married, and was rich
As I could wish to be;

Of sheep I numbered a full score,
And every year increased my store.

IV.

Year after year my stock it grew;
And from this one, this single ewe,
Full fifty comely sheep I raised,
As fine a flock as ever grazed!
Upon the Quantock hills they fed;
They throve, and we at home did thrive:
— This lusty Lamb of all my store
Is all that is alive;
And now I care not if we die,
And perish all of poverty.

V.

Six Children, Sir! had I to feed;
Hard labour in a time of need!
My pride was tamed, and in our grief
I of the Parish asked relief.
They said, I was a wealthy man;
My sheep upon the uplands fed,
And it was fit that thence I took
Whereof to buy us bread.
"Do this: how can we give to you,"
They cried, "what to the poor is due?"

VI.

I sold a sheep, as they had said,
And bought my little children bread,
And they were healthy with their food;
For me — it never did me good.
A woeful time it was for me,
To see the end of all my gains,
The pretty flock which I had reared
With all my care and pains,
To see it melt like snow away —
For me it was a woeful day.

VII.

Another still! and still another!
A little lamb, and then its mother!
It was a vein that never stopped —
Like blood-drops from my heart they dropped.
'Till thirty were not left alive
They dwindled, dwindled, one by one;
And I may say, that many a time
I wished they all were gone —
Reckless of what might come at last
Were but the bitter struggle past.

VIII.

To wicked deeds I was inclined,
And wicked fancies crossed my mind;
And every man I chanced to see,
I thought he knew some ill of me:
No peace, no comfort could I find,
No ease, within doors or without;
And, crazily and wearily
I went my work about;
And oft was moved to flee from home,
And hide my head where wild beasts roam.

IX.

Sir! 'twas a precious flock to me,
As dear as my own children be;
For daily with my growing store
I loved my children more and more.
Alas! it was an evil time;
God cursed me in my sore distress;
I prayed, yet every day I thought
I loved my children less;
And every week, and every day,
My flock it seemed to melt away.

X.

They dwindled, Sir, sad sight to see!
From ten to five, from five to three,

>   A lamb, a wether, and a ewe; —
>   And then at last from three to two;
>   And, of my fifty, yesterday
>   I had but only one:
>   And here it lies upon my arm,
>   Alas! and I have none; —
>   To-day I fetched it from the rock;
>   It is the last of all my flock."

1798.

XXII.
REPENTANCE.
A PASTORAL BALLAD.

The fields which with covetous spirit we sold,
Those beautiful fields, the delight of the day,
Would have brought us more good than a burthen of gold,
Could we but have been as contented as they.

When the troublesome Tempter beset us, said I,
"Let him come, with his purse proudly grasped in his hand;
But, Allan, be true to me, Allan, — we'll die
Before he shall go with an inch of the land!"

There dwelt we, as happy as birds in their bowers;
Unfettered as bees that in gardens abide;
We could do what we liked with the land, it was ours;
And for us the brook murmured that ran by its side.

But now we are strangers, go early or late;
And often, like one overburthened with sin,
With my hand on the latch of the half-opened gate,
I look at the fields, but I cannot go in!

When I walk by the hedge on a bright summer's day,
Or sit in the shade of my grandfather's tree,
A stern face it puts on, as if ready to say,
"What ails you, that you must come creeping to me!"

With our pastures about us, we could not be sad;
Our comfort was near if we ever were crost;
But the comfort, the blessings, and wealth that we had,
We slighted them all, — and our birth-right was lost.

Oh, ill-judging sire of an innocent son
Who must now be a wanderer! but peace to that strain!
Think of evening's repose when our labour was done,
The sabbath's return, and its leisure's soft chain!

And in sickness, if night had been sparing of sleep,
How cheerful, at sunrise, the hill where I stood,
Looking down on the kine, and our treasure of sheep
That besprinkled the field; 'twas like youth in my blood!

Now I cleave to the house, and am dull as a snail;
And, oftentimes, hear the church-bell with a sigh,
That follows the thought — We've no land in the vale,
Save six feet of earth where our forefathers lie!

1804.

XXIII.
THE AFFLICTION OF MARGARET —.

I.

Where art thou, my beloved Son,
Where art thou, worse to me than dead?
Oh find me, prosperous or undone!
Or, if the grave be now thy bed,
Why am I ignorant of the same,
That I may rest; and neither blame
Nor sorrow may attend thy name?

II.

Seven years, alas! to have received
No tidings of an only child;
To have despaired, have hoped, believed,
And been for evermore beguiled;

Sometimes with thoughts of very bliss!
I catch at them, and then I miss;
Was ever darkness like to this?

III.

He was among the prime in worth,
An object beauteous to behold;
Well born, well bred; I sent him forth
Ingenuous, innocent, and bold:
If things ensued that wanted grace,
As hath been said, they were not base;
And never blush was on my face.

IV.

Ah! little doth the young-one dream,
When full of play and childish cares,
What power is in his wildest scream,
Heard by his mother unawares!
He knows it not, he cannot guess:
Years to a mother bring distress;
But do not make her love the less.

V.

Neglect me! no, I suffered long
From that ill thought; and, being blind,
Said, "Pride shall help me in my wrong:
Kind mother have I been, as kind
As ever breathed:" and that is true;
I've wet my path with tears like dew,
Weeping for him when no one knew.

VI.

My Son, if thou be humbled, poor,
Hopeless of honour and of gain,
Oh! do not dread thy mother's door;
Think not of me with grief and pain:
I now can see with better eyes;
And worldly grandeur I despise,
And fortune with her gifts and lies.

THE AFFLICTION OF MARGARET.

VII.

Alas! the fowls of heaven have wings,
And blasts of heaven will aid their flight;
They mount — how short a voyage brings
The wanderers back to their delight!
Chains tie us down by land and sea;
And wishes, vain as mine, may be
All that is left to comfort thee.

VIII.

Perhaps some dungeon hears thee groan,
Maimed, mangled by inhuman men;
Or thou upon a desert thrown
Inheritest the lion's den;
Or hast been summoned to the deep,
Thou, thou and all thy mates, to keep
An incommunicable sleep.

IX.

I look for ghosts; but none will force
Their way to me: 'tis falsely said
That there was ever intercourse
Between the living and the dead;
For, surely, then I should have sight
Of him I wait for day and night,
With love and longings infinite.

X.

My apprehensions come in crowds;
I dread the rustling of the grass;
The very shadows of the clouds
Have power to shake me as they pass:
I question things and do not find
One that will answer to my mind;
And all the world appears unkind.

XI.

Beyond participation lie
My troubles, and beyond relief:
If any chance to heave a sigh,
They pity me, and not my grief.
Then come to me, my Son, or send
Some tidings that my woes may end;
I have no other earthly friend!

1804.

XXIV.
MATERNAL GRIEF.

Departed Child! I could forget thee once
Though at my bosom nursed; this woeful gain
Thy dissolution brings, that in my soul
Is present and perpetually abides
A shadow, never, never to be displaced
By the returning substance, seen or touched,
Seen by mine eyes, or clasped in my embrace.
Absence and death how differ they! and how
Shall I admit that nothing can restore
What one short sigh so easily removed? —
Death, life, and sleep, reality and thought,
Assist me, God, their boundaries to know,
O teach me calm submission to thy Will!

   The Child she mourned had overstepped the pale
Of infancy, but still did breathe the air
That sanctifies its confines, and partook
Reflected beams of that celestial light
To all the Little-ones on sinful earth
Not unvouchsafed — a light that warmed and cheered
Those several qualities of heart and mind
Which, in her own blest nature, rooted deep,
Daily before the Mother's watchful eye,

And not hers only, their peculiar charms
Unfolded, — beauty, for its present self,
And for its promises to future years,
With not unfrequent rapture fondly hailed.

  Have you espied upon a dewy lawn
A pair of Leverets each provoking each
To a continuance of their fearless sport,
Two separate Creatures in their several gifts
Abounding, but so fashioned that, in all
That Nature prompts them to display, their looks,
Their starts of motion and their fits of rest,
An undistinguishable style appears
And character of gladness, as if Spring
Lodged in their innocent bosoms, and the spirit
Of the rejoicing morning were their own.

  Such union, in the lovely Girl maintained
And her twin Brother, had the parent seen,
Ere, pouncing like a ravenous bird of prey,
Death in a moment parted them, and left
The Mother, in her turns of anguish, worse
Than desolate; for oft-times from the sound
Of the survivor's sweetest voice (dear child,
He knew it not) and from his happiest looks,
Did she extract the food of self-reproach,
As one that lived ungrateful for the stay
By Heaven afforded to uphold her maimed
And tottering spirit. And full oft the Boy,
Now first acquainted with distress and grief,
Shrunk from his Mother's presence, shunned with fear
Her sad approach, and stole away to find,
In his known haunts of joy where'er he might,
A more congenial object. But, as time
Softened her pangs and reconciled the child
To what he saw, he gradually returned,
Like a scared Bird encouraged to renew

A broken intercourse; and, while his eyes
Were yet with pensive fear and gentle awe
Turned upon her who bore him, she would stoop
To imprint a kiss that lacked not power to spread
Faint colour over both their pallid cheeks,
And stilled his tremulous lip. Thus they were calmed
And cheered; and now together breathe fresh air
In open fields; and when the glare of day
Is gone, and twilight to the Mother's wish
Befriends the observance, readily they join
In walks whose boundary is the lost One's grave,
Which he with flowers hath planted, finding there
Amusement, where the Mother does not miss
Dear consolation, kneeling on the turf
In prayer, yet blending with that solemn rite
Of pious faith the vanities of grief;
For such, by pitying Angels and by Spirits
Transferred to regions upon which the clouds
Of our weak nature rest not, must be deemed
Those willing tears, and unforbidden sighs,
And all those tokens of a cherished sorrow,
Which, soothed and sweetened by the grace of Heaven
As now it is, seems to her own fond heart,
Immortal as the love that gave it being.

XXV.

THE SAILOR'S MOTHER.

One morning (raw it was and wet —
A foggy day in winter time)
A Woman on the road I met,
Not old, though something past her prime:
Majestic in her person, tall and straight;
And like a Roman matron's was her mien and gait.

THE SAILOR'S MOTHER.

The ancient spirit is not dead;
Old times, thought I, are breathing there;
Proud was I that my country bred
Such strength, a dignity so fair:
She begged an alms, like one in poor estate;
I looked at her again, nor did my pride abate.

When from these lofty thoughts I woke,
"What is it," said I, "that you bear,
Beneath the covert of your Cloak,
Protected from this cold damp air?"
She answered, soon as she the question heard,
"A simple burthen, Sir, a little Singing-bird."

And, thus continuing, she said,
"I had a Son, who many a day
Sailed on the seas, but he is dead;
In Denmark he was cast away:
And I have travelled weary miles to see
If aught which he had owned might still remain for me.

The bird and cage they both were his:
'Twas my Son's bird; and neat and trim
He kept it: many voyages
The singing-bird had gone with him;
When last he sailed, he left the bird behind;
From bodings, as might be, that hung upon his mind.

He to a fellow-lodger's care
Had left it, to be watched and fed,
And pipe its song in safety; — there
I found it when my Son was dead;
And now, God help me for my little wit!
I bear it with me, Sir; — he took so much delight in it."

1800.

XXVI.
THE CHILDLESS FATHER.

"Up, Timothy, up with your staff and away!
Not a soul in the village this morning will stay;
The hare has just started from Hamilton's grounds,
And Skiddaw is glad with the cry of the hounds."

— Of coats and of jackets grey, scarlet, and green,
On the slopes of the pastures all colours were seen;
With their comely blue aprons, and caps white as snow,
The girls on the hills made a holiday show.

Fresh sprigs of green box-wood, not six months before,
Filled the funeral basin* at Timothy's door;
A coffin through Timothy's threshold had past;
One Child did it bear, and that Child was his last.

Now fast up the dell came the noise and the fray,
The horse and the horn, and the hark! hark away!
Old Timothy took up his staff, and he shut
With a leisurely motion the door of his hut.

Perhaps to himself at that moment he said;
"The key I must take, for my Ellen is dead."
But of this in my ears not a word did he speak;
And he went to the chase with a tear on his cheek.   1800.

XXVII.
THE EMIGRANT MOTHER.

Once in a lonely hamlet I sojourned
In which a Lady driven from France did dwell;
The big and lesser griefs with which she mourned,
In friendship she to me would often tell.

* In several parts of the North of England, when a funeral takes place, a basin full of sprigs of box-wood is placed at the door of the house from which the coffin is taken up, and each person who attends the funeral ordinarily takes a sprig of this box-wood, and throws it into the grave of the deceased.

THE EMIGRANT MOTHER.

This Lady, dwelling upon British ground,
Where she was childless, daily would repair
To a poor neighbouring cottage; as I found,
For sake of a young Child whose home was there.

Once having seen her clasp with fond embrace
This Child, I chanted to myself a lay,
Endeavouring, in our English tongue, to trace
Such things as she unto the Babe might say:
And thus, from what I heard and knew, or guessed,
My song the workings of her heart expressed.

I.

"Dear Babe, thou daughter of another,
One moment let me be thy mother!
An infant's face and looks are thine
And sure a mother's heart is mine:
Thy own dear mother's far away,
At labour in the harvest field:
Thy little sister is at play; —
What warmth, what comfort would it yield
To my poor heart, if thou wouldst be
One little hour a child to me!

II.

Across the waters I am come,
And I have left a babe at home:
A long, long way of land and sea!
Come to me — I 'm no enemy:
I am the same who at thy side
Sate yesterday, and made a nest
For thee, sweet Baby! — thou hast tried,
Thou know'st the pillow of my breast;
Good, good art thou: — alas! to me
Far more than I can be to thee.

III.

Here, little Darling, dost thou lie;
An infant thou, a mother I!

Mine wilt thou be, thou hast no fears;
Mine art thou — spite of these my tears.
Alas! before I left the spot,
My baby and its dwelling-place,
The nurse said to me, 'Tears should not
Be shed upon an infant's face,
It was unlucky' — no, no, no;
No truth is in them who say so!

IV.

My own dear Little-one will sigh,
Sweet Babe! and they will let him die.
'He pines,' they 'll say, 'it is his doom,
And you may see his hour is come.'
Oh! had he but thy cheerful smiles,
Limbs stout as thine, and lips as gay,
Thy looks, thy cunning, and thy wiles,
And countenance like a summer's day,
They would have hopes of him; — and then
I should behold his face again!

V.

'Tis gone — like dreams that we forget;
There was a smile or two — yet — yet
I can remember them, I see
The smiles, worth all the world to me.
Dear Baby! I must lay thee down;
Thou troublest me with strange alarms;
Smiles hast thou, bright ones of thy own;
I cannot keep thee in my arms;
For they confound me; — where — where is
That last, that sweetest smile of his?

VI.

Oh! how I love thee! — we will stay
Together here this one half day.
My sister's child, who bears my name,
From France to sheltering England came;

She with her mother crossed the sea;
The babe and mother near me dwell:
Yet does my yearning heart to thee
Turn rather, though I love her well:
Rest, little Stranger, rest thee here!
Never was any child more dear!

VII.

— I cannot help it; ill intent
I've none, my pretty Innocent!
I weep — I know they do thee wrong,
These tears — and my poor idle tongue.
Oh, what a kiss was that! my cheek
How cold it is! but thou art good;
Thine eyes are on me — they would speak,
I think, to help me if they could.
Blessings upon that soft, warm face,
My heart again is in its place!

VIII.

While thou art mine, my little Love,
This cannot be a sorrowful grove;
Contentment, hope, and mother's glee,
I seem to find them all in thee:
Here's grass to play with, here are flowers;
I'll call thee by my darling's name;
Thou hast, I think, a look of ours,
Thy features seem to me the same;
His little sister thou shalt be;
And, when once more my home I see,
I'll tell him many tales of Thee."

1802.

XXVIII.
VAUDRACOUR AND JULIA.

The following tale was written as an Episode, in a work from which its length may perhaps exclude it. The facts are true; no invention as to these has been exercised, as none was needed.

O HAPPY time of youthful lovers (thus
My story may begin) O balmy time,
In which a love-knot on a lady's brow
Is fairer than the fairest star in heaven!
To such inheritance of blessed fancy
(Fancy that sports more desperately with minds
Than ever fortune hath been known to do)
The high-born Vaudracour was brought, by years
Whose progress had a little overstepped
His stripling prime. A town of small repute,
Among the vine-clad mountains of Auvergne,
Was the Youth's birth-place. There he wooed a Maid
Who heard the heart-felt music of his suit
With answering vows. Plebeian was the stock,
Plebeian, though ingenuous, the stock,
From which her graces and her honours sprung:
And hence the father of the enamoured Youth,
With haughty indignation, spurned the thought
Of such alliance. — From their cradles up,
With but a step between their several homes,
Twins had they been in pleasure; after strife
And petty quarrels, had grown fond again;
Each other's advocate, each other's stay;
And, in their happiest moments, not content,
If more divided than a sportive pair
Of sea-fowl, conscious both that they are hovering
Within the eddy of a common blast,
Or hidden only by the concave depth
Of neighbouring billows from each other's sight.

Thus, not without concurrence of an age
Unknown to memory, was an earnest given

By ready nature for a life of love,
For endless constancy, and placid truth;
But whatsoe'er of such rare treasure lay
Reserved, had fate permitted, for support
Of their maturer years, his present mind
Was under fascination; — he beheld
A vision, and adored the thing he saw.
Arabian fiction never filled the world
With half the wonders that were wrought for him.
Earth breathed in one great presence of the spring;
Life turned the meanest of her implements,
Before his eyes, to price above all gold;
The house she dwelt in was a sainted shrine;
Her chamber-window did surpass in glory
The portals of the dawn; all paradise
Could, by the simple opening of a door,
Let itself in upon him: — pathways, walks,
Swarmed with enchantment, till his spirit sank,
Surcharged, within him, overblest to move
Beneath a sun that wakes a weary world
To its dull round of ordinary cares;
A man too happy for mortality!

   So passed the time, till whether through effect
Of some unguarded moment that dissolved
Virtuous restraint — ah, speak it, think it, not!
Deem rather that the fervent Youth, who saw
So many bars between his present state
And the dear haven where he wished to be
In honourable wedlock with his Love,
Was in his judgment tempted to decline
To perilous weakness, and entrust his cause
To nature for a happy end of all;
Deem that by such fond hope the Youth was swayed,
And bear with their transgression, when I add
That Julia, wanting yet the name of wife,
Carried about her for a secret grief

The promise of a mother.
                              To conceal
The threatened shame, the parents of the Maid
Found means to hurry her away by night,
And unforewarned, that in some distant spot
She might remain shrouded in privacy,
Until the babe was born. When morning came,
The Lover, thus bereft, stung with his loss,
And all uncertain whither he should turn,
Chafed like a wild beast in the toils; but soon
Discovering traces of the fugitives,
Their steps he followed to the Maid's retreat.
Easily may the sequel be divined —
Walks to and fro — watchings at every hour;
And the fair Captive, who, whene'er she may,
Is busy at her casement as the swallow
Fluttering its pinions, almost within reach,
About the pendent nest, did thus espy;
Her Lover! — thence a stolen interview,
Accomplished under friendly shade of night.

   I pass the raptures of the pair; — such theme
Is, by innumerable poets, touched
In more delightful verse than skill of mine
Could fashion; chiefly by that darling bard
Who told of Juliet and her Romeo,
And of the lark's note heard before its time,
And of the streaks that laced the severing clouds
In the unrelenting east. — Through all her courts
The vacant city slept; the busy winds,
That keep no certain intervals of rest,
Moved not; meanwhile the galaxy displayed
Her fires, that like mysterious pulses beat
Aloft; — momentous but uneasy bliss!
To their full hearts the universe seemed hung
On that brief meeting's slender filament!

They parted; and the generous Vaudracour
Reached speedily the native threshold, bent
On making (so the Lovers had agreed)
A sacrifice of birthright to attain
A final portion from his father's hand;
Which granted, Bride and Bridegroom then would flee
To some remote and solitary place,
Shady as night, and beautiful as heaven,
Where they may live, with no one to behold
Their happiness, or to disturb their love.
But *now* of this no whisper; not the less,
If ever an obtrusive word were dropped
Touching the matter of his passion, still,
In his stern father's hearing, Vaudracour
Persisted openly that death alone
Should abrogate his human privilege
Divine, of swearing everlasting truth,
Upon the altar, to the Maid he loved.

"You shall be baffled in your mad intent
If there be justice in the court of France,"
Muttered the Father. — From these words the Youth
Conceived a terror; and, by night or day,
Stirred nowhere without weapons, that full soon
Found dreadful provocation: for at night
When to his chamber he retired, attempt
Was made to seize him by three armèd men,
Acting, in furtherance of the father's will,
Under a private signet of the State.
One the rash Youth's ungovernable hand
Slew, and as quickly to a second gave
A perilous wound — he shuddered to behold
The breathless corse; then peacefully resigned
His person to the law, was lodged in prison,
And wore the fetters of a criminal.

Have you observed a tuft of wingèd seed
That, from the dandelion's naked stalk,

Mounted aloft, is suffered not to use
Its natural gifts for purposes of rest,
Driven by the autumnal whirlwind to and fro
Through the wide element? or have you marked
The heavier substance of a leaf-clad bough,
Within the vortex of a foaming flood,
Tormented? by such aid you may conceive
The perturbation that ensued; — ah, no!
Desperate the Maid — the Youth is stained with blood;
Unmatchable on earth is their disquiet!
Yet as the troubled seed and tortured bough
Is Man, subjected to despotic sway.

For him, by private influence with the Court,
Was pardon gained, and liberty procured;
But not without exaction of a pledge,
Which liberty and love dispersed in air.
He flew to her from whom they would divide him —
He clove to her who could not give him peace —
Yea, his first word of greeting was, — "All right
Is gone from me; my lately-towering hopes,
To the least fibre of their lowest root,
Are withered; thou no longer canst be mine,
I thine — the conscience-striken must not woo
The unruffled Innocent, — I see thy face,
Behold thee, and my misery is complete!"

"One, are we not?" exclaimed the Maiden — "One,
For innocence and youth, for weal and woe?"
Then with the father's name she coupled words
Of vehement indignation; but the Youth
Checked her with filial meekness; for no thought
Uncharitable crossed his mind, no sense
Of hasty anger rising in the eclipse
Of true domestic loyalty, did e'er
Find place within his bosom. — Once again
The persevering wedge of tyranny
Achieved their separation: and once more

Were they united, — to be yet again
Disparted, pitiable lot! But here
A portion of the tale may well be left
In silence, though my memory could add
Much how the Youth, in scanty space of time,
Was traversed from without; much, too, of thoughts
That occupied his days in solitude
Under privation and restraint; and what,
Through dark and shapeless fear of things to come,
And what, through strong compunction for the past,
He suffered — breaking down in heart and mind!

Doomed to a third and last captivity,
His freedom he recovered on the eve
Of Julia's travail. When the babe was born,
Its presence tempted him to cherish schemes
Of future happiness. "You shall return,
Julia," said he, "and to your father's house
Go with the child. — You have been wretched; yet
The silver shower, whose reckless burthen weighs
Too heavily upon the lily's head,
Oft leaves a saving moisture at its root.
Malice, beholding you, will melt away.
Go! — 'tis a town where both of us were born;
None will reproach you, for our truth is known;
And if, amid those once-bright bowers, our fate
Remain unpitied, pity is not in man.
With ornaments — the prettiest nature yields
Or art can fashion, shall you deck our boy,
And feed his countenance with your own sweet looks
Till no one can resist him. — Now, even now,
I see him sporting on the sunny lawn;
My father from the window sees him too;
Startled, as if some new-created thing
Enriched the earth, or Faery of the woods
Bounded before him; — but the unweeting Child
Shall by his beauty win his grandsire's heart

So that it shall be softened, and our loves
End happily, as they began!"
                            These gleams
Appeared but seldom; oftener was he seen
Propping a pale and melancholy face
Upon the Mother's bosom; resting thus
His head upon one breast, while from the other
The Babe was drawing in its quiet food.
— That pillow is no longer to be thine,
Fond Youth! that mournful solace now must pass
Into the list of things that cannot be!
Unwedded Julia, terror-smitten, hears
The sentence, by her mother's lip pronounced,
That dooms her to a convent. — Who shall tell,
Who dares report, the tidings to the lord
Of her affections? so they blindly asked
Who knew not to what quiet depths a weight
Of agony had pressed the sufferer down:
The word, by others dreaded, he can hear
Composed and silent, without visible sign
Of even the least emotion. Noting this,
When the impatient object of his love
Upbraided him with slackness, he returned
No answer, only took the mother's hand
And kissed it; seemingly devoid of pain,
Or care, that what so tenderly he pressed,
Was a dependant on the obdurate heart
Of one who came to disunite their lives
For ever — sad alternative! preferred,
By the unbending Parents of the Maid,
To secret 'spousals meanly disavowed.
— So be it!
            In the city he remained
A season after Julia had withdrawn
To those religious walls. He, too, departs —
Who with him? — even the senseless Little-one.
With that sole charge he passed the city-gates,

For the last time, attendant by the side
Of a close chair, a litter, or sedan,
In which the Babe was carried. To a hill,
That rose a brief league distant from the town,
The dwellers in that house where he had lodged
Accompanied his steps, by anxious love
Impelled; — they parted from him there, and stood
Watching below till he had disappeared
On the hill top. His eyes he scarcely took,
Throughout that journey, from the vehicle
(Slow-moving ark of all his hopes!) that veiled
The tender infant: and at every inn,
And under every hospitable tree
At which the bearers halted or reposed,
Laid him with timid care upon his knees,
And looked, as mothers ne'er were known to look,
Upon the nursling which his arms embraced.

This was the manner in which Vaudracour
Departed with his infant; and thus reached
His father's house, where to the innocent child
Admittance was denied. The young man spake
No word of indignation or reproof,
But of his father begged, a last request,
That a retreat might be assigned to him
Where in forgotten quiet he might dwell,
With such allowance as his wants required;
For wishes he had none. To a lodge that stood
Deep in a forest, with leave given, at the age
Of four-and-twenty summers he withdrew;
And thither took with him his motherless Babe,
And one domestic for their common needs,
An aged woman. It consoled him here
To attend upon the orphan, and perform
Obsequious service to the precious child,
Which, after a short time, by some mistake
Or indiscretion of the Father, died. —

9*

The Tale I follow to its last recess
Of suffering or of peace, I know not which:
Theirs be the blame who caused the woe, not mine!

   From this time forth he never shared a smile
With mortal creature. An Inhabitant
Of that same town in which the pair had left
So lively a remembrance of their griefs,
By chance of business, coming within reach
Of his retirement, to the forest lodge
Repaired, but only found the matron there,
Who told him that his pains were thrown away,
For that her Master never uttered word
To living thing — not even to her. — Behold!
While they were speaking, Vaudracour approached;
But, seeing some one near, as on the latch
Of the garden-gate his hand was laid, he shrunk —
And, like a shadow, glided out of view.
Shocked at his savage aspect, from the place
The visitor retired.
                Thus lived the Youth
Cut off from all intelligence with man,
And shunning even the light of common day;
Nor could the voice of Freedom, which through France
Full speedily resounded, public hope,
Or personal memory of his own deep wrongs,
Rouse him: but in those solitary shades
His days he wasted, an imbecile mind!

                                          1805.

XXIX.
THE IDIOT BOY.

'Tis eight o'clock, — a clear March night,
The moon is up, — the sky is blue,
The owlet, in the moonlight air,
Shouts from nobody knows where;
He lengthens out his lonely shout,
Halloo! halloo! a long halloo!

— Why bustle thus about your door,
What means this bustle, Betty Foy?
Why are you in this mighty fret?
And why on horseback have you set
Him whom you love, your Idiot Boy?

Scarcely a soul is out of bed;
Good Betty, put him down again;
His lips with joy they burr at you;
But, Betty! what has he to do
With stirrup, saddle, or with rein?

But Betty's bent on her intent;
For her good neighbour, Susan Gale,
Old Susan, she who dwells alone,
Is sick, and makes a piteous moan,
As if her very life would fail.

There's not a house within a mile,
No hand to help them in distress;
Old Susan lies a-bed in pain,
And sorely puzzled are the twain,
For what she ails they cannot guess.

And Betty's husband's at the wood,
Where by the week he doth abide,
A woodman in the distant vale;
There's none to help poor Susan Gale;
What must be done? what will betide?

And Betty from the lane has fetched
Her Pony, that is mild and good;
Whether he be in joy or pain,
Feeding at will along the lane,
Or bringing faggots from the wood.

And he is all in travelling trim, —
And, by the moonlight, Betty Foy
Has on the well-girt saddle set
(The like was never heard of yet)
Him whom she loves, her Idiot Boy.

And he must post without delay
Across the bridge and through the dale,
And by the church, and o'er the down,
To bring a Doctor from the town,
Or she will die, old Susan Gale.

There is no need of boot or spur,
There is no need of whip or wand;
For Johnny has his holly-bough,
And with a *hurly-burly* now
He shakes the green bough in his hand.

And Betty o'er and o'er has told
The Boy, who is her best delight,
Both what to follow, what to shun,
What do, and what to leave undone,
How turn to left, and how to right.

And Betty's most especial charge,
Was, "Johnny! Johnny! mind that you
Come home again, nor stop at all, —
Come home again, whate'er befal,
My Johnny, do, I pray you do."

To this did Johnny answer make,
Both with his head and with his hand,
And proudly shook the bridle too;
And then! his words were not a few,
Which Betty well could understand.

And now that Johnny is just going,
Though Betty's in a mighty flurry,
She gently pats the Pony's side,
On which her Idiot Boy must ride,
And seems no longer in a hurry.

But when the Pony moved his legs,
Oh! then for the poor Idiot Boy!
For joy he cannot hold the bridle,
For joy his head and heels are idle,
He's idle all for very joy.

And while the Pony moves his legs,
In Johnny's left hand you may see
The green bough motionless and dead:
The Moon that shines above his head
Is not more still and mute than he.

His heart it was so full of glee,
That till full fifty yards were gone,
He quite forgot his holly whip,
And all his skill in horsemanship:
Oh! happy, happy, happy John.

And while the Mother, at the door,
Stands fixed, her face with joy o'erflows,
Proud of herself, and proud of him,
She sees him in his travelling trim,
How quietly her Johnny goes.

The silence of her Idiot Boy,
What hopes it sends to Betty's heart!
He's at the guide-post — he turns right;
She watches till he 's out of sight,
And Betty will not then depart.

Burr, burr — now Johnny's lips they burr,
As loud as any mill, or near it;
Meek as a lamb the Pony moves,
And Johnny makes the noise he loves,
And Betty listens, glad to hear it.

Away she hies to Susan Gale:
Her Messenger's in merry tune;
The owlets hoot, the owlets curr,
And Johnny's lips they burr, burr, burr,
As on he goes beneath the moon.

His steed and he right well agree;
For of this Pony there's a rumour,
That, should he lose his eyes and ears,
And should he live a thousand years,
He never will be out of humour.

But then he is a horse that thinks;
And when he thinks, his pace is slack;
Now, though he knows poor Johnny well,
Yet, for his life, he cannot tell
What he has got upon his back.

So through the moonlight lanes they go,
And far into the moonlight dale,
And by the church, and o'er the down,
To bring a Doctor from the town,
To comfort poor old Susan Gale.

And Betty, now at Susan's side,
Is in the middle of her story,
What speedy help her Boy will bring,
With many a most diverting thing,
Of Johnny's wit, and Johnny's glory.

And Betty, still at Susan's side,
By this time is not quite so flurried:
Demure with porringer and plate
She sits, as if in Susan's fate
Her life and soul were buried.

But Betty, poor good woman! she,
You plainly in her face may read it,
Could lend out of that moment's store
Five years of happiness or more
To any that might need it.

But yet I guess that now and then
With Betty all was not so well;
And to the road she turns her ears,
And thence full many a sound she hears,
Which she to Susan will not tell.

Poor Susan moans, poor Susan groans;
"As sure as there's a moon in heaven,"
Cries Betty, "he 'll be back again;
They'll both be here — 'tis almost ten —
Both will be here before eleven."

Poor Susan moans, poor Susan groans;
The clock gives warning for eleven;
'Tis on the stroke — "He must be near,"
Quoth Betty, "and will soon be here,
As sure as there's a moon in heaven."

The clock is on the stroke of twelve,
And Johnny is not yet in sight:
— The Moon 's in heaven, as Betty sees,
But Betty is not quite at ease;
And Susan has a dreadful night.

And Betty, half an hour ago,
On Johnny vile reflections cast:
"A little idle sauntering Thing!"
With other names, an endless string;
But now that time is gone and past.

And Betty's drooping at the heart,
That happy time all past and gone,
"How can it be he is so late?
The Doctor, he has made him wait;
Susan! they 'll both be here anon."

And Susan's growing worse and worse,
And Betty's in a sad *quandary*;
And then there's nobody to say
If she must go, or she must stay!
— She's in a sad *quandary*.

The clock is on the stroke of one;
But neither Doctor nor his Guide
Appears along the moonlight road;
There's neither horse nor man abroad,
And Betty's still at Susan's side.

And Susan now begins to fear
Of sad mischances not a few,
That Johnny may perhaps be drowned;
Or lost, perhaps, and never found;
Which they must both for ever rue.

She prefaced half a hint of this
With, "God forbid it should be true!"
At the first word that Susan said
Cried Betty, rising from the bed,
"Susan, I'd gladly stay with you.

I must be gone, I must away:
Consider, Johnny's but half-wise;
Susan, we must take care of him,
If he is hurt in life or limb" —
"Oh God forbid!" poor Susan cries.

"What can I do?" says Betty, going,
"What can I do to ease your pain?
Good Susan tell me, and I'll stay:
I fear you're in a dreadful way,
But I shall soon be back again."

"Nay, Betty, go! good Betty, go!
There's nothing that can ease my pain."
Then off she hies; but with a prayer
That God poor Susan's life would spare,
Till she comes back again.

So, through the moonlight lane she goes,
And far into the moonlight dale;
And how she ran, and how she walked,
And all that to herself she talked,
Would surely be a tedious tale.

In high and low, above, below,
In great and small, in round and square,
In tree and tower was Johnny seen,
In bush and brake, in black and green;
'Twas Johnny, Johnny, every where.

And while she crossed the bridge, there came
A thought with which her heart is sore —
Johnny perhaps his horse forsook,
To hunt the moon within the brook,
And never will be heard of more.

Now is she high upon the down,
Alone amid a prospect wide;
There's neither Johnny nor his Horse
Among the fern or in the gorse;
There's neither Doctor nor his Guide.

"Oh saints! what is become of him?
Perhaps he's climbed into an oak,
Where he will stay till he is dead;
Or, sadly he has been misled,
And joined the wandering gipsy-folk.

Or him that wicked Pony's carried
To the dark cave, the goblin's hall;
Or in the castle he 's pursuing
Among the ghosts his own undoing;
Or playing with the waterfall."

At poor old Susan then she railed,
While to the town she posts away;
"If Susan had not been so ill,
Alas! I should have had him still,
My Johnny, till my dying day."

Poor Betty, in this sad distemper,
The Doctor's self could hardly spare:
Unworthy things she talked, and wild;
Even he, of cattle the most mild,
The Pony had his share.

But now she's fairly in the town,
And to the Doctor's door she hies;
'Tis silence all on every side;
The town so long, the town so wide,
Is silent as the skies.

And now she's at the Doctor's door,
She lifts the knocker, rap, rap, rap;
The Doctor at the casement shows
His glimmering eyes that peep and doze!
And one hand rubs his old night-cap.

"Oh Doctor! Doctor! where 's my Johnny?"
"I'm here, what is't you want with me?"
"Oh Sir! you know I'm Betty Foy,
And I have lost my poor dear Boy,
You know him — him you often see;

He's not so wise as some folks be:"
"The devil take his wisdom!" said
The Doctor, looking somewhat grim,
"What, Woman! should I know of him?"
And, grumbling, he went back to bed!

"O woe is me! O woe is me!
Here will I die; here will I die;
I thought to find my lost one here,
But he is neither far nor near,
Oh! what a wretched Mother I!"

She stops, she stands, she looks about;
Which way to turn she cannot tell.
Poor Betty! it would ease her pain
If she had heart to knock again;
— The clock strikes three — a dismal knell!

Then up along the town she hies,
No wonder if her senses fail;
This piteous news so much it shocked her,
She quite forgot to send the Doctor,
To comfort poor old Susan Gale.

And now she's high upon the down,
And she can see a mile of road:
"O cruel! I'm almost threescore;
Such night as this was ne'er before,
There's not a single soul abroad."

She listens, but she cannot hear
The foot of horse, the voice of man;
The streams with softest sound are flowing,
The grass you almost hear it growing,
You hear it now, if e'er you can.

The owlets through the long blue night
Are shouting to each other still:
Fond lovers! yet not quite hob nob,
They lengthen out the tremulous sob,
That echoes far from hill to hill.

Poor Betty now has lost all hope,
Her thoughts are bent on deadly sin,
A green-grown pond she just has past,
And from the brink she hurries fast,
Lest she should drown herself therein.

And now she sits her down and weeps;
Such tears she never shed before;
"Oh dear, dear Pony! my sweet joy!
Oh carry back my Idiot Boy!
And we will ne'er o'erload thee more."

A thought is come into her head:
The Pony he is mild and good,
And we have always used him well;
Perhaps he's gone along the dell,
And carried Johnny to the wood.

Then up she springs as if on wings;
She thinks no more of deadly sin;
If Betty fifty ponds should see,
The last of all her thoughts would be
To drown herself therein.

O Reader! now that I might tell
What Johnny and his Horse are doing!
What they've been doing all this time,
Oh could I put it into rhyme,
A most delightful tale pursuing!

Perhaps, and no unlikely thought!
He with his Pony now doth roam
The cliffs and peaks so high that are,
To lay his hands upon a star,
And in his pocket bring it home.

Perhaps he's turned himself about,
His face unto his horse's tail,
And, still and mute, in wonder lost,
All silent as a horseman-ghost,
He travels slowly down the vale.

And now, perhaps, is hunting sheep,
A fierce and dreadful hunter he;
Yon valley, now so trim and green,
In five months' time, should he be seen,
A desert wilderness will be!

Perhaps, with head and heels on fire,
And like the very soul of evil,
He's galloping away, away,
And so will gallop on for aye,
The bane of all that dread the devil!

I to the Muses have been bound
These fourteen years, by strong indentures:
O gentle Muses! let me tell
But half of what to him befel;
He surely met with strange adventures.

O gentle Muses! is this kind?
Why will ye thus my suit repel?
Why of your further aid bereave me?
And can ye thus unfriended leave me:
Ye Muses! whom I love so well?

THE IDIOT BOY.

Who's yon, that, near the waterfall,
Which thunders down with headlong force,
Beneath the moon, yet shining fair,
As careless as if nothing were,
Sits upright on a feeding horse?

Unto his horse — there feeding free,
He seems, I think, the rein to give;
Of moon or stars he takes no heed;
Of such we in romances read:
— 'Tis Johnny! Johnny! as I live.

And that's the very Pony, too!
Where is she, where is Betty Foy?
She hardly can sustain her fears;
The roaring waterfall she hears,
And cannot find her Idiot Boy.

Your Pony's worth his weight in gold:
Then calm your terrors, Betty Foy!
She's coming from among the trees,
And now all full in view she sees
Him whom she loves, her Idiot Boy.

And Betty sees the Pony too:
Why stand you thus, good Betty Foy?
It is no goblin, 'tis no ghost,
'Tis he whom you so long have lost,
He whom you love, your Idiot Boy.

She looks again — her arms are up —
She screams — she cannot move for joy;
She darts, as with a torrent's force,
She almost has o'erturned the Horse,
And fast she holds her Idiot Boy.

And Johnny burrs, and laughs aloud;
Whether in cunning or in joy
I cannot tell; but while he laughs,
Betty a drunken pleasure quaffs
To hear again her Idiot Boy.

And now she's at the Pony's tail,
And now is at the Pony's head, —
On that side now, and now on this;
And, almost stifled with her bliss,
A few sad tears does Betty shed.

She kisses o'er and o'er again
Him whom she loves, her Idiot Boy;
She's happy here, is happy there,
She is uneasy every where;
Her limbs are all alive with joy.

She pats the Pony, where or when
She knows not, happy Betty Foy!
The little Pony glad may be,
But he is milder far than she,
You hardly can perceive his joy.

"Oh! Johnny, never mind the Doctor;
You 've done your best, and that is all:"
She took the reins, when this was said,
And gently turned the Pony's head
From the loud waterfall.

By this the stars were almost gone,
The moon was setting on the hill,
So pale you scarcely looked at her:
The little birds began to stir,
Though yet their tongues were still.

The Pony, Betty, and her Boy,
Wind slowly through the woody dale;
And who is she, betimes abroad,
That hobbles up the steep rough road?
Who is it, but old Susan Gale?

Long time lay Susan lost in thought;
And many dreadful fears beset her,
Both for her Messenger and Nurse;
And, as her mind grew worse and worse,
Her body — it grew better.

THE IDIOT BOY.

She turned, she tossed herself in bed,
On all sides doubts and terrors met her;
Point after point did she discuss;
And, while her mind was fighting thus,
Her body still grew better.

"Alas! what is become of them?
These fears can never be endured;
I'll to the wood." — The word scarce said,
Did Susan rise up from her bed,
As if by magic cured.

Away she goes up hill and down,
And to the wood at length is come;
She spies her Friends, she shouts a greeting;
Oh me! it is a merry meeting
As ever was in Christendom.

The owls have hardly sung their last,
While our four travellers homeward wend;
The owls have hooted all night long,
And with the owls began my song,
And with the owls must end.

For while they all were travelling home,
Cried Betty, "Tell us, Johnny, do,
Where all this long night you have been,
What you have heard, what you have seen:
And, Johnny, mind you tell us true."

Now Johnny all night long had heard
The owls in tuneful concert strive;
No doubt too he the moon had seen;
For in the moonlight he had been
From eight o'clock till five.

And thus, to Betty's question, he
Made answer, like a traveller bold,
(His very words I give to you,)
"The cocks did crow to-whoo, to-whoo,
And the sun did shine so cold!"

— Thus answered Johnny in his glory,
And that was all his travel's story.

1798.

XXX.
MICHAEL.
A PASTORAL POEM.

If from the public way you turn your steps
Up the tumultuous brook of Green-head Ghyll,
You will suppose that with an upright path
Your feet must struggle; in such bold ascent
The pastoral mountains front you, face to face.
But, courage! for around that boisterous brook
The mountains have all opened out themselves,
And made a hidden valley of their own.
No habitation can be seen; but they
Who journey thither find themselves alone
With a few sheep, with rocks and stones, and kites
That overhead are sailing in the sky.
It is in truth an utter solitude;
Nor should I have made mention of this Dell
But for one object which you might pass by,
Might see and notice not. Beside the brook
Appears a straggling heap of unhewn stones!
And to that simple object appertains
A story — unenriched with strange events,
Yet not unfit, I deem, for the fireside,
Or for the summer shade. It was the first
Of those domestic tales that spake to me
Of Shepherds, dwellers in the valleys, men
Whom I already loved; — not verily
For their own sakes, but for the fields and hills
Where was their occupation and abode.
And hence this Tale, while I was yet a Boy
Careless of books, yet having felt the power
Of Nature, by the gentle agency

Of natural objects, led me on to feel
For passions that were not my own, and think
(At random and imperfectly indeed)
On man, the heart of man, and human life.
Therefore, although it be a history
Homely and rude, I will relate the same
For the delight of a few natural hearts;
And, with yet fonder feeling, for the sake
Of youthful Poets, who among these hills
Will be my second self when I am gone.

Upon the forest-side in Grassmere Vale
There dwelt a Shepherd, Michael was his name;
An old man, stout of heart, and strong of limb.
His bodily frame had been from youth to age
Of an unusual strength: his mind was keen,
Intense, and frugal, apt for all affairs,
And in his shepherd's calling he was prompt
And watchful more than ordinary men.
Hence had he learned the meaning of all winds,
Of blasts of every tone; and, oftentimes,
When others heeded not, he heard the South
Make subterraneous music, like the noise
Of bagpipers on distant Highland hills.
The Shepherd, at such warning, of his flock
Bethought him, and he to himself would say,
"The winds are now devising work for me!"
And, truly, at all times, the storm, that drives
The traveller to a shelter, summoned him
Up to the mountains: he had been alone
Amid the heart of many thousand mists,
That came to him, and left him, on the heights.
So lived he till his eightieth year was past.
And grossly that man errs, who should suppose
That the green valleys, and the streams and rocks,
Were things indifferent to the Shepherd's thoughts.
Fields, where with cheerful spirits he had breathed

The common air; hills, which with vigorous step
He had so often climbed; which had impressed
So many incidents upon his mind
Of hardship, skill or courage, joy or fear;
Which, like a book, preserved the memory
Of the dumb animals whom he had saved,
Had fed or sheltered, linking to such acts
The certainty of honourable gain;
Those fields, those hills — what could they less? had laid
Strong hold on his affections, were to him
A pleasurable feeling of blind love,
The pleasure which there is in life itself.

   His days had not been passed in singleness.
His Helpmate was a comely matron, old —
Though younger than himself full twenty years.
She was a woman of a stirring life,
Whose heart was in her house: two wheels she had
Of antique form; this large, for spinning wool;
That small, for flax; and if one wheel had rest,
It was because the other was at work.
The Pair had but one inmate in their house,
An only Child, who had been born to them
When Michael, telling o'er his years, began
To deem that he was old, — in shepherd's phrase,
With one foot in the grave. This only Son,
With two brave sheep-dogs tried in many a storm,
The one of an inestimable worth,
Made all their household. I may truly say,
That they were as a proverb in the vale
For endless industry. When day was gone,
And from their occupations out of doors
The Son and Father were come home, even then,
Their labour did not cease; unless when all
Turned to the cleanly supper-board, and there,
Each with a mess of pottage and skimmed milk,
Sat round the basket piled with oaten cakes,

And their plain home-made cheese. Yet when the meal
Was ended, Luke (for so the Son was named)
And his old Father both betook themselves
To such convenient work as might employ
Their hands by the fire-side; perhaps to card
Wool for the Housewife's spindle, or repair
Some injury done to sickle, flail, or scythe,
Or other implement of house or field.

Down from the ceiling, by the chimney's edge,
That in our ancient uncouth country style
With huge and black projection overbrowed
Large space beneath, as duly as the light
Of day grew dim the Housewife hung a lamp;
An aged utensil, which had performed
Service beyond all others of its kind.
Early at evening did it burn — and late,
Surviving comrade of uncounted hours,
Which, going by from year to year, had found,
And left the couple neither gay perhaps
Nor cheerful, yet with objects and with hopes,
Living a life of eager industry.
And now, when Luke had reached his eighteenth year,
There by the light of this old lamp they sate,
Father and Son, while far into the night
The Housewife plied her own peculiar work,
Making the cottage through the silent hours
Murmur as with the sound of summer flies.
This light was famous in its neighbourhood,
And was a public symbol of the life
That thrifty Pair had lived. For, as it chanced,
Their cottage on a plot of rising ground
Stood single, with large prospect, north and south,
High into Easedale, up to Dunmail-Raise,
And westward to the village near the lake;
And from this constant light, so regular
And so far seen, the House itself, by all

Who dwelt within the limits of the vale,
Both old and young, was named THE EVENING STAR.

Thus living on through such a length of years,
The Shepherd, if he loved himself, must needs
Have loved his Helpmate; but to Michael's heart
This son of his old age was yet more dear —
Less from instinctive tenderness, the same
Fond spirit that blindly works in the blood of all —
Than that a child, more than all other gifts
That earth can offer to declining man,
Brings hope with it, and forward-looking thoughts,
And stirrings of inquietude, when they
By tendency of nature needs must fail.
Exceeding was the love he bare to him,
His heart and his heart's joy! For oftentimes
Old Michael, while he was a babe in arms,
Had done him female service, not alone
For pastime and delight, as is the use
Of fathers, but with patient mind enforced
To acts of tenderness; and he had rocked
His cradle, as with a woman's gentle hand.

And, in a later time, ere yet the Boy
Had put on boy's attire, did Michael love,
Albeit of a stern unbending mind,
To have the Young-one in his sight, when he
Wrought in the field, or on his shepherd's stool
Sate with a fettered sheep before him stretched
Under the large old oak, that near his door
Stood single, and, from matchless depth of shade,
Chosen for the Shearer's covert from the sun,
Thence in our rustic dialect was called
The CLIPPING TREE,* a name which yet it bears.
There, while they two were sitting in the shade,
With others round them, earnest all and blithe,

* Clipping is the word used in the North of England for shearing.

Would Michael exercise his heart with looks
Of fond correction and reproof bestowed
Upon the Child, if he disturbed the sheep
By catching at their legs, or with his shouts
Scared them, while they lay still beneath the shears.

   And when by Heaven's good grace the boy grew up
A healthy Lad, and carried in his cheek
Two steady roses that were five years old;
Then Michael from a winter coppice cut
With his own hand a sapling, which he hooped
With iron, making it throughout in all
Due requisites a perfect shepherd's staff,
And gave it to the Boy; wherewith equipt
He as a watchman oftentimes was placed
At gate or gap, to stem or turn the flock;
And, to his office prematurely called,
There stood the urchin, as you will divine,
Something between a hindrance and a help;
And for this cause not always, I believe,
Receiving from his Father hire of praise;
Though nought was left undone which staff, or voice,
Or looks, or threatening gestures, could perform.

   But soon as Luke, full ten years old, could stand
Against the mountain blasts; and to the heights,
Not fearing toil, nor length of weary ways,
He with his Father daily went, and they
Were as companions, why should I relate
That objects which the Shepherd loved before
Were dearer now? that from the Boy there came
Feelings and emanations — things which were
Light to the sun and music to the wind;
And that the old Man's heart seemed born again?

   Thus in his Father's sight the Boy grew up:
And now, when he had reached his eighteenth year,
He was his comfort and his daily hope.

While in this sort the simple household lived
From day to day, to Michael's ear there came
Distressful tidings. Long before the time
Of which I speak, the Shepherd had been bound
In surety for his brother's son, a man
Of an industrious life, and ample means;
But unforeseen misfortunes suddenly
Had prest upon him; and old Michael now
Was summoned to discharge the forfeiture,
A grievous penalty, but little less
Than half his substance. This unlooked-for claim,
At the first hearing, for a moment took
More hope out of his life than he supposed
That any old man ever could have lost.
As soon as he had armed himself with strength
To look his trouble in the face, it seemed
The Shepherd's sole resource to sell at once
A portion of his patrimonial fields.
Such was his first resolve; he thought again,
And his heart failed him. "Isabel," said he,
Two evenings after he had heard the news,
"I have been toiling more than seventy years,
And in the open sunshine of God's love
Have we all lived; yet if these fields of ours
Should pass into a stranger's hand, I think
That I could not lie quiet in my grave.
Our lot is a hard lot; the sun himself
Has scarcely been more diligent than I;
And I have lived to be a fool at last
To my own family. An evil man
That was, and made an evil choice, if he
Were false to us; and if he were not false,
There are ten thousand to whom loss like this
Had been no sorrow. I forgive him; — but
'Twere better to be dumb than to talk thus.

When I began, my purpose was to speak
Of remedies and of a cheerful hope.
Our Luke shall leave us, Isabel; the land
Shall not go from us, and it shall be free;
He shall possess it, free as is the wind
That passes over it. We have, thou know'st,
Another kinsman — he will be our friend
In this distress. He is a prosperous man,
Thriving in trade — and Luke to him shall go,
And with his kinsman's help and his own thrift
He quickly will repair this loss, and then
He may return to us. If here he stay,
What can be done? Where every one is poor,
What can be gained?"
      At this the old Man paused,
And Isabel sat silent, for her mind
Was busy, looking back into past times.
There's Richard Bateman, thought she to herself,
He was a parish-boy — at the church-door
They made a gathering for him, shillings, pence
And halfpennies, wherewith the neighbours bought
A basket, which they filled with pedlar's wares;
And, with this basket on his arm, the lad
Went up to London, found a master there,
Who, out of many, chose the trusty boy
To go and overlook his merchandise
Beyond the seas; where he grew wondrous rich,
And left estates and monies to the poor,
And, at his birth-place, built a chapel floored
With marble, which he sent from foreign lands.
These thoughts, and many others of like sort,
Passed quickly through the mind of Isabel,
And her face brightened. The old Man was glad,
And thus resumed: — "Well, Isabel! this scheme
These two days, has been meat and drink to me.
Far more than we have lost is left us yet.
— We have enough — I wish indeed that I

Were younger; — but this hope is a good hope.
Make ready Luke's best garments, of the best
Buy for him more, and let us send him forth
To-morrow, or the next day, or to-night:
— If he *could* go, the Boy should go to-night."

   Here Michael ceased, and to the fields went forth
With a light heart. The Housewife for five days
Was restless morn and night, and all day long
Wrought on with her best fingers to prepare
Things needful for the journey of her son.
But Isabel was glad when Sunday came
To stop her in her work: for, when she lay
By Michael's side, she through the last two nights
Heard him, how he was troubled in his sleep:
And when they rose at morning she could see
That all his hopes were gone. That day at noon
She said to Luke, while they two by themselves
Were sitting at the door, "Thou must not go:
We have no other Child but thee to lose,
None to remember — do not go away,
For if thou leave thy Father he will die."
The Youth made answer with a jocund voice;
And Isabel, when she had told her fears,
Recovered heart. That evening her best fare
Did she bring forth, and all together sat
Like happy people round a Christmas fire.

   With daylight Isabel resumed her work;
And all the ensuing week the house appeared
As cheerful as a grove in Spring: at length
The expected letter from their kinsman came,
With kind assurances that he would do
His utmost for the welfare of the Boy;
To which, requests were added, that forthwith
He might be sent to him. Ten times or more
The letter was read over; Isabel
Went forth to show it to the neighbours round;

Nor was there at that time on English land
A prouder heart than Luke's. When Isabel
Had to her house returned, the old Man said,
"He shall depart to-morrow." To this word
The Housewife answered, talking much of things
Which, if at such short notice he should go,
Would surely be forgotten. But at length
She gave consent, and Michael was at ease.

Near the tumultuous brook of Green-head Ghyll,
In that deep valley, Michael had designed
To build a Sheep-fold; and, before he heard
The tidings of his melancholy loss,
For this same purpose he had gathered up
A heap of stones, which by the streamlet's edge
Lay thrown together, ready for the work.
With Luke that evening thitherward he walked:
And soon as they had reached the place he stopped,
And thus the old Man spake to him: — "My Son,
To-morrow thou wilt leave me: with full heart
I look upon thee, for thou art the same
That wert a promise to me ere thy birth,
And all thy life hast been my daily joy.
I will relate to thee some little part
Of our two histories; 'twill do thee good
When thou art from me, even if I should touch
On things thou canst not know of. — After thou
First cam'st into the world — as oft befals
To new-born infants — thou didst sleep away
Two days, and blessings from thy Father's tongue
Then fell upon thee. Day by day passed on,
And still I loved thee with increasing love.
Never to living ear came sweeter sounds
Than when I heard thee by our own fire-side
First uttering, without words, a natural tune;
While thou, a feeding babe, didst in thy joy
Sing at thy Mother's breast. Month followed month,

And in the open fields my life was passed
And on the mountains; else I think that thou
Hadst been brought up upon thy Father's knees.
But we were playmates, Luke: among these hills,
As well thou knowest, in us the old and young
Have played together, nor with me didst thou
Lack any pleasure which a boy can know."
Luke had a manly heart; but at these words
He sobbed aloud. The old Man grasped his hand,
And said, "Nay, do not take it so — I see
That these are things of which I need not speak.
— Even to the utmost I have been to thee
A kind and a good Father: and herein
I but repay a gift which I myself
Received at others' hands; for, though now old
Beyond the common life of man, I still
Remember them who loved me in my youth.
Both of them sleep together; here they lived,
As all their Forefathers had done; and when
At length their time was come, they were not loth
To give their bodies to the family mould.
I wished that thou should'st live the life they lived:
But, 'tis a long time to look back, my Son,
And see so little gain from threescore years.
These fields were burthened when they came to me:
Till I was forty years of age, not more
Than half of my inheritance was mine.
I toiled and toiled; God blessed me in my work,
And till these three weeks past the land was free.
— It looks as if it never could endure
Another Master. Heaven forgive me, Luke,
If I judge ill for thee, but it seems good
That thou should'st go."
                        At this the old Man paused;
Then, pointing to the stones near which they stood,
Thus, after a short silence, he resumed:
"This was a work for us; and now, my Son,

It is a work for me. But, lay one stone —
Here, lay it for me, Luke, with thine own hands.
Nay, Boy, be of good hope; — we both may live
To see a better day. At eighty-four
I still am strong and hale; — do thou thy part;
I will do mine. — I will begin again
With many tasks that were resigned to thee:
Up to the heights, and in among the storms,
Will I without thee go again, and do
All works which I was wont to do alone,
Before I knew thy face. — Heaven bless thee, Boy!
Thy heart these two weeks has been beating fast
With many hopes; it should be so — yes — yes —
I knew that thou could'st never have a wish
To leave me, Luke: thou hast been bound to me
Only by links of love: when thou art gone,
What will be left to us! — But, I forget
My purposes. Lay now the corner-stone,
As I requested; and hereafter, Luke,
When thou art gone away, should evil men
Be thy companions, think of me, my Son,
And of this moment; hither turn thy thoughts,
And God will strengthen thee: amid all fear
And all temptation, Luke, I pray that thou
May'st bear in mind the life thy Fathers lived,
Who, being innocent, did for that cause
Bestir them in good deeds. Now, fare thee well —
When thou return'st, thou in this place wilt see
A work which is not here: a covenant
'Twill be between us; but, whatever fate
Befal thee, I shall love thee to the last,
And bear thy memory with me to the grave."

   The Shepherd ended here; and Luke stooped down,
And, as his Father had requested, laid
The first stone of the Sheep-fold. At the sight
The old Man's grief broke from him; to his heart
He pressed his Son, he kissèd him and wept;

And to the house together they returned.
— Hushed was that House in peace, or seeming peace,
Ere the night fell: — with morrow's dawn the Boy
Began his journey, and when he had reached
The public way, he put on a bold face;
And all the neighbours, as he passed their doors,
Came forth with wishes and with farewell prayers,
That followed him till he was out of sight.

 A good report did from their Kinsman come,
Of Luke and his well doing: and the Boy
Wrote loving letters, full of wondrous news,
Which, as the Housewife phrased it, were throughout
"The prettiest letters that were ever seen."
Both parents read them with rejoicing hearts.
So, many months passed on: and once again
The Shepherd went about his daily work
With confident and cheerful thoughts; and now
Sometimes when he could find a leisure hour
He to that valley took his way, and there
Wrought at the Sheep-fold. Meantime Luke began
To slacken in his duty; and, at length,
He in the dissolute city gave himself
To evil courses: ignominy and shame
Fell on him, so that he was driven at last
To seek a hiding-place beyond the seas.

 There is a comfort in the strength of love;
'Twill make a thing endurable, which else
Would overset the brain, or break the heart:
I have conversed with more than one who well
Remember the old Man, and what he was
Years after he had heard this heavy news.
His bodily frame had been from youth to age
Of an unusual strength. Among the rocks
He went, and still looked up to sun and cloud,
And listened to the wind; and, as before,
Performed all kinds of labour for his sheep,

And for the land, his small inheritance.
And to that hollow dell from time to time
Did he repair, to build the Fold of which
His flock had need. 'Tis not forgotten yet
The pity which was then in every heart
For the old Man — and 'tis believed by all
That many and many a day he thither went,
And never lifted up a single stone.

  There, by the Sheep-fold, sometimes was he seen
Sitting alone, or with his faithful Dog,
Then old, beside him, lying at his feet.
The length of full seven years, from time to time,
He at the building of this Sheep-fold wrought,
And left the work unfinished when he died.
Three years, or little more, did Isabel
Survive her Husband: at her death the estate
Was sold, and went into a stranger's hand.
The Cottage which was named the EVENING STAR
Is gone — the ploughshare has been through the ground
On which it stood; great changes have been wrought
In all the neighbourhood: — yet the oak is left
That grew beside their door; and the remains
Of the unfinished Sheep-fold may be seen
Beside the boisterous brook of Green-head Ghyll.   1800.

XXXI.
THE WIDOW ON WINDERMERE SIDE.
I.

How beautiful when up a lofty height
Honour ascends among the humblest poor,
And feeling sinks as deep! See there the door
Of One, a Widow, left beneath a weight
Of blameless debt. On evil Fortune's spite
She wasted no complaint, but strove to make
A just repayment, both for conscience-sake
And that herself and hers should stand upright

In the world's eye.   Her work when daylight failed
Paused not, and through the depth of night she kept
Such earnest vigils, that belief prevailed
With some, the noble Creature never slept;
But, one by one, the hand of death assailed
Her children, from her inmost heart bewept.

II.

The Mother mourned, nor ceased her tears to flow,
Till a winter's noon-day placed her buried Son
Before her eyes, last child of many gone —
His raiment of angelic white, and lo!
His very feet bright as the dazzling snow
Which they are touching; yea far brighter, even
As that which comes, or seems to come, from heaven,
Surpasses aught these elements can show.
Much she rejoiced, trusting that from that hour
Whate'er befel she could not grieve or pine;
But the Transfigured, in and out of season,
Appeared, and spiritual presence gained a power
Over material forms that mastered reason.
Oh, gracious Heaven, in pity make her thine!

III.

But why that prayer? as if to her could come
No good but by the way that leads to bliss
Through Death, — so judging we should judge amiss.
Since reason failed want is her threatened doom,
Yet frequent transports mitigate the gloom:
Nor of those maniacs is she one that kiss
The air or laugh upon a precipice;
No, passing through strange sufferings toward the tomb,
She smiles as if a martyr's crown were won:
Oft, when light breaks through clouds or waving trees,
With outspread arms and fallen upon her knees
The Mother hails in her descending Son
An Angel, and in earthly ecstacies
Her own angelic glory seems begun.

XXXII.
FAREWELL LINES.

'High bliss is only for a higher state,'
But, surely, if severe afflictions borne
With patience merit the reward of peace,
Peace ye deserve; and may the solid good,
Sought by a wise though late exchange, and here
With bounteous hand beneath a cottage-roof
To you accorded, never be withdrawn,
Nor for the world's best promises renounced.
Most soothing was it for a welcome Friend,
Fresh from the crowded city, to behold
That lonely union, privacy so deep,
Such calm employments, such entire content.
So when the rain is over, the storm laid,
A pair of herons oft-times have I seen,
Upon a rocky islet, side by side,
Drying their feathers in the sun, at ease;
And so, when night with grateful gloom had fallen,
Two glow-worms in such nearness that they shared,
As seemed, their soft self-satisfying light,
Each with the other, on the dewy ground,
Where He that made them blesses their repose. —
When wandering among lakes and hills I note,
Once more, those creatures thus by nature paired,
And guarded in their tranquil state of life,
Even, as your happy presence to my mind
Their union brought, will they repay the debt,
And send a thankful spirit back to you,
With hope that we, dear Friends! shall meet again.

XXXIII.
THE REDBREAST.
(SUGGESTED IN A WESTMORELAND COTTAGE.)

Driven in by Autumn's sharpening air
From half-stripped woods and pastures bare,
Brisk Robin seeks a kindlier home:
Not like a beggar is he come,
But enters as a looked-for guest,
Confiding in his ruddy breast,
As if it were a natural shield
Charged with a blazon on the field,
Due to that good and pious deed
Of which we in the Ballad read.
But pensive fancies putting by,
And wild-wood sorrows, speedily
He plays the expert ventriloquist;
And, caught by glimpses now — now missed,
Puzzles the listener with a doubt
If the soft voice he throws about
Comes from within doors or without!
Was ever such a sweet confusion,
Sustained by delicate illusion?
He's at your elbow — to your feeling
The notes are from the floor or ceiling;
And there's a riddle to be guessed,
'Till you have marked his heaving chest,
And busy throat whose sink and swell,
Betray the Elf that loves to dwell
In Robin's bosom, as a chosen cell.

Heart-pleased we smile upon the Bird
If seen, and with like pleasure stirred
Commend him, when he's only heard.
But small and fugitive our gain
Compared with *hers* who long hath lain,

With languid limbs and patient head
Reposing on a lone sick-bed;
Where now, she daily hears a strain
That cheats her of too busy cares,
Eases her pain, and helps her prayers.
And who but this dear Bird beguiled
The fever of that pale-faced Child;
Now cooling, with his passing wing,
Her forehead, like a breeze of Spring:
Recalling now, with descant soft
Shed round her pillow from aloft,
Sweet thoughts of angels hovering nigh,
And the invisible sympathy
Of 'Matthew, Mark, and Luke, and John,
Blessing the bed she lies upon*?'
And sometimes, just as listening ends
In slumber, with the cadence blends
A dream of that low-warbled hymn
Which old folk, fondly pleased to trim
Lamps of faith, now burning dim,
Say that the Cherubs carved in stone,
When clouds gave way at dead of night
And the ancient church was filled with light,
Used to sing in heavenly tone
Above and round the sacred places
They guard, with winged baby-faces.

Thrice happy Creature! in all lands
Nurtured by hospitable hands:
Free entrance to this cot has he,
Entrance and exit both *yet* free;
And, when the keen unruffled weather
That thus brings man and bird together,

---

* The words —
    'Matthew, Mark, and Luke, and John,
      Bless the bed that I lie on,'
are part of a child's prayer, still in general use through the northern counties.

Shall with its pleasantness be past,
And casement closed and door made fast,
To keep at bay the howling blast,
He needs not fear the season's rage,
For the whole house is Robin's cage.
Whether the bird flit here or there,
O'er table *lilt*, or perch on chair,
Though some may frown and make a stir
To scare him as a trespasser,
And he belike will flinch or start,
Good friends he has to take his part;
One chiefly, who with voice and look
Pleads for him from the chimney-nook,
Where sits the Dame, and wears away
Her long and vacant holiday;
With images about her heart,
Reflected from the years gone by,
On human nature's second infancy.

1834.

XXXIV.
HER EYES ARE WILD.

I.

Her eyes are wild, her head is bare,
The sun has burnt her coal-black hair;
Her eyebrows have a rusty stain,
And she came far from over the main.
She has a baby on her arm,
Or else she were alone:
And underneath the hay-stack warm,
And on the greenwood stone,
She talked and sung the woods among,
And it was in the English tongue.

II.

"Sweet babe! they say that I am mad;
But nay, my heart is far too glad;
And I am happy when I sing
Full many a sad and doleful thing:
Then, lovely baby, do not fear!
I pray thee have no fear of me;
But safe as in a cradle, here
My lovely baby! thou shalt be:
To thee I know too much I owe;
I cannot work thee any woe.

III.

A fire was once within my brain;
And in my head a dull, dull pain;
And fiendish faces, one, two, three,
Hung at my breast, and pulled at me;
But then there came a sight of joy;
It came at once to do me good;
I waked, and saw my little boy,
My little boy of flesh and blood;
Oh joy for me that sight to see!
For he was here, and only he.

IV.

Suck, little babe, oh suck again!
It cools my blood; it cools my brain;
Thy lips I feel them, baby! they
Draw from my heart the pain away.
Oh! press me with thy little hand;
It loosens something at my chest;
About that tight and deadly band
I feel thy little fingers prest.
The breeze I see is in the tree:
It comes to cool my babe and me.

V.

Oh! love me, love me, little boy!
Thou art thy mother's only joy;
And do not dread the waves below,
When o'er the sea-rock's edge we go;
The high crag cannot work me harm,
Nor leaping torrents when they howl;
The babe I carry on my arm,
He saves for me my precious soul;
Then happy lie; for blest am I;
Without me my sweet babe would die.

VI.

Then do not fear, my boy! for thee
Bold as a lion will I be;
And I will always be thy guide,
Through hollow snows and rivers wide.
I'll build an Indian bower; I know
The leaves that make the softest bed:
And, if from me thou wilt not go,
But still be true till I am dead,
My pretty thing! then thou shalt sing
As merry as the birds in spring.

VII.

Thy father cares not for my breast,
'Tis thine, sweet baby, there to rest;
'Tis all thine own! — and, if its hue
Be changed, that was so fair to view,
'Tis fair enough for thee, my dove!
My beauty, little child, is flown,
But thou wilt live with me in love;
And what if my poor cheek be brown?
'Tis well for me, thou canst not see
How pale and wan it else would be.

VIII.

Dread not their taunts, my little Life;
I am thy father's wedded wife;
And underneath the spreading tree
We two will live in honesty.
If his sweet boy he could forsake,
With me he never would have stayed:
From him no harm my babe can take;
But he, poor man! is wretched made;
And every day we two will pray
For him that's gone and far away.

IX.

I'll teach my boy the sweetest things:
I'll teach him how the owlet sings.
My little babe! thy lips are still,
And thou hast almost sucked thy fill.
— Where art thou gone, my own dear child?
What wicked looks are those I see?
Alas! alas! that look so wild,
It never, never came from me:
If thou art mad, my pretty lad,
Then I must be for ever sad.

X.

Oh! smile on me, my little lamb!
For I thy own dear mother am:
My love for thee has well been tried;
I've sought thy father far and wide.
I know the poisons of the shade;
I know the earth-nuts fit for food:
Then, pretty dear, be not afraid:
We'll find thy father in the wood.
Now laugh and be gay, to the woods away!
And there, my babe, we'll live for aye."   1798.

POEMS OF THE FANCY.

I.

A WHIRL-BLAST from behind the hill
Rushed o'er the wood with startling sound;
Then — all at once the air was still,
And showers of hailstones pattered round.
Where leafless oaks towered high above,
I sat within an undergrove
Of tallest hollies, tall and green;
A fairer bower was never seen.
From year to year the spacious floor
With withered leaves is covered o'er,
And all the year the bower is green.
But see! where'er the hailstones drop
The withered leaves all skip and hop;
There's not a breeze — no breath of air —
Yet here, and there, and every where
Along the floor, beneath the shade
By those embowering hollies made,
The leaves in myriads jump and spring,
As if with pipes and music rare
Some Robin Good-fellow were there,
And all those leaves, in festive glee,
Were dancing to the minstrelsy.

1799.

II.
THE WATERFALL AND THE EGLANTINE.

I.

"BEGONE, thou fond presumptuous Elf,"
Exclaimed an angry Voice,
"Nor dare to thrust thy foolish self
Between me and my choice!"
A small Cascade fresh swoln with snows
Thus threatened a poor Briar-rose,
That, all bespattered with his foam,
And dancing high and dancing low,
Was living, as a child might know,
In an unhappy home.

II.

"Dost thou presume my course to block?
Off, off! or, puny Thing!
I'll hurl thee headlong with the rock
To which thy fibres cling."
The Flood was tyrannous and strong;
The patient Briar suffered long,
Nor did he utter groan or sigh,
Hoping the danger would be past;
But, seeing no relief, at last,
He ventured to reply.

III.

"Ah!" said the Briar, "blame me not;
Why should we dwell in strife?
We who in this sequestered spot
Once lived a happy life!
You stirred me on my rocky bed —
What pleasure through my veins you spread
The summer long, from day to day,
My leaves you freshened and bedewed;
Nor was it common gratitude
That did your cares repay.

IV.

When spring came on with bud and bell,
Among these rocks did I
Before you hang my wreaths to tell
That gentle days were nigh!
And in the sultry summer hours,
I sheltered you with leaves and flowers;
And in my leaves — now shed and gone,
The linnet lodged, and for us two
Chanted his pretty songs, when you
Had little voice or none.

V.

But now proud thoughts are in your breast —
What grief is mine you see,
Ah! would you think, even yet how blest
Together we might be!
Though of both leaf and flower bereft,
Some ornaments to me are left —
Rich store of scarlet hips is mine,
With which I, in my humble way,
Would deck you many a winter day,
A happy Eglantine!"

VI.

What more he said I cannot tell,
The Torrent down the rocky dell
Came thundering loud and fast;
I listened, nor aught else could hear;
The Briar quaked — and much I fear
Those accents were his last.

1800.

III.
THE OAK AND THE BROOM.
A PASTORAL.

I.

His simple truths did Andrew glean
Beside the babbling rills;
A careful student he had been
Among the woods and hills.
One winter's night, when through the trees
The wind was roaring, on his knees
His youngest born did Andrew hold:
And while the rest, a ruddy quire,
Were seated round their blazing fire,
This Tale the Shepherd told.

II.

"I saw a crag, a lofty stone
As ever tempest beat!
Out of its head an Oak had grown,
A Broom out of its feet.
The time was March, a cheerful noon —
The thaw-wind, with the breath of June,
Breathed gently from the warm south-west:
When, in a voice sedate with age,
This Oak, a giant and a sage,
His neighbour thus addressed: —

III.

'Eight weary weeks, through rock and clay,
Along this mountain's edge,
The Frost hath wrought both night and day,
Wedge driving after wedge.
Look up! and think, above your head
What trouble, surely, will be bred;
Last night I heard a crash — 'tis true,
The splinters took another road —
I see them yonder — what a load
For such a Thing as you!

IV.

You are preparing as before,
To deck your slender shape;
And yet, just three years back — no more —
You had a strange escape:
Down from yon cliff a fragment broke;
It thundered down, with fire and smoke,
And hitherward pursued its way;
This ponderous block was caught by me,
And o'er your head, as you may see,
'Tis hanging to this day!

V.

If breeze or bird to this rough steep
Your kind's first seed did bear;
The breeze had better been asleep,
The bird caught in a snare:
For you and your green twigs decoy
The little witless shepherd-boy
To come and slumber in your bower;
And, trust me, on some sultry noon,
Both you and he, Heaven knows how soon!
Will perish in one hour.

VI.

From me this friendly warning take' —
The Broom began to doze,
And thus, to keep herself awake,
Did gently interpose;
'My thanks for your discourse are due;
That more than what you say is true,
I know, and I have known it long;
Frail is the bond by which we hold
Our being, whether young or old,
Wise, foolish, weak, or strong.

VII.

'Disasters, do the best we can,
Will reach both great and small;
And he is oft the wisest man,
Who is not wise at all.
For me, why should I wish to roam?
This spot is my paternal home,
It is my pleasant heritage;
My father many a happy year,
Spread here his careless blossoms, here
Attained a good old age.

VIII.

Even such as his may be my lot.
What cause have I to haunt
My heart with terrors? Am I not
In truth a favoured plant!
On me such bounty Summer pours,
That I am covered o'er with flowers;
And, when the Frost is in the sky,
My branches are so fresh and gay
That you might look at me and say,
This Plant can never die.

IX.

The butterfly, all green and gold,
To me hath often flown,
Here in my blossoms to behold
Wings lovely as his own.
When grass is chill with rain or dew,
Beneath my shade, the mother-ewe
Lies with her infant lamb; I see
The love they to each other make,
And the sweet joy which they partake,
It is a joy to me.'

X.

Her voice was blithe, her heart was light;
The Broom might have pursued
Her speech, until the stars of night
Their journey had renewed;
But in the branches of the oak
Two ravens now began to croak
Their nuptial song, a gladsome air;
And to her own green bower the breeze
That instant brought two stripling bees
To rest, or murmur there.

XI.

One night, my Children! from the north
There came a furious blast;
At break of day I ventured forth,
And near the cliff I passed.
The storm had fallen upon the Oak,
And struck him with a mighty stroke,
And whirled, and whirled him far away;
And, in one hospitable cleft,
The little careless Broom was left
To live for many a day."

1800.

IV.

TO A SEXTON.

Let thy wheel-barrow alone —
Wherefore, Sexton, piling still
In thy bone-house bone on bone?
'Tis already like a hill
In a field of battle made,
Where three thousand skulls are laid;
These died in peace each with the other, —
Father, sister, friend, and brother.

TO A SEXTON.

Mark the spot to which I point!
From this platform, eight feet square,
Take not even a finger-joint:
Andrew's whole fire-side is there.
Here, alone, before thine eyes,
Simon's sickly daughter lies,
From weakness now, and pain defended,
Whom he twenty winters tended.

Look but at the gardener's pride —
How he glories, when he sees
Roses, lilies, side by side,
Violets in families!
By the heart of Man, his tears,
By his hopes and by his fears,
Thou, too heedless, art the Warden
Of a far superior garden.

Thus then, each to other dear,
Let them all in quiet lie,
Andrew there, and Susan here,
Neighbours in mortality.
And, should I live through sun and rain
Seven widowed years without my Jane,
O Sexton, do not then remove her,
Let one grave hold the Loved and Lover!

1799.

V.

TO THE DAISY.

"Her* divine skill taught me this,
That from every thing I saw
I could some instruction draw,
And raise pleasure to the height
Through the meanest object's sight.
By the murmur of a spring,
Or the least bough's rustelling;
By a Daisy whose leaves spread
Shut when Titan goes to bed;
Or a shady bush or tree;
She could more infuse in me
Than all Nature's beauties can
In some other wiser man."

G. WITHER.

In youth from rock to rock I went,
From hill to hill in discontent
Of pleasure high and turbulent,
   Most pleased when most uneasy;
But now my own delights I make, —
My thirst at every rill can slake,
And gladly Nature's love partake,
   Of Thee, sweet Daisy!

Thee Winter in the garland wears
That thinly decks his few grey hairs;
Spring parts the clouds with softest airs,
   That she may sun thee;
Whole Summer-fields are thine by right;
And Autumn, melancholy Wight!
Doth in thy crimson head delight
   When rains are on thee.

* His muse.

TO THE DAISY.

In shoals and bands, a morrice train,
Thou greet'st the traveller in the lane;
Pleased at his greeting thee again;
   Yet nothing daunted,
Nor grieved if thou be set at nought:
And oft alone in nooks remote
We meet thee, like a pleasant thought,
   When such are wanted.

Be violets in their secret mews
The flowers the wanton Zephyrs choose;
Proud be the rose, with rains and dews
   Her head impearling,
Thou liv'st with less ambitious aim,
Yet hast not gone without thy fame;
Thou art indeed by many a claim
   The Poet's darling.

If to a rock from rains he fly,
Or, some bright day of April sky,
Imprisoned by hot sunshine lie
   Near the green holly,
And wearily at length should fare;
He needs but look about, and there
Thou art! — a friend at hand, to scare
   His melancholy.

A hundred times, by rock or bower,
Ere thus I have lain couched an hour,
Have I derived from thy sweet power
   Some apprehension;
Some steady love; some brief delight;
Some memory that had taken flight;
Some chime of fancy wrong or right;
   Or stray invention.

If stately passions in me burn,
And one chance look to thee should turn,
I drink out of an humbler urn

  A lowlier pleasure;
The homely sympathy that heeds
The common life, our nature breeds;
A wisdom fitted to the needs
  Of hearts at leisure.

Fresh-smitten by the morning ray,
When thou art up, alert and gay,
Then, cheerful Flower! my spirits play
  With kindred gladness:
And when, at dusk, by dews opprest
Thou sink'st, the image of thy rest
Hath often eased my pensive breast
  Of careful sadness.

And all day long I number yet,
All seasons through, another debt,
Which I, wherever thou art met,
  To thee am owing;
An instinct call it, a blind sense;
A happy, genial influence,
Coming one knows not how, nor whence,
  Nor whither going.

Child of the Year! that round dost run
Thy pleasant course,—when day's begun
As ready to salute the sun
  As lark or leveret,
Thy long-lost praise thou shalt regain;
Nor be less dear to future men
Than in old time;—thou not in vain
  Art Nature's favourite.* 1802.

---

* See, in Chaucer and the elder Poets, the honours formerly paid to this flower.

VI.
THE GREEN LINNET.

Beneath these fruit-tree boughs that shed
Their snow-white blossoms on my head,
With brightest sunshine round me spread
   Of spring's unclouded weather,
In this sequestered nook how sweet
To sit upon my orchard-seat!
And birds and flowers once more to greet,
   My last year's friends together.

One have I marked, the happiest guest
In all this covert of the blest:
Hail to Thee, far above the rest
   In joy of voice and pinion!
Thou, Linnet! in thy green array,
Presiding Spirit here to-day,
Dost lead the revels of the May;
   And this is thy dominion.

While birds, and butterflies, and flowers,
Make all one band of paramours,
Thou, ranging up and down the bowers,
   Art sole in thy employment:
A Life, a Presence like the Air,
Scattering thy gladness without care,
Too blest with any one to pair;
   Thyself thy own enjoyment.

Amid yon tuft of hazel trees,
That twinkle to the gusty breeze,
Behold him perched in ecstacies,
   Yet seeming still to hover;
There! where the flutter of his wings
Upon his back and body flings
Shadows and sunny glimmerings,
   That cover him all over.

My dazzled sight he oft deceives,
A Brother of the dancing leaves;
Then flits, and from the cottage-eaves
    Pours forth his song in gushes;
As if by that exulting strain
He mocked and treated with disdain
The voiceless Form he chose to feign,
    While fluttering in the bushes.   1803.

VII.
TO A SKY-LARK.

Up with me! up with me into the clouds!
    For thy song, Lark, is strong;
Up with me, up with me into the clouds!
    Singing, singing,
With clouds and sky about thee ringing,
    Lift me, guide me till I find
That spot which seems so to thy mind!

I have walked through wildernesses dreary,
And to-day my heart is weary;
Had I now the wings of a Faery,
Up to thee would I fly.
There is madness about thee, and joy divine
In that song of thine;
Lift me, guide me high and high
To thy banqueting-place in the sky.

    Joyous as morning,
Thou art laughing and scorning;
Thou hast a nest for thy love and thy rest,
And, though little troubled with sloth,
Drunken Lark! thou would'st be loth
To be such a traveller as I.
Happy, happy Liver,
With a soul as strong as a mountain river
Pouring out praise to the almighty Giver,
    Joy and jollity be with us both!

Alas! my journey, rugged and uneven,
Through prickly moors or dusty ways must wind;
But hearing thee, or others of thy kind,
As full of gladness and as free of heaven,
I, with my fate contented, will plod on,
And hope for higher raptures, when life's day is done.

1805.

VIII.
TO THE SMALL CELANDINE.*

Pansies, lilies, kingcups, daisies,
Let them live upon their praises;
Long as there's a sun that sets,
Primroses will have their glory;
Long as there are violets,
They will have a place in story:
There's a flower that shall be mine,
'Tis the little Celandine.

Eyes of some men travel far
For the finding of a star;
Up and down the heavens they go,
Men that keep a mighty rout!
I'm as great as they, I trow,
Since the day I found thee out,
Little Flower! — I'll make a stir,
Like a sage astronomer.

Modest, yet withal an Elf
Bold, and lavish of thyself;
Since we needs must first have met
I have seen thee, high and low,
Thirty years or more, and yet
'Twas a face I did not know;
Thou hast now, go where I may,
Fifty greetings in a day.

* Common Pilewort.

Ere a leaf is on a bush,
In the time before the thrush
Has a thought about her nest,
Thou wilt come with half a call,
Spreading out thy glossy breast
Like a careless Prodigal;
Telling tales about the sun,
When we've little warmth, or none.

Poets, vain men in their mood!
Travel with the multitude:
Never heed them; I aver
That they all are wanton wooers;
But the thrifty cottager,
Who stirs little out of doors,
Joys to spy thee near her home;
Spring is coming, thou art come!

Comfort have thou of thy merit,
Kindly, unassuming Spirit!
Careless of thy neighbourhood,
Thou dost show thy pleasant face
On the moor, and in the wood,
In the lane; — there's not a place,
Howsoever mean it be,
But 'tis good enough for thee.

Ill befal the yellow flowers,
Children of the flaring hours!
Buttercups, that will be seen,
Whether we will see or no;
Others, too, of lofty mien;
They have done as worldlings do,
Taken praise that should be thine,
Little, humble Celandine!

Prophet of delight and mirth,
Ill-requited upon earth;

Herald of a mighty band,
Of a joyous train ensuing,
Serving at my heart's command,
Tasks that are no tasks renewing,
I will sing, as doth behove,
Hymns in praise of what I love!

1803.

IX.
TO THE SAME FLOWER.

Pleasures newly found are sweet
When they lie about our feet:
February last, my heart
First at sight of thee was glad;
All unheard of as thou art,
Thou must needs, I think, have had,
Celandine! and long ago,
Praise of which I nothing know.

I have not a doubt but he,
Whosoe'er the man might be,
Who the first with pointed rays
(Workman worthy to be sainted)
Set the sign-board in a blaze,
When the rising sun he painted,
Took the fancy from a glance
At thy glittering countenance.

Soon as gentle breezes bring
News of winter's vanishing,
And the children build their bowers,
Sticking 'kerchief-plots of mould
All about with full-blown flowers,
Thick as sheep in shepherd's fold!
With the proudest thou art there,
Mantling in the tiny square.

Often have I sighed to measure
By myself a lonely pleasure,
Sighed to think, I read a book
Only read, perhaps, by me;
Yet I long could overlook
Thy bright coronet and thee,
And thy arch and wily ways,
And thy store of other praise.

Blithe of heart, from week to week
Thou dost play at hide-and-seek;
While the patient primrose sits
Like a beggar in the cold,
Thou, a flower of wiser wits,
Slip'st into thy sheltering hold;
Liveliest of the vernal train
When ye all are out again.

Drawn by what peculiar spell,
By what charm of sight or smell,
Does the dim-eyed curious Bee,
Labouring for her waxen cells,
Fondly settle upon thee
Prized above all buds and bells
Opening daily at thy side;
By the season multiplied?

Thou art not beyond the moon,
But a thing "beneath our shoon:"
Let the bold Discoverer thrid
In his bark the Polar Sea;
Rear who will a pyramid;
Praise it is enough for me,
If there be but three or four
Who will love my little Flower.

1803.

X.
THE SEVEN SISTERS;
OR,
THE SOLITUDE OF BINNORIE.

I.
Seven Daughters had Lord Archibald,
All children of one mother:
You could not say in one short day
What love they bore each other.
A garland, of seven lilies, wrought!
Seven Sisters that together dwell;
But he, bold Knight as ever fought,
Their Father, took of them no thought,
He loved the wars so well.
Sing, mournfully, oh! mournfully,
The solitude of Binnorie!

II.
Fresh blows the wind, a western wind,
And from the shores of Erin,
Across the wave, a Rover brave
To Binnorie is steering:
Right onward to the Scottish strand
The gallant ship is borne;
The warriors leap upon the land,
And hark! the Leader of the band
Hath blown his bugle horn.
Sing, mournfully, oh! mournfully,
The solitude of Binnorie.

III.
Beside a grotto of their own,
With boughs above them closing,
The Seven are laid, and in the shade
They lie like fawns reposing.

But now, upstarting with affright
At noise of man and steed,
Away they fly to left, to right —
Of your fair household, Father-knight,
Methinks you take small heed!
Sing, mournfully, oh! mournfully,
The solitude of Binnorie.

IV.

Away the seven fair Campbells fly,
And, over hill and hollow,
With menace proud, and insult loud,
The youthful Rovers follow.
Cried they, "Your Father loves to roam:
Enough for him to find
The empty house when he comes home;
For us your yellow ringlets comb,
For us be fair and kind!"
Sing, mournfully, oh! mournfully,
The solitude of Binnorie.

V.

Some close behind, some side by side,
Like clouds in stormy weather;
They run, and cry, "Nay, let us die,
And let us die together."
A lake was near; the shore was steep;
There never foot had been;
They ran, and with a desperate leap
Together plunged into the deep,
Nor ever more were seen.
Sing, mournfully, oh! mournfully,
The solitude of Binnorie.

VI.

The stream that flows out of the lake,
As through the glen it rambles,
Repeats a moan o'er moss and stone,
For those seven lovely Campbells.

Seven little Islands, green and bare,
Have risen from out the deep:
The fishers say, those sisters fair,
By faeries all are buried there,
And there together sleep.
Sing, mournfully, oh! mournfully,
The solitude of Binnorie.

1804.

XI.

Who fancied what a pretty sight
This Rock would be if edged around
With living snow-drops? circlet bright!
How glorious to this orchard-ground!
Who loved the little Rock, and set
Upon its head this coronet?

Was it the humour of a child?
Or rather of some gentle maid,
Whose brows, the day that she was styled
The shepherd-queen, were thus arrayed?
Of man mature, or matron sage?
Or old man toying with his age?

I asked — 'twas whispered; The device
To each and all might well belong:
It is the Spirit of Paradise
That prompts such work, a Spirit strong,
That gives to all the self-same bent
Where life is wise and innocent.

1803.

XII.
SONG FOR THE SPINNING WHEEL.

FOUNDED UPON A BELIEF PREVALENT AMONG THE PASTORAL VALES OF WESTMORELAND.

Swiftly turn the murmuring wheel!
Night has brought the welcome hour,
When the weary fingers feel
Help, as if from faery power;
Dewy night o'ershades the ground;
Turn the swift wheel round and round!

Now, beneath the starry sky,
Couch the widely-scattered sheep; —
Ply the pleasant labour, ply!
For the spindle, while they sleep,
Runs with speed more smooth and fine,
Gathering up a trustier line.

Short-lived likings may be bred
By a glance from fickle eyes;
But true love is like the thread
Which the kindly wool supplies,
When the flocks are all at rest
Sleeping on the mountain's breast.   1812.

XIII.
HINT FROM THE MOUNTAINS.

FOR CERTAIN POLITICAL PRETENDERS.

"Who but hails the sight with pleasure
 When the wings of genius rise,
Their ability to measure
    With great enterprise;
But in man was ne'er such daring
As yon Hawk exhibits, pairing
His brave spirit with the war in
    The stormy skies!

Mark him, how his power he uses,
  Lays it by, at will resumes!
Mark, ere for his haunt he chooses
  Clouds and utter glooms!
There, he wheels in downward mazes;
Sunward now his flight he raises,
Catches fire, as seems, and blazes
  With uninjured plumes!" —

ANSWER.

"Stranger, 'tis no act of courage
  Which aloft thou dost discern;
No bold *bird* gone forth to forage
  'Mid the tempest stern;
But such mockery as the nations
See, when public perturbations
Lift men from their native stations,
  Like yon TUFT OF FERN;

Such it is; the aspiring creature
  Soaring on undaunted wing,
(So you fancied) is by nature
  A dull helpless thing,
Dry and withered, light and yellow; —
That to be the tempest's fellow!
Wait — and you shall see how hollow
  Its endeavouring!"

1817.

XIV.
ON SEEING A NEEDLECASE IN THE FORM OF A HARP.

THE WORK OF E. M. S.

FROWNS are on every Muse's face,
  Reproaches from their lips are sent,
That mimicry should thus disgrace
  The noble Instrument.

A very Harp in all but size!
 Needles for strings in apt gradation!
Minerva's self would stigmatize
 The unclassic profanation.

Even her *own* needle that subdued
 Arachne's rival spirit,
Though wrought in Vulcan's happiest mood,
 Such honour could not merit.

And this, too, from the Laureate's Child,
 A living lord of melody!
How will her Sire be reconciled
 To the refined indignity?

I spake, when whispered a low voice,
 "Bard! moderate your ire;
Spirits of all degrees rejoice
 In presence of the lyre.

The Minstrels of Pygmean bands,
 Dwarf Genii, moonlight-loving Fays,
Have shells to fit their tiny hands
 And suit their slender lays.

Some, still more delicate of ear,
 Have lutes (believe my words)
Whose framework is of gossamer,
 While sunbeams are the chords.

Gay Sylphs this miniature will court,
 Made vocal by their brushing wings,
And sullen Gnomes will learn to sport
 Around its polished strings;

Whence strains to love-sick maiden dear,
 While in her lonely bower she tries
To cheat the thought she cannot cheer,
 By fanciful embroideries.

Trust, angry Bard! a knowing Sprite,
  Nor think the Harp her lot deplores;
Though 'mid the stars the Lyre shine bright,
  Love *stoops* as fondly as he soars."

1827.

XV.

GLAD sight wherever new with old
Is joined through some dear homeborn tie;
The life of all that we behold
Depends upon that mystery.
Vain is the glory of the sky,
The beauty vain of field and grove
Unless, while with admiring eye
We gaze, we also learn to love.

XVI.
THE DANISH BOY.
A FRAGMENT.

I.

BETWEEN two sister moorland rills
There is a spot that seems to lie
Sacred to flowerets of the hills,
And sacred to the sky.
And in this smooth and open dell
There is a tempest-stricken tree;
A corner-stone by lightning cut,
The last stone of a lonely hut;
And in this dell you see
A thing no storm can e'er destroy,
The shadow of a Danish Boy.

II.

In clouds above, the lark is heard,
But drops not here to earth for rest;
Within this lonesome nook the bird
Did never build her nest.
No beast, no bird hath here his home;
Bees, wafted on the breezy air,
Pass high above those fragrant bells
To other flowers: — to other dells
Their burthens do they bear;
The Danish Boy walks here alone:
The lovely dell is all his own.

III.

A Spirit of noon-day is he;
Yet seems a form of flesh and blood;
Nor piping shepherd shall he be,
Nor herd-boy of the wood.
A regal vest of fur he wears,
In colour like a raven's wing;
It fears not rain, nor wind, nor dew;
But in the storm 'tis fresh and blue
As budding pines in spring;
His helmet has a vernal grace,
Fresh as the bloom upon his face.

IV.

A harp is from his shoulder slung;
Resting the harp upon his knee;
To words of a forgotten tongue
He suits its melody.
Of flocks upon the neighbouring hill
He is the darling and the joy;
And often, when no cause appears,
The mountain-ponies prick their ears,
— They hear the Danish Boy,
While in the dell he sings alone
Beside the tree and corner-stone.

V.

There sits he; in his face you spy
No trace of a ferocious air,
Nor ever was a cloudless sky
So steady or so fair.
The lovely Danish Boy is blest
And happy in his flowery cove:
From bloody deeds his thoughts are far;
And yet he warbles songs of war,
That seem like songs of love,
For calm and gentle is his mien;
Like a dead Boy he is serene.

1799.

XVII.
SONG
FOR THE WANDERING JEW.

Though the torrents from their fountains
Roar down many a craggy steep,
Yet they find among the mountains
Resting-places calm and deep.

Clouds that love through air to hasten,
Ere the storm its fury stills,
Helmet-like themselves will fasten
On the heads of towering hills.

What, if through the frozen centre
Of the Alps the Chamois bound,
Yet he has a home to enter
In some nook of chosen ground:

And the Sea-horse, though the ocean
Yield him no domestic cave,
Slumbers without sense of motion,
Couched upon the rocking wave.

If on windy days the Raven
Gambol like a dancing skiff,
Not the less she loves her haven
In the bosom of the cliff.

The fleet Ostrich, till day closes,
Vagrant over desert sands,
Brooding on her eggs reposes
When chill night that care demands.

Day and night my toils redouble,
Never nearer to the goal;
Night and day, I feel the trouble
Of the Wanderer in my soul. 1800.

XVIII.
STRAY PLEASURES.

*"— Pleasure is spread through the earth
In stray gifts to be claimed by whoever shall find."*

By their floating mill,
That lies dead and still,
Behold yon Prisoners three,
The Miller with two Dames, on the breast of the Thames!
The platform is small, but gives room for them all;
And they're dancing merrily.

From the shore come the notes
To their mill where it floats,
To their house and their mill tethered fast:
To the small wooden isle where, their work to beguile,
They from morning to even take whatever is given; —
And many a blithe day they have past.

In sight of the spires,
All alive with the fires
Of the sun going down to his rest,
In the broad open eye of the solitary sky,
They dance, — there are three, as jocund as free,
While they dance on the calm river's breast.

  Man and Maidens wheel,
   They themselves make the reel,
And their music 's a prey which they seize;
It plays not for them, — what matter? 'tis theirs;
And if they had care, it has scattered their cares
While they dance, crying, "Long as ye please."

  They dance not for me,
   Yet mine is their glee!
Thus pleasure is spread through the earth
In stray gifts to be claimed by whoever shall find;
Thus a rich loving-kindness, redundantly kind,
Moves all nature to gladness and mirth.

  The showers of the spring
   Rouse the birds, and they sing;
If the wind do but stir for his proper delight,
Each leaf, that and this, his neighbour will kiss;
Each wave, one and t'other, speeds after his brother;
They are happy, for that is their right!

1806.

XIX.

THE PILGRIM'S DREAM;

OR,

THE STAR AND THE GLOW-WORM.

A Pilgrim, when the summer day
Had closed upon his weary way,
A lodging begged beneath a castle's roof;
But him the haughty Warder spurned;
And from the gate the Pilgrim turned,
To seek such covert as the field
Or heath-besprinkled copse might yield,
Or lofty wood, shower-proof.

He paced along; and, pensively,
Halting beneath a shady tree,
Whose moss-grown root might serve for couch or seat,
Fixed on a Star his upward eye;
Then, from the tenant of the sky
He turned, and watched with kindred look,
A Glow-worm, in a dusky nook, .
Apparent at his feet.

The murmur of a neighbouring stream
Induced a soft and slumbrous dream,
A pregnant dream, within whose shadowy bounds
He recognised the earth-born Star,
And *That* which glittered from afar;
And (strange to witness!) from the frame
Of the ethereal Orb, there came
Intelligible sounds.

Much did it taunt the humble Light
That now, when day was fled, and night
Hushed the dark earth, fast closing weary eyes,
A very reptile could presume
To show her taper in the gloom,
As if in rivalship with One
Who sate a ruler on his throne
Erected in the skies.

"Exalted Star!" the Worm replied,
"Abate this unbecoming pride,
Or with a less uneasy lustre shine;
Thou shrink'st as momently thy rays
Are mastered by the breathing haze;
While neither mist, nor thickest cloud
That shapes in heaven its murky shroud,
Hath power to injure mine.

But not for this do I aspire
To match the spark of local fire,

That at my will burns on the dewy lawn,
With thy acknowledged glories; — No!
Yet, thus upbraided, I may show
What favours do attend me here,
Till, like thyself, I disappear
Before the purple dawn."

When this in modest guise was said,
Across the welkin seemed to spread
A boding sound — for aught but sleep unfit!
Hills quaked, the rivers backward ran;
That Star, so proud of late, looked wan;
And reeled with visionary stir
In the blue depth, like Lucifer
Cast headlong to the pit!

Fire raged: and, when the spangled floor
Of ancient ether was no more,
New heavens succeeded, by the dream brought forth:
And all the happy Souls that rode
Transfigured through that fresh abode,
Had heretofore, in humble trust,
Shone meekly 'mid their native dust,
The Glow-worms of the earth!

This knowledge, from an Angel's voice
Proceeding, made the heart rejoice
Of Him who slept upon the open lea:
Waking at morn he murmured not;
And, till life's journey closed, the spot
Was to the Pilgrim's soul endeared,
Where by that dream he had been cheered
Beneath the shady tree.

1818.

XX.
A WREN'S NEST.

Among the dwellings framed by birds
   In field or forest with nice care,
Is none that with the little Wren's
   In snugness may compare.

No door the tenement requires,
   And seldom needs a laboured roof;
Yet is it to the fiercest sun
   Impervious, and storm-proof.

So warm, so beautiful withal,
   In perfect fitness for its aim,
That to the Kind by special grace
   Their instinct surely came.

And when for their abodes they seek
   An opportune recess,
The hermit has no finer eye
   For shadowy quietness.

These find, 'mid ivied abbey-walls,
   A canopy in some still nook;
Others are pent-housed by a brae
   That overhangs a brook.

There to the brooding bird her mate
   Warbles by fits his low clear song;
And by the busy streamlet both
   Are sung to all day long.

Or in sequestered lanes they build,
   Where, till the flitting bird's return,
Her eggs within the nest repose,
   Like relics in an urn.

A WREN'S NEST.

But still, where general choice is good,
    There is a better and a best;
And, among fairest objects, some
    Are fairer than the rest;

This, one of those small builders proved
    In a green covert, where, from out
The forehead of a pollard oak,
    The leafy antlers sprout;

For She who planned the mossy lodge,
    Mistrusting her evasive skill,
Had to a Primrose looked for aid
    Her wishes to fulfil.

High on the trunk's projecting brow,
    And fixed an infant's span above
The budding flowers, peeped forth the nest
    The prettiest of the grove!

The treasure proudly did I show
    To some whose minds without disdain
Can turn to little things; but once
    Looked up for it in vain:

'Tis gone — a ruthless spoiler's prey,
    Who heeds not beauty, love, or song,
'Tis gone! (so seemed it) and we grieved
    Indignant at the wrong.

Just three days after, passing by
    In clearer light the moss-built cell
I saw, espied its shaded mouth;
    And felt that all was well.

The Primrose for a veil had spread
    The largest of her upright leaves;
And thus, for purposes benign,
    A simple flower deceives.

Concealed from friends who might disturb
   Thy quiet with no ill intent,
Secure from evil eyes and hands
   On barbarous plunder bent,

Rest, Mother-bird! and when thy young
   Take flight, and thou art free to roam,
When withered is the guardian Flower,
   And empty thy late home,

Think how ye prospered, thou and thine,
   Amid the unviolated grove
Housed near the growing Primrose-tuft
   In foresight, or in love. 1833.

XXI.
LOVE LIES BLEEDING.

You call it, "Love lies bleeding,"— so you may,
Though the red Flower, not prostrate, only droops,
As we have seen it here from day to day,
From month to month, life passing not away:
A flower how rich in sadness! Even thus stoops,
(Sentient by Grecian sculpture's marvellous power)
Thus leans, with hanging brow and body bent
Earthward in uncomplaining languishment,
The dying Gladiator. So, sad Flower!
('Tis Fancy guides me willing to be led,
Though by a slender thread,)
So drooped Adonis bathed in sanguine dew
Of his death-wound, when he from innocent air
The gentlest breath of resignation drew;
While Venus in a passion of despair
Rent, weeping over him, her golden hair
Spangled with drops of that celestial shower.
She suffered, as Immortals sometimes do;
But pangs more lasting far, *that* Lover knew
Who first, weighed down by scorn, in some lone bower

Did press this semblance of unpitied smart
Into the service of his constant heart,
His own dejection, downcast Flower! could share
With thine, and gave the mournful name which thou wilt ever
    bear.

XXII.
COMPANION TO THE FOREGOING.

Never enlivened with the liveliest ray
That fosters growth or checks or cheers decay,
Nor by the heaviest rain-drops more deprest,
This Flower, that first appeared as summer's guest,
Preserves her beauty 'mid autumnal leaves
And to her mournful habits fondly cleaves.
When files of stateliest plants have ceased to bloom,
One after one submitting to their doom,
When her coevals each and all are fled,
What keeps her thus reclined upon her lonesome bed?

    The old mythologists, more impress'd than we
Of this late day by character in tree
Or herb, that claimed peculiar sympathy,
Or by the silent lapse of fountain clear,
Or with the language of the viewless air
By bird or beast made vocal, sought a cause
To solve the mystery, not in Nature's laws
But in Man's fortunes. Hence a thousand tales
Sung to the plaintive lyre in Grecian vales.
Nor doubt that something of their spirit swayed
The fancy-stricken Youth or heart-sick Maid,
Who, while each stood companionless and eyed
This undeparting Flower in crimson dyed,
Thought of a wound which death is slow to cure,
A fate that has endured and will endure,
And, patience coveting yet passion feeding,
Called the dejected Lingerer, *Love lies Bleeding.*

XXIII.
RURAL ILLUSIONS.

Sylph was it? or a Bird more bright
    Than those of fabulous stock?
A second darted by; — and lo!
    Another of the flock,
Through sunshine flitting from the bough
    To nestle in the rock.
Transient deception! a gay freak
    Of April's mimicries!
Those brilliant strangers, hailed with joy
    Among the budding trees,
Proved last year's leaves, pushed from the spray
    To frolic on the breeze.

Maternal Flora! show thy face,
    And let thy hand be seen,
Thy hand here sprinkling tiny flowers,
    That, as they touch the green,
Take root (so seems it) and look up
    In honour of their Queen.
Yet, sooth, those little starry specks,
    That not in vain aspired
To be confounded with live growths,
    Most dainty, most admired,
Were only blossoms dropped from twigs
    Of their own offspring tired.

Not such the World's illusive shows;
    Her wingless flutterings,
Her blossoms which, though shed, outbrave
    The floweret as it springs,
For the undeceived, smile as they may,
    Are melancholy things:

But gentle Nature plays her part
  With ever-varying wiles,
And transient feignings with plain truth
  So well she reconciles,
That those fond Idlers most are pleased
  Whom oftenest she beguiles.

1832.

XXIV.

THE KITTEN AND FALLING LEAVES.

That way look, my Infant, lo!
What a pretty baby-show!
See the Kitten on the wall,
Sporting with the leaves that fall,
Withered leaves — one — two — and three —
From the lofty elder-tree!
Through the calm and frosty air
Of this morning bright and fair,
Eddying round and round they sink
Softly, slowly: one might think,
From the motions that are made,
Every little leaf conveyed
Sylph or Faery hither tending, —
To this lower world descending,
Each invisible and mute,
In his wavering parachute.
— But the Kitten, how she starts,
Crouches, stretches, paws and darts!
First at one, and then its fellow
Just as light and just as yellow;
There are many now — now one —
Now they stop and there are none:
What intenseness of desire
In her upward eye of fire!
With a tiger-leap half-way
Now she meets the coming prey,

Lets it go as fast, and then
Has it in her power again:
Now she works with three or four,
Like an Indian conjurer;
Quick as he in feats of art,
Far beyond in joy of heart.
Were her antics played in the eye
Of a thousand standers-by,
Clapping hands with shout and stare,
What would little Tabby care
For the plaudits of the crowd?
Over happy to be proud,
Over wealthy in the treasure
Of her own exceeding pleasure!

'Tis a pretty baby-treat;
Nor, I deem, for me unmeet;
Here, for neither Babe nor me,
Other play-mate can I see.
Of the countless living things,
That with stir of feet and wings
(In the sun or under shade,
Upon bough or grassy blade)
And with busy revellings,
Chirp and song, and murmurings,
Made this orchard's narrow space,
And this vale so blithe a place;
Multitudes are swept away
Never more to breathe the day:
Some are sleeping; some in bands
Travelled into distant lands;
Others slunk to moor and wood,
Far from human neighbourhood;
And, among the Kinds that keep
With us closer fellowship,
With us openly abide,
All have laid their mirth aside.

Where is he that giddy Sprite,
Blue-cap, with his colours bright,
Who was blest as bird could be,
Feeding in the apple-tree;
Made such wanton spoil and rout,
Turning blossoms inside out;
Hung — head pointing towards the ground —
Fluttered, perched, into a round
Bound himself, and then unbound;
Lithest, gaudiest Harlequin!
Prettiest tumbler ever seen!
Light of heart and light of limb;
What is now become of Him?
Lambs, that through the mountains went
Frisking, bleating merriment,
When the year was in its prime,
They are sobered by this time.
If you look to vale or hill,
If you listen, all is still,
Save a little neighbouring rill,
That from out the rocky ground
Strikes a solitary sound.
Vainly glitter hill and plain,
And the air is calm in vain;
Vainly Morning spreads the lure
Of a sky serene and pure;
Creature none can she decoy
Into open sign of joy:
Is it that they have a fear
Of the dreary season near?
Or that other pleasures be
Sweeter even than gaiety?

   Yet, whate'er enjoyments dwell
In the impenetrable cell
Of the silent heart which Nature
Furnishes to every creature;

Whatsoe'er we feel and know
Too sedate for outward show,
Such a light of gladness breaks,
Pretty Kitten! from thy freaks, —
Spreads with such a living grace
O'er my little Dora's face;
Yes, the sight so stirs and charms
Thee, Baby, laughing in my arms,
That almost I could repine
That your transports are not mine,
That I do not wholly fare
Even as ye do, thoughtless pair!
And I will have my careless season
Spite of melancholy reason,
Will walk through life in such a way
That, when time brings on decay,
Now and then I may possess
Hours of perfect gladsomeness.
— Pleased by any random toy;
By a kitten's busy joy,
Or an infant's laughing eye
Sharing in the ecstasy;
I would fare like that or this,
Find my wisdom in my bliss;
Keep the sprightly soul awake,
And have faculties to take,
Even from things by sorrow wrought,
Matter for a jocund thought,
Spite of care, and spite of grief,
To gambol with Life's falling Leaf.

1804.

XXV.
THE WAGGONER.

"In Cairo's crowded streets
The impatient Merchant, wondering, waits in vain,
And Mecca saddens at the long delay."
THOMSON.

TO CHARLES LAMB, ESQ.

MY DEAR FRIEND,

When I sent you, a few weeks ago, the Tale of Peter Bell, you asked 'why THE WAGGONER was not added?' — To say the truth, — from the higher tone of imagination, and the deeper touches of passion aimed at in the former, I apprehended this little Piece could not accompany it without disadvantage. In the year 1806, if I am not mistaken, THE WAGGONER was read to you in manuscript, and, as you have remembered it for so long a time, I am the more encouraged to hope, that, since the localities on which the Poem partly depends did not prevent its being interesting to you, it may prove acceptable to others. Being therefore in some measure the cause of its present appearance, you must allow me the gratification of inscribing it to you; in acknowledgment of the pleasure I have derived from your Writings, and of the high esteem with which

I am very truly yours,
WILLIAM WORDSWORTH.

RYDAL MOUNT, *May* 20, 1819.

CANTO FIRST.

'Tis spent — this burning day of June!
Soft darkness o'er its latest gleams is stealing;
The buzzing dor-hawk, round and round, is wheeling, —
That solitary bird
Is all that can be heard
In silence deeper far than that of deepest noon!

Confiding Glow-worms, 'tis a night
Propitious to your earth-born light!
But, where the scattered stars are seen
In hazy straits the clouds between,
Each, in his station twinkling not,
Seems changed into a pallid spot.
The mountains against heaven's grave weight
Rise up, and grow to wondrous height.

The air, as in a lion's den,
Is close and hot; — and now and then
Comes a tired and sultry breeze
With a haunting and a panting,
Like the stifling of disease;
But the dews allay the heat,
And the silence makes it sweet.

Hush, there is some one on the stir!
'Tis Benjamin the Waggoner;
Who long hath trod this toilsome way,
Companion of the night and day.
That far-off tinkling's drowsy cheer,
Mix'd with a faint yet grating sound
In a moment lost and found,
The Wain announces — by whose side
Along the banks of Rydal Mere
He paces on, a trusty Guide, —
Listen! you can scarcely hear!
Hither he his course is bending; —
Now he leaves the lower ground
And up the craggy hill ascending
Many a stop and stay he makes,
Many a breathing-fit he takes; —
Steep the way and wearisome,
Yet all the while his whip is dumb!

The Horses have worked with right good-will,
And so have gained the top of the hill;
He was patient, they were strong,
And now they smoothly glide along,
Recovering breath, and pleased to win
The praises of mild Benjamin.
Heaven shield him from mishap and snare!
But why so early with this prayer?
Is it for threatenings in the sky?
Or for some other danger nigh?

No; none is near him yet, though he
Be one of much infirmity;
For at the bottom of the brow,
Where once the DOVE and OLIVE-BOUGH
Offered a greeting of good ale
To all who entered Grasmere Vale;
And called on him who must depart
To leave it with a jovial heart;
There, where the DOVE and OLIVE-BOUGH
Once hung, a Poet harbours now,
A simple water-drinking Bard;
Why need our Hero then (though frail
His best resolves) be on his guard?
He marches by, secure and bold;
Yet while he thinks on times of old,
It seems that all looks wondrous cold;
He shrugs his shoulders, shakes his head,
And, for the honest folk within,
It is a doubt with Benjamin
Whether they be alive or dead!

Here is no danger, — none at all!
Beyond his wish he walks secure;
But pass a mile — and *then* for trial, —
Then for the pride of self-denial;
If he resist that tempting door,
Which with such friendly voice will call;
If he resist those casement panes,
And that bright gleam which thence will fall
Upon his leaders' bells and manes,
Inviting him with cheerful lure:
For still, though all be dark elsewhere,
Some shining notice will be *there*,
Of open house and ready fare.

The place to Benjamin right well
Is known, and by as strong a spell

As used to be that sign of love
And hope — the OLIVE-BOUGH and DOVE;
He knows it to his cost, good Man!
Who does not know the famous SWAN?
Object uncouth! and yet our boast,
For it was painted by the Host;
His own conceit the figure planned,
'Twas coloured all by his own hand;
And that frail Child of thirsty clay,
Of whom I sing this rustic lay,
Could tell with self-dissatisfaction
Quaint stories of the bird's attraction!

Well! that is past — and in despite
Of open door and shining light.
And now the conqueror essays
The long ascent of Dunmail-raise;
And with his team is gentle here
As when he clomb from Rydal Mere;
His whip they do not dread — his voice
They only hear it to rejoice.
To stand or go is at *their* pleasure;
Their efforts and their time they measure
By generous pride within the breast;
And, while they strain, and while they rest,
He thus pursues his thoughts at leisure.

Now am I fairly safe to-night —
And with proud cause my heart is light:
I trespassed lately worse than ever —
But Heaven has blest a good endeavour;
And, to my soul's content, I find
The evil One is left behind.
Yes, let my master fume and fret,
Here am I — with my horses yet!
My jolly team, he finds that ye
Will work for nobody but me!

Full proof of this the Country gained;
It knows how ye were vexed and strained,
And forced unworthy stripes to bear,
When trusted to another's care.
Here was it — on this rugged slope,
Which now ye climb with heart and hope,
I saw you, between rage and fear,
Plunge, and fling back a spiteful ear,
And ever more and more confused,
As ye were more and more abused:
As chance would have it, passing by
I saw you in that jeopardy:
A word from me was like a charm;
Ye pulled together with one mind;
And your huge burthen, safe from harm,
Moved like a vessel in the wind!
— Yes, without me, up hills so high
'Tis vain to strive for mastery.
Then grieve not, jolly team! though tough
The road we travel, steep, and rough;
Though Rydal-heights and Dunmail-raise,
And all their fellow banks and braes,
Full often make you stretch and strain,
And halt for breath and halt again,
Yet to their sturdiness 'tis owing
That side by side we still are going!

While Benjamin in earnest mood
His meditations thus pursued,
A storm, which had been smothered long,
Was growing inwardly more strong;
And, in its struggles to get free,
Was busily employed as he.
The thunder had begun to growl —
He heard not, too intent of soul;
The air was now without a breath —
He marked not that 'twas still as death

But soon large rain-drops on his head
Fell with the weight of drops of lead; —
He starts — and takes, at the admonition,
A sage survey of his condition.
The road is black before his eyes,
Glimmering faintly where it lies;
Black is the sky — and every hill,
Up to the sky, is blacker still —
Sky, hill, and dale, one dismal room,
Hung round and overhung with gloom;
Save that above a single height
Is to be seen a lurid light,
Above Helm-crag* — a streak half dead,
A burning of portentous red;
And near that lurid light, full well
The ASTROLOGER, sage Sidrophel,
Where at his desk and book he sits,
Puzzling aloft his curious wits;
He whose domain is held in common
With no one but the ANCIENT WOMAN,
Cowering beside her rifted cell,
As if intent on magic spell; —
Dread pair, that, spite of wind and weather,
Still sit upon Helm-crag together!

The ASTROLOGER was not unseen
By solitary Benjamin;
But total darkness came anon,
And he and every thing was gone:
And suddenly a ruffling breeze,
(That would have rocked the sounding trees
Had aught of sylvan growth been there)
Swept through the Hollow long and bare:
The rain rushed down — the road was battered,
As with the force of billows shattered;

* A mountain of Grasmere, the broken summit of which presents two figures, full as distinctly shaped as that of the famous Cobbler near Arroquhar in Scotland.

The horses are dismayed, nor know
Whether they should stand or go;
And Benjamin is groping near them,
Sees nothing, and can scarcely hear them.
He is astounded, — wonder not, —
With such a charge in such a spot;
Astounded in the mountain gap
With thunder-peals, clap after clap,
Close-treading on the silent flashes —
And somewhere, as he thinks, by crashes
Among the rocks; with weight of rain,
And sullen motions long and slow,
That to a dreary distance go —
Till, breaking in upon the dying strain,
A rending o'er his head begins the fray again.

Meanwhile, uncertain what to do,
And oftentimes compelled to halt,
The horses cautiously pursue
Their way, without mishap or fault;
And now have reached that pile of stones,
Heaped over brave King Dunmail's bones,
He who had once supreme command,
Last king of rocky Cumberland;
His bones, and those of all his Power,
Slain here in a disastrous hour!

When, passing through this narrow strait,
Stony, and dark, and desolate,
Benjamin can faintly hear
A voice that comes from some one near,
A female voice: — "Whoe'er you be,
Stop," it exclaimed, "and pity me!"
And, less in pity than in wonder,
Amid the darkness and the thunder,
The Waggoner, with prompt command,
Summons his horses to a stand.

While, with increasing agitation,
The Woman urged her supplication,
In rueful words, with sobs between —
The voice of tears that fell unseen;
There came a flash — a startling glare,
And all Seat-Sandal was laid bare!
'Tis not a time for nice suggestion,
And Benjamin, without a question,
Taking her for some way-worn rover,
Said, "Mount, and get you under cover!"

Another voice, in tone as hoarse
As a swoln brook with rugged course,
Cried out, "Good brother, why so fast?
I've had a glimpse of you — *avast!*
Or, since it suits you to be civil,
Take her at once — for good and evil!"

"It is my Husband," softly said
The Woman, as if half afraid:
By this time she was snug within,
Through help of honest Benjamin;
She and her Babe, which to her breast
With thankfulness the Mother pressed;
And now the same strong voice more near
Said cordially, "My Friend, what cheer?
Rough doings these! as God's my judge,
The sky owes somebody a grudge!
We've had in half an hour or less
A twelvemonth's terror and distress!"

Then Benjamin entreats the Man
Would mount, too, quickly as he can:
The Sailor — Sailor now no more,
But such he had been heretofore —
To courteous Benjamin replied,
"Go you your way, and mind not me;

For I must have, whate'er betide,
My ass and fifty things beside, —
Go, and I 'll follow speedily!"

   The Waggon moves — and with its load
Descends along the sloping road;
And the rough Sailor instantly
Turns to a little tent hard by:
For when, at closing-in of day,
The family had come that way,
Green pasture and the soft warm air
Tempted them to settle there. —
Green is the grass for beast to graze,
Around the stones of Dunmail-raise!

   The Sailor gathers up his bed,
Takes down the canvas overhead;
And, after farewell to the place,
A parting word — though not of grace,
Pursues, with Ass and all his store,
The way the Waggon went before.

CANTO SECOND.

If Wytheburn's modest House of prayer,
As lowly as the lowliest dwelling,
Had, with its belfry's humble stock,
A little pair that hang in air,
Been mistress also of a clock,
(And one, too, not in crazy plight)
Twelve strokes that clock would have been telling
Under the brow of old Helvellyn —
Its bead-roll of midnight,
Then, when the Hero of my tale
Was passing by, and, down the vale
(The vale now silent, hushed I ween
As if a storm had never been)
Proceeding with a mind at ease;
While the old Familiar of the seas

Intent to use his utmost haste,
Gained ground upon the Waggon fast,
And gives another lusty cheer;
For spite of rumbling of the wheels,
A welcome greeting he can hear; —
It is a fiddle in its glee
Dinning from the Cherry Tree!

Thence the sound — the light is there —
As Benjamin is now aware,
Who, to his inward thoughts confined,
Had almost reached the festive door,
When, startled by the Sailor's roar,
He hears a sound and sees the light,
And in a moment calls to mind
That 'tis the village Merry-night!*

Although before in no dejection,
At this insidious recollection
His heart with sudden joy is filled, —
His ears are by the music thrilled,
His eyes take pleasure in the road
Glittering before him bright and broad;
And Benjamin is wet and cold,
And there are reasons manifold
That make the good, tow'rds which he's yearning,
Look fairly like a lawful earning.

Nor has thought time to come and go,
To vibrate between yes and no;
For, cries the Sailor, "Glorious chance
That blew us hither! — let him dance,
Who can or will! — my honest soul,
Our treat shall be a friendly bowl!"

---

* A term well known in the North of England, and applied to rural Festivals where young persons meet in the evening for the purpose of dancing.

He draws him to the door — "Come in,
Come, come," cries he to Benjamin!
And Benjamin — ah, woe is me!
Gave the word — the horses heard
And halted, though reluctantly.

"Blithe souls and lightsome hearts have we,
Feasting at the Cherry Tree!"
This was the outside proclamation,
This was the inside salutation;
What bustling — jostling — high and low!
A universal overflow!
What tankards foaming from the tap!
What store of cakes in every lap!
What thumping — stumping — overhead!
The thunder had not been more busy:
With such a stir you would have said,
This little place may well be dizzy!
'Tis who can dance with greatest vigour —
'Tis what can be most prompt and eager;
As if it heard the fiddle's call,
The pewter clatters on the wall;
The very bacon shows it feeling,
Swinging from the smoky ceiling!

A steaming bowl, a blazing fire,
What greater good can heart desire?
'Twere worth a wise man's while to try
The utmost anger of the sky!
To *seek* for thoughts of a gloomy cast,
If such the bright amends at last.
Now should you say I judge amiss,
The Cherry Tree shows proof of this;
For soon of all the happy there,
Our Travellers are the happiest pair;
All care with Benjamin is gone —
A Cæsar past the Rubicon!

He thinks not of his long, long, strife; —
The Sailor, Man by nature gay,
Hath no resolves to throw away;
And he hath now forgot his Wife,
Hath quite forgotten her — or may be
Thinks her the luckiest soul on earth,
Within that warm and peaceful berth,
      Under cover,
      Terror over,
Sleeping by her sleeping Baby.

With bowl that sped from hand to hand,
The gladdest of the gladsome band,
Amid their own delight and fun,
They hear — when every dance is done,
When every whirling bout is o'er —
The fiddle's *squeak* * — that call to bliss,
Ever followed by a kiss;
They envy not the happy lot,
But enjoy their own the more!

While thus our jocund Travellers fare,
Up springs the Sailor from his chair —
Limps (for I might have told before
That he was lame) across the floor —
Is gone — returns — and with a prize;
With what? — a Ship of lusty size;
A gallant stately Man-of-war,
Fixed on a smoothly-sliding car.
Surprise to all, but most surprise
To Benjamin, who rubs his eyes,
Not knowing that he had befriended
A Man so gloriously attended!

"This," cries the Sailor, "a Third-rate is —
Stand back, and you shall see her gratis!

* At the close of each strathspey, or jig, a particular note from the fiddle summons the Rustic to the agreeable duty of saluting his partner.

This was the Flag-ship at the Nile,
The Vanguard — you may smirk and smile,
But, pretty Maid, if you look near,
You'll find you've much in little here!
A nobler ship did never swim,
And you shall see her in full trim:
I'll set, my friends, to do you honour,
Set every inch of sail upon her."
So said, so done; and masts, sails, yards,
He names them all; and interlards
His speech with uncouth terms of art,
Accomplished in the showman's part;
And then, as from a sudden check,
Cries out — " 'Tis there, the quarter-deck
On which brave Admiral Nelson stood —
A sight that would have roused your blood!
One eye he had, which, bright as ten,
Burned like a fire among his men;
Let this be land, and that be sea,
Here lay the French — and *thus* came we!"

Hushed was by this the fiddle's sound,
The dancers all were gathered round,
And, such the stillness of the house,
You might have heard a nibbling mouse;
While, borrowing helps where'er he may,
The Sailor through the story runs
Of ships to ships and guns to guns;
And does his utmost to display
The dismal conflict, and the might
And terror of that marvellous night!
"A bowl, a bowl of double measure,"
Cries Benjamin, " a draught of length,
To Nelson, England's pride and treasure,
Her bulwark and her tower of strength!"
When Benjamin had seized the bowl,

The mastiff, from beneath the waggon,
Where he lay, watchful as a dragon,
Rattled his chain; — 'twas all in vain,
For Benjamin, triumphant soul!
He heard the monitory growl;
Heard — and in opposition quaffed
A deep, determined, desperate draught!
Nor did the battered Tar forget,
Or flinch from what he deemed his debt:
Then, like a hero crowned with laurel,
Back to her place the ship he led;
Wheeled her back in full apparel;
And so, flag flying at mast head,
Re-yoked her to the Ass: — anon,
Cries Benjamin, "We must be gone."
Thus, after two hours' hearty stay,
Again behold them on their way!

CANTO THIRD.

Right gladly had the horses stirred,
When they the wished-for greeting heard,
The whip's loud notice from the door,
That they were free to move once more.
You think those doings must have bred
In them disheartening doubts and dread;
No, not a horse of all the eight,
Although it be a moonless night,
Fears either for himself or freight;
For this they know (and let it hide,
In part, the offences of their guide)
That Benjamin, with clouded brains,
Is worth the best with all their pains;
And, if they had a prayer to make,
The prayer would be that they may take
With him whatever comes in course,
The better fortune or the worse;

That no one else may have business near them,
And, drunk or sober, he may steer them.

So, forth in dauntless mood they fare,
And with them goes the guardian pair.

Now, heroes, for the true commotion,
The triumph of your late devotion!
Can aught on earth impede delight,
Still mounting to a higher height;
And higher still — a greedy flight!
Can any low-born care pursue her,
Can any mortal clog come to her?
No notion have they — not a thought,
That is from joyless regions brought!
And, while they coast the silent lake,
Their inspiration I partake;
Share their empyreal spirits — yea,
With their enraptured vision, see —
O fancy — what a jubilee!
What shifting pictures — clad in gleams
Of colour bright as feverish dreams!
Earth, spangled sky, and lake serene,
Involved and restless all — a scene
Pregnant with mutual exaltation,
Rich change, and multiplied creation!
This sight to me the Muse imparts; —
And then, what kindness in their hearts!
What tears of rapture, what vow-making,
Profound entreaties, and hand-shaking!
What solemn, vacant, interlacing,
As if they'd fall asleep embracing!
Then, in the turbulence of glee,
And in the excess of amity,
Says Benjamin, "That Ass of thine,
He spoils thy sport, and hinders mine:
If he were tethered to the waggon,
He'd drag as well what he is dragging;

And we, as brother should with brother,
Might trudge it alongside each other!"

Forthwith, obedient to command,
The horses made a quiet stand;
And to the waggon's skirts was tied
The Creature, by the Mastiff's side,
The Mastiff wondering, and perplext
With dread of what will happen next;
And thinking it but sorry cheer,
To have such company so near!

This new arrangement made, the Wain
Through the still night proceeds again;
No Moon hath risen her light to lend;
But indistinctly may be kenned
The Vanguard, following close behind,
Sails spread, as if to catch the wind!

"Thy wife and child are snug and warm,
Thy ship will travel without harm;
I like," said Benjamin, "her shape and stature:
And this of mine — this bulky creature
Of which I have the steering — this,
Seen fairly, is not much amiss!
We want your streamers, friend, you know;
But, altogether as we go,
We make a kind of handsome show!
Among these hills, from first to last,
We've weathered many a furious blast;
Hard passage forcing on, with head
Against the storm, and canvass spread.
I hate a boaster; but to thee
Will say 't, who know'st both land and sea,
The unluckiest hulk that stems the brine
Is hardly worse beset than mine,
When cross-winds on her quarter beat;
And, fairly lifted from my feet,

I stagger onward — heaven knows how;
But not so pleasantly as now:
Poor pilot I, by snows confounded,
And many a foundrous pit surrounded!
Yet here we are, by night and day
Grinding through rough and smooth our way;
Through foul and fair our task fulfilling;
And long shall be so yet — God willing!"

"Ay," said the Tar, "through fair and foul —
But save us from yon screeching owl!"
That instant was begun a fray
Which called their thoughts another way:
The mastiff, ill-conditioned carl!
What must he do but growl and snarl,
Still more and more dissatisfied
With the meek comrade at his side!
Till, not incensed though put to proof,
The Ass, uplifting a hind hoof,
Salutes the Mastiff on the head;
And so were better manners bred,
And all was calmed and quieted.

"Yon screech-owl," says the Sailor, turning
Back to his former cause of mourning,
"Yon owl! — pray God that all be well!
'Tis worse than any funeral bell;
As sure as I've the gift of sight,
We shall be meeting ghosts to-night!"
— Said Benjamin, "This whip shall lay
A thousand, if they cross our way.
I know that Wanton's noisy station,
I know him and his occupation;
The jolly bird hath learned his cheer
Upon the banks of Windermere;
Where a tribe of them make merry,
Mocking the man that keeps the ferry;

Hallooing from an open throat,
Like travellers shouting for a boat.
— The tricks he learned at Windermere
This vagrant owl is playing here —
That is the worst of his employment:
He's at the top of his enjoyment!"

This explanation stilled the alarm,
Cured the foreboder like a charm;
This, and the manner, and the voice,
Summoned the Sailor to rejoice;
His heart is up — he fears no evil
From life or death, from man or devil;
He wheels — and, making many stops,
Brandished his crutch against the mountain tops;
And, while he talked of blows and scars,
Benjamin, among the stars,
Beheld a dancing — and a glancing;
Such retreating and advancing
As, I ween, was never seen
In bloodiest battle since the days of Mars!

CANTO FOURTH.

Thus they, with freaks of proud delight,
Beguile the remnant of the night;
And many a snatch of jovial song
Regales them as they wind along;
While to the music, from on high,
The echoes make a glad reply. —
But the sage Muse the revel heeds
No farther than her story needs;
Nor will she servilely attend
The loitering journey to its end.
— Blithe spirits of her own impel
The Muse, who scents the morning air,
To take of this transported pair

A brief and unreproved farewell;
To quit the slow-paced waggon's side,
And wander down yon hawthorn dell,
With murmuring Greta for her guide.
— There doth she ken the awful form
Of Raven-crag — black as a storm —
Glimmering through the twilight pale;
And Ghimmer-crag,* his tall twin brother,
Each peering forth to meet the other: —
And, while she roves through St. John's Vale,
Along the smooth unpathwayed plain,
By sheep-track or through cottage lane,
Where no disturbance comes to intrude
Upon the pensive solitude,
Her unsuspecting eye, perchance,
With the rude shepherd's favoured glance,
Beholds the faeries in array,
Whose party-coloured garments gay
The silent company betray:
Red, green, and blue; a moment's sight!
For Skiddaw-top with rosy light
Is touched — and all the band take flight.
— Fly also, Muse! and from the dell
Mount to the ridge of Nathdale Fell;
Thence, look thou forth o'er wood and lawn
Hoar with the frost-like dews of dawn;
Across yon meadowy bottom look,
Where close fogs hide their parent brook;
And see, beyond that hamlet small,
The ruined towers of Threlkeld-hall,
Lurking in a double shade,
By trees and lingering twilight made!
There, at Blencathara's rugged feet,
Sir Lancelot gave a safe retreat
To noble Clifford; from annoy
Concealed the persecuted boy,

* The crag of the ewe lamb.

Well pleased in rustic garb to feed
His flock, and pipe on shepherd's reed
Among this multitude of hills,
Crags, woodlands, waterfalls, and rills;
Which soon the morning shall enfold,
From east to west, in ample vest
Of massy gloom and radiance bold.

   The mists, that o'er the streamlet's bed
Hung low, begin to rise and spread;
Even while I speak their skirts of grey
Are smitten by a silver ray;
And lo! — up Castrigg's naked steep
(Where, smoothly urged, the vapours sweep
Along — and scatter and divide,
Like fleecy clouds self-multiplied)
The stately waggon is ascending,
With faithful Benjamin attending,
Apparent now beside his team —
Now lost amid a glittering steam:
And with him goes his Sailor-friend,
By this time near their journey's end;
And, after their high-minded riot,
Sickening into thoughtful quiet;
As if the morning's pleasant hour,
Had for their joys a killing power.
And, sooth, for Benjamin a vein
Is opened of still deeper pain,
As if his heart by notes were stung
From out the lowly hedge-rows flung;
As if the warbler lost in light
Reproved his soarings of the night,
In strains of rapture pure and holy
Upbraided his distempered folly.

   Drooping is he, his step is dull;
But the horses stretch and pull;

With increasing vigour climb,
Eager to repair lost time;
Whether, by their own desert,
Knowing what cause there is for shame,
They are labouring to avert
As much as may be of the blame,
Which, they foresee, must soon alight
Upon *his* head, whom, in despite
Of all his failings, they love best;
Whether for him they are distrest;
Or, by length of fasting roused,
Are impatient to be housed:
Up against the hill they strain
Tugging at the iron chain,
Tugging all with might and main,
Last and foremost, every horse
To the utmost of his force!
And the smoke and respiration,
Rising like an exhalation,
Blend with the mist — a moving shroud
To form, an undissolving cloud;
Which, with slant ray, the merry sun
Takes delight to play upon.
Never golden-haired Apollo,
Pleased some favourite chief to follow
Through accidents of peace or war,
In a perilous moment threw
Around the object of his care
Veil of such celestial hue;
Interposed so bright a screen —
Him and his enemies between!

Alas! what boots it? — who can hide,
When the malicious Fates are bent
On working out an ill intent?
Can destiny be turned aside?

No — sad progress of my story!
Benjamin, this outward glory
Cannot shield thee from thy Master,
Who from Keswick has pricked forth,
Sour and surly as the north;
And, in fear of some disaster,
Comes to give what help he may,
And to hear what thou canst say;
If, as needs he must forbode,
Thou hast been loitering on the road!
His fears, his doubts, may now take flight —
The wished-for object is in sight;
Yet, trust the Muse, it rather hath
Stirred him up to livelier wrath;
Which he stifles, moody man!
With all the patience that he can;
To the end that, at your meeting,
He may give thee decent greeting.

   There he is — resolved to stop,
Till the waggon gains the top;
But stop he cannot — must advance:
Him Benjamin, with lucky glance,
Espies — and instantly is ready,
Self-collected, poised, and steady:
And, to be the better seen,
Issues from his radiant shroud,
From his close-attending cloud,
With careless air and open mien.
Erect his port and firm his going;
So struts yon cock that now is crowing;
And the morning light in grace
Strikes upon his lifted face,
Hurrying the pallid hue away
That might his trespasses betray.
But what can all avail to clear him,

Or what need of explanation,
Parley or interrogation?
For the Master sees, alas!
That unhappy Figure near him,
Limping o'er the dewy grass,
Where the road it fringes, sweet,
Soft and cool to way-worn feet;
And, O indignity! an Ass,
By his noble Mastiff's side,
Tethered to the waggon's tail:
And the ship, in all her pride,
Following after in full sail!
Not to speak of babe and mother;
Who, contented with each other,
And snug as birds in leafy arbour,
Find, within, a blessed harbour!

With eager eyes the Master pries;
Looks in and out, and through and through;
Says nothing — till at last he spies
A wound upon the Mastiff's head,
A wound, where plainly might be read
What feats an Ass's hoof can do!
But drop the rest: — this aggravation,
This complicated provocation,
A hoard of grievances unsealed;
All past forgiveness is repealed;
And thus, and through distempered blood
On both sides, Benjamin the good,
The patient, and the tender-hearted,
Was from his team and waggon parted;
When duty of that day was o'er,
Laid down his whip — and served no more. —
Nor could the waggon long survive,
Which Benjamin had ceased to drive:
It lingered on; — guide after guide
Ambitiously the office tried;

But each unmanageable hill
Called for *his* patience and *his* skill; —
And sure it is, that through this night,
And what the morning brought to light,
Two losses had we to sustain,
We lost both WAGGONER and WAIN!

Accept, O Friend, for praise or blame,
The gift of this adventurous song;
A record which I dared to frame,
Though timid scruples checked me long;
They checked me — and I left the theme
Untouched; — in spite of many a gleam
Of fancy which thereon was shed,
Like pleasant sunbeams shifting still
Upon the side of a distant hill:
But Nature might not be gainsaid;
For what I have and what I miss
I sing of these; — it makes my bliss!
Nor is it I who play the part,
But a shy spirit in my heart,
That comes and goes — will sometimes leap
From hiding-places ten years deep;
Or haunts me with familiar face,
Returning, like a ghost unlaid,
Until the debt I owe be paid.
Forgive me, then; for I had been
On friendly terms with this Machine:
In him, while he was wont to trace
Our roads, through many a long year's space,
A living almanack had we;
We had a speaking diary,
That in this uneventful place,
Gave to the days a mark and name
By which we knew them when they came.
— Yes, I, and all about me here,
Through all the changes of the year,

Had seen him through the mountains go,
In pomp of mist or pomp of snow,
Majestically huge and slow:
Or, with a milder grace adorning
The landscape of a summer's morning;
While Grasmere smoothed her liquid plain
The moving image to detain;
And mighty Fairfield, with a chime
Of echoes, to his march kept time;
When little other business stirred,
And little other sound was heard;
In that delicious hour of balm,
Stillness, solitude, and calm,
While yet the valley is arrayed,
On this side with a sober shade;
On that is prodigally bright —
Crag, lawn, and wood — with rosy light.
— But most of all, thou lordly Wain!
I wish to have thee here again,
When windows flap and chimney roars,
And all is dismal out of doors;
And, sitting by my fire, I see
Eight sorry carts, no less a train!
Unworthy successors of thee,
Come straggling through the wind and rain:
And oft, as they pass slowly on,
Beneath my windows, one by one,
See, perched upon the naked height
The summit of a cumbrous freight,
A single traveller — and there
Another; then perhaps a pair —
The lame, the sickly, and the old;
Men, women, heartless with the cold;
And babes in wet and starveling plight;
Which once, be weather as it might,
Had still a nest within a nest,
Thy shelter — and their mother's breast!

Then most of all, then far the most,
Do I regret what we have lost;
Am grieved for that unhappy sin
Which robbed us of good Benjamin;—
And of his stately Charge, which none
Could keep alive when He was gone!

1805.

POEMS OF THE IMAGINATION.

I.
THERE WAS A BOY.

There was a Boy; ye knew him well, ye cliffs
And islands of Winander! — many a time,
At evening, when the earliest stars began
To move along the edges of the hills,
Rising or setting, would he stand alone,
Beneath the trees, or by the glimmering lake;
And there, with fingers interwoven, both hands
Pressed closely palm to palm and to his mouth
Uplifted, he, as through an instrument,
Blew mimic hootings to the silent owls,
That they might answer him. — And they would shout
Across the watery vale, and shout again,
Responsive to his call, — with quivering peals,
And long halloos, and screams, and echoes loud
Redoubled and redoubled; concourse wild
Of jocund din! And, when there came a pause
Of silence such as baffled his best skill:
Then, sometimes, in that silence, while he hung
Listening, a gentle shock of mild surprise
Has carried far into his heart the voice
Of mountain-torrents; or the visible scene
Would enter unawares into his mind
With all its solemn imagery, its rocks,
Its woods, and that uncertain heaven received
Into the bosom of the steady lake.

This boy was taken from his mates, and died
In childhood, ere he was full twelve years old.
Pre-eminent in beauty is the vale
Where he was born and bred: the church-yard hangs
Upon a slope above the village-school;
And, through that church-yard when my way has led
On summer-evenings, I believe, that there
A long half-hour together I have stood
Mute — looking at the grave in which he lies!

1799.

II.
TO THE CUCKOO.

O BLITHE New-comer! I have heard,
I hear thee and rejoice.
O Cuckoo! shall I call thee Bird,
Or but a wandering Voice?

While I am lying on the grass
Thy twofold shout I hear,
From hill to hill it seems to pass,
At once far off, and near.

Though babbling only to the Vale,
Of sunshine and of flowers,
Thou bringest unto me a tale
Of visionary hours.

Thrice welcome, darling of the Spring!
Even yet thou art to me
No bird, but an invisible thing,
A voice, a mystery;

The same whom in my school-boy days
I listened to; that Cry
Which made me look a thousand ways
In bush, and tree, and sky.

To seek thee did I often rove
Through woods and on the green;
And thou wert still a hope, a love;
Still longed for, never seen.

And I can listen to thee yet;
Can lie upon the plain
And listen, till I do beget
That golden time again.

O blessed Bird! the earth we pace
Again appears to be
An unsubstantial, faery place;
That is fit home for Thee!

1804.

III.
A NIGHT-PIECE.

  — The sky is overcast,
With a continuous cloud of texture close,
Heavy and wan, all whitened by the Moon,
Which through that veil is indistinctly seen,
A dull contracted circle, yielding light
So feebly spread, that not a shadow falls,
Chequering the ground — from rock, plant, tree, or tower.
At length a pleasant instantaneous gleam
Startles the pensive traveller while he treads
His lonesome path, with unobserving eye
Bent earthwards; he looks up — the clouds are split
Asunder, — and above his head he sees
The clear Moon, and the glory of the heavens.
There, in a black-blue vault she sails along,
Followed by multitudes of stars, that, small
And sharp, and bright, along the dark abyss
Drive as she drives: how fast they wheel away,
Yet vanish not! — the wind is in the tree,
But they are silent; — still they roll along
Immeasurably distant; and the vault,

Built round by those white clouds, enormous clouds,
Still deepens its unfathomable depth.
At length the Vision closes; and the mind,
Not disturbed by the delight it feels,
Which slowly settles into peaceful calm,
Is left to muse upon the solemn scene.

1798.

IV.
YEW-TREES.

THERE is a Yew-tree, pride of Lorton Vale,
Which to this day stands single, in the midst
Of its own darkness, as it stood of yore:
Not loth to furnish weapons for the bands
Of Umfraville or Percy ere they marched
To Scotland's heaths; or those that crossed the sea
And drew their sounding bows at Azincour,
Perhaps at earlier Crecy, or Poictiers.
Of vast circumference and gloom profound
This solitary Tree! a living thing
Produced too slowly ever to decay;
Of form and aspect too magnificent
To be destroyed. But worthier still of note
Are those fraternal Four of Borrowdale,
Joined in one solemn and capacious grove;
Huge trunks! and each particular trunk a growth
Of intertwisted fibres serpentine
Up-coiling, and inveterately convolved;
Nor uninformed with Phantasy, and looks
That threaten the profane; — a pillared shade,
Upon whose grassless floor of red-brown hue,
By sheddings from the pining umbrage tinged
Perennially — beneath whose sable roof
Of boughs, as if for festal purpose, decked
With unrejoicing berries — ghostly Shapes
May meet at noontide; Fear and trembling Hope,
Silence and Foresight; Death the Skeleton

And time the Shadow; — there to celebrate,
As in a natural temple scattered o'er
With altars undisturbed of mossy stone,
United worship; or in mute repose
To lie, and listen to the mountain flood
Murmuring from Glaramara's inmost caves.

1803.

V.
NUTTING.

———— It seems a day
(I speak of one from many singled out),
One of those heavenly days that cannot die;
When, in the eagerness of boyish hope,
I left our cottage-threshold, sallying forth
With a huge wallet o'er my shoulders slung,
A nutting-crook in hand; and turned my steps
Tow'rd some far-distant wood, a Figure quaint,
Tricked out in proud disguise of cast-off weeds
Which for that service had been husbanded,
By exhortation of my frugal Dame —
Motley accoutrement, of power to smile
At thorns, and brakes, and brambles, — and, in truth,
More ragged than need was! O'er pathless rocks,
Through beds of matted fern, and tangled thickets,
Forcing my way, I came to one dear nook
Unvisited, where not a broken bough
Drooped with its withered leaves, ungracious sign
Of devastation; but the hazels rose
Tall and erect, with tempting clusters hung,
A virgin scene! — A little while I stood,
Breathing with such suppression of the heart
As joy delights in; and, with wise restraint
Voluptuous, fearless of a rival, eyed
The banquet; — or beneath the trees I sate
Among the flowers, and with the flowers I played;
A temper known to those, who, after long

And weary expectation, have been blest
With sudden happiness beyond all hope.
Perhaps it was a bower beneath whose leaves
The violets of five seasons re-appear
And fade, unseen by any human eye;
Where fairy water-breaks do murmur on
For ever; and I saw the sparkling foam,
And — with my cheek on one of those green stones
That, fleeced with moss, under the shady trees,
Lay round me, scattered like a flock of sheep —
I heard the murmur and the murmuring sound,
In that sweet mood when pleasure loves to pay
Tribute to ease; and, of its joy secure,
The heart luxuriates with indifferent things,
Wasting its kindliness on stocks and stones,
And on the vacant air. Then up I rose,
And dragged to earth both branch and bough, with crash
And merciless ravage: and the shady nook
Of hazels, and the green and mossy bower,
Deformed and sullied, patiently gave up
Their quiet being: and, unless I now
Confound my present feelings with the past;
Ere from the mutilated bower I turned
Exulting, rich beyond the wealth of kings,
I felt a sense of pain when I beheld
The silent trees, and saw the intruding sky. —
Then, dearest Maiden, move along these shades
In gentleness of heart; with gentle hand
Touch — for there is a spirit in the woods.

1799.

VI.

She was a Phantom of delight
When first she gleamed upon my sight;
A lovely Apparition, sent
To be a moment's ornament;

Her eyes as stars of Twilight fair;
Like Twilight's, too, her dusky hair;
But all things else about her drawn
From May-time and the cheerful Dawn;
A dancing Shape, an Image gay,
To haunt, to startle, and way-lay.

I saw her upon nearer view,
A Spirit, yet a Woman too!
Her household motions light and free,
And steps of virgin-liberty;
A countenance in which did meet
Sweet records, promises as sweet;
A Creature not too bright or good
For human nature's daily food;
For transient sorrows, simple wiles,
Praise, blame, love, kisses, tears, and smiles.

And now I see with eye serene
The very pulse of the machine;
A Being breathing thoughtful breath,
A Traveller between life and death;
The reason firm, the temperate will,
Endurance, foresight, strength, and skill;
A perfect Woman, nobly planned,
To warn, to comfort, and command;
And yet a Spirit still, and bright
With something of angelic light.

1804.

VII.

O NIGHTINGALE! thou surely art
A creature of a "fiery heart": —
These notes of thine — they pierce and pierce;
Tumultuous harmony and fierce!
Thou sing'st as if the God of wine
Had helped thee to a Valentine;

A song in mockery and despite
Of shades, and dews, and silent night;
And steady bliss, and all the loves
Now sleeping in these peaceful groves.

I heard a Stock-dove sing or say
His homely tale, this very day;
His voice was buried among trees,
Yet to be come-at by the breeze:
He did not cease; but cooed — and cooed;
And somewhat pensively he wooed:
He sang of love, with quiet blending,
Slow to begin, and never ending;
Of serious faith, and inward glee;
That was the song — the song for me!

1806.

VIII.

Three years she grew in sun and shower,
Then Nature said, "A lovelier flower
On earth was never sown;
This Child I to myself will take;
She shall be mine, and I will make
A Lady of my own.

Myself will to my darling be
Both law and impulse: and with me
The Girl, in rock and plain,'
In earth and heaven, in glade and bower,
Shall feel an overseeing power
To kindle or restrain.

She shall be sportive as the fawn
That wild with glee across the lawn
Or up the mountain springs;
And her's shall be the breathing balm,
And her's the silence and the calm
Of mute insensate things.

The floating clouds their state shall lend
To her; for her the willow bend;
Nor shall she fail to see
Even in the motions of the Storm
Grace that shall mould the Maiden's form
By silent sympathy.

The stars of midnight shall be dear
To her; and she shall lean her ear
In many a secret place
Where rivulets dance their wayward round,
And beauty born of murmuring sound
Shall pass into her face.

And vital feelings of delight
Shall rear her form to stately height,
Her virgin bosom swell;
Such thoughts to Lucy I will give
While she and I together live
Here in this happy dell."

Thus Nature spake — The work was done —
How soon my Lucy's race was run!
She died, and left to me
This heath, this calm, and quiet scene;
The memory of what has been,
And never more will be.   1799.

IX.

A SLUMBER did my spirit seal;
  I had no human fears;
She seemed a thing that could not feel
  The touch of earthly years.

No motion has she now, no force;
  She neither hears nor sees;
Rolled round in earth's diurnal course,
  With rocks, and stones, and trees.   1799.

X.

I WANDERED lonely as a cloud
That floats on high o'er vales and hills,
When all at once I saw a crowd,
A host, of golden daffodils;
Beside the lake, beneath the trees,
Fluttering and dancing in the breeze.

Continuous as the stars that shine
And twinkle on the milky way,
They stretched in never-ending line
Along the margin of a bay:
Ten thousand saw I at a glance,
Tossing their heads in sprightly dance.

The waves beside them danced; but they
Out-did the sparkling waves in glee:
A poet could not but be gay,
In such a jocund company:
I gazed — and gazed — but little thought
What wealth the show to me had brought:

For oft, when on my couch I lie
In vacant or in pensive mood,
They flash upon that inward eye
Which is the bliss of solitude;
And then my heart with pleasure fills,
And dances with the daffodils.

1804.

XI.
THE REVERIE OF POOR SUSAN.

AT the corner of Wood Street, when daylight appears,
Hangs a Thrush that sings loud, it has sung for three years:
Poor Susan has passed by the spot, and has heard
In the silence of morning the song of the Bird.

'Tis a note of enchantment; what ails her? She sees
A mountain ascending, a vision of trees;
Bright volumes of vapour through Lothbury glide,
And a river flows on through the vale of Cheapside.

Green pastures she views in the midst of the dale,
Down which she so often has tripped with her pail;
And a single small cottage, a nest like a dove's,
The one only dwelling on earth that she loves.

She looks, and her heart is in heaven: but they fade,
The mist and the river, the hill and the shade:
The stream will not flow, and the hill will not rise,
And the colours have all passed away from her eyes!

1797.

XII.
POWER OF MUSIC.

An Orpheus! an Orpheus! yes, Faith may grow bold,
And take to herself all the wonders of old; —
Near the stately Pantheon you'll meet with the same
In the street that from Oxford hath borrowed its name.

His station is there; and he works on the crowd,
He sways them with harmony merry and loud;
He fills with his power all their hearts to the brim —
Was aught ever heard like his fiddle and him?

What an eager assembly! what an empire is this!
The weary have life, and the hungry have bliss;
The mourner is cheered, and the anxious have rest;
And the guilt-burthened soul is no longer opprest.

As the Moon brightens round her the clouds of the night,
So He, where he stands, is a centre of light;
It gleams on the face, there, of dusky-browed Jack,
And the pale-visaged Baker's, with basket on back.

That errand-bound 'Prentice was passing in haste —
What matter! he's caught — and his time runs to waste;
The Newsman is stopped, though he stops on the fret;
And the half-breathless Lamplighter — he's in the net!

The Porter sits down on the weight which he bore;
The Lass with her barrow wheels hither her store; —
If a thief could be here he might pilfer at ease;
She sees the Musician, 'tis all that she sees!

He stands, backed by the wall; — he abates not his din;
His hat gives him vigour, with boons dropping in,
From the old and the young, from the poorest; and there!
The one-pennied Boy has his penny to spare.

O blest are the hearers, and proud be the hand
Of the pleasure it spreads through so thankful a band;
I am glad for him, blind as he is! — all the while
If they speak 'tis to praise, and they praise with a smile.

That tall Man, a giant in bulk and in height,
Not an inch of his body is free from delight;
Can he keep himself still, if he would? oh, not he!
The music stirs in him like wind through a tree.

Mark that Cripple who leans on his crutch; like a tower
That long has leaned forward, leans hour after hour! —
That Mother, whose spirit in fetters is bound,
While she dandles the Babe in her arms to the sound.

Now, coaches and chariots! roar on like a stream;
Here are twenty souls happy as souls in a dream:
They are deaf to your murmurs — they care not for you,
Nor what ye are flying, nor what ye pursue!

1806.

XIII.

STAR-GAZERS.

What crowd is this? what have we here! we must not pass it by;
A Telescope upon its frame, and pointed to the sky:
Long is it as a barber's pole, or mast of little boat,
Some little pleasure skiff, that doth on Thames's waters float.

The Show-man chooses well his place, 'tis Leicester's busy Square;
And is as happy in his night, for the heavens are blue and fair;
Calm, though impatient, is the crowd; each stands ready with the fee,
And envies him that's looking; — what an insight must it be!

Yet, Show-man, where can lie the cause? Shall thy Implement have blame,
A boaster, that when he is tried, fails, and is put to shame?
Or is it good as others are, and be their eyes in fault?
Their eyes, or minds? or, finally, is yon resplendent vault?

Is nothing of that radiant pomp so good as we have here?
Or gives a thing but small delight that never can be dear?
The silver moon with all her vales, and hills of mightiest fame,
Doth she betray us when they're seen? or are they but a name?

Or is it rather that Conceit rapacious is and strong,
And bounty never yields so much but it seems to do her wrong?
Or is it, that when human Souls a journey long have had
And are returned into themselves, they cannot but be sad?

Or must we be constrained to think that these Spectators
    rude,
Poor in estate, of manners base, men of the multitude,
Have souls which never yet have risen, and therefore pro-
    strate lie?
No, no, this cannot be; — men thirst for power and majesty!

Does, then, a deep and earnest thought the blissful mind
    employ
Of him who gazes, or has gazed? a grave and steady joy,
That doth reject all show of pride, admits no outward sign,
Because not of this noisy world, but silent and divine!

Whatever be the cause, 'tis sure that they who pry and pore
Seem to meet with little gain, seem less happy than before:
One after One they take their turn, nor have I once espied
That doth not slackly go away, as if dissatisfied.

1806.

XIV.
WRITTEN IN MARCH,
WHILE RESTING ON THE BRIDGE AT THE FOOT OF BROTHER'S WATER.

    The Cock is crowing,
    The stream is flowing,
    The small birds twitter,
    The lake doth glitter,
The green field sleeps in the sun;
    The oldest and youngest
    Are at work with the strongest;
    The cattle are grazing,
    Their heads never raising;
There are forty feeding like one!

    Like an army defeated
    The snow hath retreated,
    And now doth fare ill
    On the top of the bare hill;

The Ploughboy is whooping — anon — anon:
  There's joy in the mountains;
  There's life in the fountains;
  Small clouds are sailing,
  Blue sky prevailing;
The rain is over and gone!

                                        1801.

XV.
BEGGARS.

She had a tall man's height or more;
Her face from summer's noontide heat
No bonnet shaded, but she wore
A mantle, to her very feet
Descending with a graceful flow,
And on her head a cap as white as new-fallen snow.

Her skin was of Egyptian brown:
Haughty, as if her eye had seen
Its own light to a distance thrown,
She towered, fit person for a Queen
To lead those ancient Amazonian files;
Or ruling Bandit's wife among the Grecian isles.

Advancing, forth she stretched her hand
And begged an alms with doleful plea
That ceased not; on our English land
Such woes, I knew, could never be;
And yet a boon I gave her, for the creature
Was beautiful to see — a weed of glorious feature.

I left her, and pursued my way;
And soon before me did espy
A pair of little Boys at play,
Chasing a crimson butterfly;
The taller followed with his hat in hand,
Wreathed round with yellow flowers the gayest of the land.

The other wore a rimless crown
With leaves of laurel stuck about;
And, while both followed up and down,
Each whooping with a merry shout,
In their fraternal features I could trace
Unquestionable lines of that wild Suppliant's face.

Yet *they*, so blithe of heart, seemed fit
For finest tasks of earth or air:
Wings let them have, and they might flit
Precursors to Aurora's car,
Scattering fresh flowers; though happier far, I ween,
To hunt their fluttering game o'er rock and level green.

They dart across my path — but lo,
Each ready with a plaintive whine!
Said I, "Not half an hour ago
Your Mother has had alms of mine."
"That cannot be," one answered — "she is dead:" —
I looked reproof — they saw — but neither hung his head.

"She has been dead, Sir, many a day." —
"Hush, boys! you're telling me a lie;
It was your Mother, as I say!"
And, in the twinkling of an eye,
"Come! come!" cried one, and without more ado,
Off to some other play the joyous Vagrants flew!

1802.

XVI.
SEQUEL TO THE FOREGOING,
COMPOSED MANY YEARS AFTER.

WHERE are they now, those wanton Boys?
For whose free range the dædal earth
Was filled with animated toys,
And implements of frolic mirth;

With tools for ready wit to guide;
And ornaments of seemlier pride,
More fresh, more bright, than princes wear;
For what one moment flung aside,
Another could repair;
What good or evil have they seen
Since I their pastime witnessed here,
Their daring wiles, their sportive cheer?
I ask — but all is dark between!

 They met me in a genial hour,
When universal nature breathed
As with the breath of one sweet flower, —
A time to overrule the power
Of discontent, and check the birth
Of thoughts with better thoughts at strife,
The most familiar bane of life
Since parting Innocence bequeathed
Mortality to Earth!
Soft clouds, the whitest of the year,
Sailed through the sky — the brooks ran clear;
The lambs from rock to rock were bounding;
With songs the budded groves resounding;
And to my heart are still endeared
The thoughts with which it then was cheered;
The faith which saw that gladsome pair
Walk through the fire with unsinged hair.
Or, if such faith must needs deceive —
Then, Spirits of beauty and of grace,
Associates in that eager chase;
Ye, who within the blameless mind
Your favourite seat of empire find —
Kind Spirits! may we not believe
That they, so happy and so fair
Through your sweet influence, and the care
Of pitying Heaven, at least were free
From touch of *deadly* injury?

Destined, whate'er their earthly doom,
For mercy and immortal bloom?   1817.

XVII.
GIPSIES.

Yet are they here the same unbroken knot
Of human Beings, in the self-same spot!
    Men, women, children, yea the frame
    Of the whole spectacle the same!
Only their fire seems bolder, yielding light,
Now deep and red, the colouring of night;
    That on their Gipsy-faces falls,
    Their bed of straw and blanket-walls.
— Twelve hours, twelve bounteous hours are gone, while I
Have been a traveller under open sky,
    Much witnessing of change and cheer,
    Yet as I left I find them here!
The weary Sun betook himself to rest; —
Then issued Vesper from the fulgent west,
    Outshining like a visible God
    The glorious path in which he trod.
And now, ascending, after one dark hour
And one night's diminution of her power,
    Behold the mighty Moon! this way
    She looks as if at them — but they
Regard not her: — oh better wrong and strife
(By nature transient) than this torpid life;
    Life which the very stars reprove
    As on their silent tasks they move!
Yet, witness all that stirs in heaven or earth!
In scorn I speak not; — they are what their birth
    And breeding suffer them to be;
    Wild outcasts of society!

1807.

XVIII.
RUTH.

When Ruth was left half desolate,
Her Father took another Mate;
And Ruth, not seven years old,
A slighted child, at her own will
Went wandering over dale and hill,
In thoughtless freedom, bold.

And she had made a pipe of straw,
And music from that pipe could draw
Like sounds of winds and floods;
Had built a bower upon the green,
As if she from her birth had been
An infant of the woods.

Beneath her father's roof, alone
She seemed to live; her thoughts her own;
Herself her own delight;
Pleased with herself, nor sad, nor gay;
And, passing thus the live-long day,
She grew to woman's height.

There came a Youth from Georgia's shore —
A military casque he wore,
With splendid feathers drest;
He brought them from the Cherokees;
The feathers nodded in the breeze
And made a gallant crest.

From Indian blood you deem him sprung:
But no! he spake the English tongue,
And bore a soldier's name;
And, when America was free
From battle and from jeopardy,
He 'cross the ocean came.

With hues of genius on his cheek
In finest tones the Youth could speak:
— While he was yet a boy,
The moon, the glory of the sun,
And streams that murmur as they run,
Had been his dearest joy.

He was a lovely Youth! I guess
The panther in the wilderness
Was not so fair as he;
And, when he chose to sport and play,
No dolphin ever was so gay
Upon the tropic sea.

Among the Indians he had fought,
And with him many tales he brought
Of pleasure and of fear;
Such tales as told to any maid
By such a Youth, in the green shade,
Were perilous to hear.

He told of girls — a happy rout!
Who quit their fold with dance and shout,
Their pleasant Indian town,
To gather strawberries all day long;
Returning with a choral song
When daylight is gone down.

He spake of plants that hourly change
Their blossoms, through a boundless range
Of intermingling hues;
With budding, fading, faded flowers
They stand the wonder of the bowers
From morn to evening dews.

He told of the magnolia, spread
High as a cloud, high over head!

The cypress and her spire;
— Of flowers that with one scarlet gleam
Cover a hundred leagues, and seem
To set the hills on fire.

The Youth of green savannahs spake,
And many an endless, endless lake,
With all its fairy crowds
Of islands, that together lie
As quietly as spots of sky
Among the evening clouds.

"How pleasant," then he said, "it were
A fisher or a hunter there,
In sunshine or in shade
To wander with an easy mind;
And build a household fire, and find
A home in every glade!

What days and what bright years! Ah me!
Our life were life indeed, with thee
So passed in quiet bliss,
And all the while," said he, "to know
That we were in a world of woe,
On such an earth as this!"

And then he sometimes interwove
Fond thoughts about a father's love:
"For there," said he, "are spun
Around the heart such tender ties,
That our own children to our eyes
Are dearer than the sun.

Sweet Ruth! and could you go with me
My helpmate in the woods to be,
Our shed at night to rear;
Or run, my own adopted bride,
A sylvan huntress at my side,
And drive the flying deer!

Beloved Ruth!" — No more he said.
The wakeful Ruth at midnight shed
A solitary tear:
She thought again — and did agree
With him to sail across the sea,
And drive the flying deer.

"And now, as fitting is and right,
We in the church our faith will plight,
A husband and a wife."
Even so they did; and I may say
That to sweet Ruth that happy day
Was more than human life.

Through dream and vision did she sink,
Delighted all the while to think
That on those lonesome floods,
And green savannahs, she should share
His board with lawful joy, and bear
His name in the wild woods.

But, as you have before been told,
This Stripling, sportive, gay, and bold,
And, with his dancing crest,
So beautiful, through savage lands
Had roamed about, with vagrant bands
Of Indians in the West.

The wind, the tempest roaring high,
The tumult of a tropic sky,
Might well be dangerous food
For him, a Youth to whom was given
So much of earth — so much of heaven,
And such impetuous blood.

Whatever in those climes he found
Irregular in sight or sound

Did to his mind impart
A kindred impulse, seemed allied
To his own powers, and justified
The workings of his heart.

Nor less, to feed voluptuous thought,
The beauteous forms of nature wrought,
Fair trees and gorgeous flowers;
The breezes their own languor lent;
The stars had feelings, which they sent
Into those favored bowers.

Yet, in his worst pursuits, I ween
That sometimes there did intervene
Pure hopes of high intent:
For passions linked to forms so fair
And stately, needs must have their share
Of noble sentiment.

But ill he lived, much evil saw,
With men to whom no better law
Nor better life was known;
Deliberately, and undeceived,
Those wild men's vices he received,
And gave them back his own.

His genius and his moral frame
Were thus impaired, and he became
The slave of low desires:
A Man who without self-control
Would seek what the degraded soul
Unworthily admires.

And yet he with no feigned delight
Had wooed the Maiden, day and night
Had loved her, night and morn:
What could he less than love a Maid
Whose heart with so much nature played?
So kind and so forlorn!

Sometimes, most earnestly, he said,
"O Ruth! I have been worse than dead;
False thoughts, thoughts bold and vain,
Encompassed me on every side
When I, in confidence and pride,
Had crossed the Atlantic main.

Before me shone a glorious world —
Fresh as a banner bright, unfurled
To music suddenly:
I looked upon those hills and plains,
And seemed as if let loose from chains,
To live at liberty.

No more of this; for now, by thee
Dear Ruth! more happily set free
With nobler zeal I burn;
My soul from darkness is released,
Like the whole sky when to the east
The morning doth return."

Full soon that better mind was gone;
No hope, no wish remained, not one, —
They stirred him now no more;
New objects did new pleasure give,
And once again he wished to live
As lawless as before.

Meanwhile, as thus with him it fared,
They for the voyage were prepared,
And went to the sea-shore,
But, when they thither came, the Youth
Deserted his poor Bride, and Ruth
Could never find him more.

God help thee, Ruth! — Such pains she had,
That she in half a year was mad,

And in a prison housed;
And there, with many a doleful song
Made of wild words, her cup of wrong
She fearfully caroused.

Yet sometimes milder hours she knew,
Nor wanted sun, nor rain, nor dew,
Nor pastimes of the May;
— They all were with her in her cell;
And a clear brook with cheerful knell
Did o'er the pebbles play.

When Ruth three seasons thus had lain,
There came a respite to her pain;
She from her prison fled;
But of the Vagrant none took thought;
And where it liked her best she sought
Her shelter and her bread.

Among the fields she breathed again:
The master-current of her brain
Ran permanent and free;
And, coming to the Banks of Tone,
There did she rest; and dwell alone
Under the greenwood tree.

The engines of her pain, the tools
That shaped her sorrow, rocks and pools,
And airs that gently stir
The vernal leaves — she loved them still;
Nor ever taxed them with the ill
Which had been done to her.

A Barn her *winter* bed supplies;
But, till the warmth of summer skies
And summer days is gone,
(And all do in this tale agree)
She sleeps beneath the greenwood tree,
And other home hath none.

An innocent life, yet far astray!
And Ruth will, long before her day,
Be broken down and old:
Sore aches she needs must have! but less
Of mind, than body's wretchedness,
From damp, and rain, and cold.

If she is prest by want of food,
She from her dwelling in the wood
Repairs to a road-side;
And there she begs at one steep place
Where up and down with easy pace
The horsemen-travellers ride.

That oaten pipe of hers is mute,
Or thrown away; but with a flute
Her loneliness she cheers;
This flute, made of a hemlock stalk,
At evening in his homeward walk
The Quantock woodman hears.

I, too, have passed her on the hills
Setting her little water-mills
By spouts and fountains wild —
Such small machinery as she turned
Ere she had wept, ere she had mourned,
A young and happy Child!

Farewell! and when thy days are told,
Ill-fated Ruth, in hallowed mould
Thy corpse shall buried be,
For thee a funeral bell shall ring,
And all the congregation sing
A Christian psalm for thee.

1799.

XIX.
RESOLUTION AND INDEPENDENCE.

I.

There was a roaring in the wind all night;
The rain came heavily and fell in floods;
But now the sun is rising calm and bright;
The birds are singing in the distant woods;
Over his own sweet voice the Stock-dove broods;
The Jay makes answer as the Magpie chatters;
And all the air is filled with pleasant noise of waters.

II.

All things that love the sun are out of doors;
The sky rejoices in the morning's birth;
The grass is bright with rain-drops; — on the moors
The hare is running races in her mirth;
And with her feet she from the plashy earth
Raises a mist, that, glittering in the sun,
Runs with her all the way, wherever she doth run.

III.

I was a Traveller then upon the moor;
I saw the hare that raced about with joy;
I heard the woods and distant waters roar;
Or heard them not, as happy as a boy:
The pleasant season did my heart employ:
My old remembrances went from me wholly;
And all the ways of men, so vain and melancholy.

IV.

But, as it sometimes chanceth, from the might
Of joy in minds that can no further go,
As high as we have mounted in delight
In our dejection do we sink as low;
To me that morning did it happen so;
And fears and fancies thick upon me came;
Dim sadness — and blind thoughts, I knew not, nor could name.

V.

I heard the sky-lark warbling in the sky;
And I bethought me of the playful hare:
Even such a happy Child of earth am I;
Even as these blissful creatures do I fare;
Far from the world I walk, and from all care;
But there may come another day to me —
Solitude, pain of heart, distress, and poverty.

VI.

My whole life I have lived in pleasant thought,
As if life's business were a summer mood;
As if all needful things would come unsought
To genial faith, still rich in genial good;
But how can He expect that others should
Build for him, sow for him, and at his call
Love him, who for himself will take no heed at all?

VII.

I thought of Chatterton, the marvellous Boy,
The sleepless Soul that perished in his pride;
Of Him who walked in glory and in joy
Following his plough, along the mountain-side:
By our own spirits are we deified;
We Poets in our youth begin in gladness;
But thereof come in the end despondency and madness.

VIII.

Now, whether it were by peculiar grace,
A leading from above, a something given,
Yet it befel, that, in this lonely place,
When I with these untoward thoughts had striven,
Beside a pool bare to the eye of heaven
I saw a Man before me unawares:
The oldest man he seemed that ever wore grey hairs.

IX.

As a huge stone is sometimes seen to lie
Couched on the bald top of an eminence;
Wonder to all who do the same espy,
By what means it could thither come, and whence;
So that it seems a thing endued with sense:
Like a sea-beast crawled forth, that on a shelf
Of rock or sand reposeth, there to sun itself;

X.

Such seemed this Man, not all alive nor dead,
Nor all asleep — in his extreme old age;
His body was bent double, feet and head
Coming together in life's pilgrimage;
As if some dire constraint of pain, or rage
Of sickness felt by him in times long past,
A more than human weight upon his frame had cast.

XI.

Himself he propped, limbs, body, and pale face,
Upon a long grey staff of shaven wood:
And, still as I drew near with gentle pace,
Upon the margin of that moorish flood
Motionless as a cloud the old man stood,
That heareth not the loud winds when they call;
And moveth all together, if it move at all.

XII.

At length, himself unsettling, he the pond
Stirred with his staff, and fixedly did look
Upon the muddy water, which he conned,
As if he had been reading in a book:
And now a stranger's privilege I took;
And, drawing to his side, to him did say,
"'This morning gives us promise of a glorious day."

XIII.

A gentle answer did the old Man make,
In courteous speech which forth he slowly drew:
And him with further words I thus bespake,
"What occupation do you there pursue?
This is a lonesome place for one like you."
Ere he replied, a flash of mild surprise
Broke from the sable orbs of his yet vivid eyes.

XIV.

His words came feebly, from a feeble chest,
But each in solemn order followed each,
With something of a lofty utterance drest —
Choice word and measured phrase, above the reach
Of ordinary men; a stately speech;
Such as grave Livers do in Scotland use,
Religious men, who give to God and man their dues.

XV.

He told, that to these waters he had come
To gather leeches, being old and poor:
Employment hazardous and wearisome!
And he had many hardships to endure:
From pond to pond he roamed, from moor to moor;
Housing, with God's good help, by choice or chance;
And in this way he gained an honest maintenance.

XVI.

The old Man still stood talking by my side;
But now his voice to me was like a stream
Scarce heard; nor word from word could I divide;
And the whole body of the Man did seem
Like one whom I had met with in a dream;
Or like a man from some far region sent,
To give me human strength, by apt admonishment.

XVII.

My former thoughts returned: the fear that kills;
And hope that is unwilling to be fed;
Cold, pain, and labour, and all fleshly ills;
And mighty Poets in their misery dead.
— Perplexed, and longing to be comforted,
My question eagerly did I renew,
"How is it that you live, and what is it you do?"

XVIII.

He with a smile did then his words repeat;
And said, that, gathering leeches, far and wide
He travelled; stirring thus about his feet
The waters of the pools where they abide.
"Once I could meet with them on every side;
But they have dwindled long by slow decay;
Yet still I persevere, and find them where I may."

XIX.

While he was talking thus, the lonely place,
The old Man's shape, and speech — all troubled me:
In my mind's eye I seemed to see him pace
About the weary moors continually,
Wandering about alone and silently.
While I these thoughts within myself pursued,
He, having made a pause, the same discourse renewed.

XX.

And soon with this he other matter blended,
Cheerfully uttered, with demeanour kind,
But stately in the main; and when he ended,
I could have laughed myself to scorn to find
In that decrepit Man so firm a mind.
"God," said I, "be my help and stay secure;
I'll think of the Leech-gatherer on the lonely moor!" 1807.

XX.
THE THORN.

I.

"There is a Thorn — it looks so old,
In truth, you'd find it hard to say
How it could ever have been young,
It looks so old and grey.
Not higher than a two years' child
It stands erect, this aged Thorn;
No leaves it has, no prickly points;
It is a mass of knotted joints,
A wretched thing forlorn.
It stands erect, and like a stone
With lichens is it overgrown.

II.

Like rock or stone, it is o'ergrown,
With lichens to the very top,
And hung with heavy tufts of moss,
A melancholy crop:
Up from the earth these mosses creep,
And this poor Thorn they clasp it round
So close, you'd say that they are bent
With plain and manifest intent
To drag it to the ground;
And all have joined in one endeavour
To bury this poor Thorn for ever.

III.

High on a mountain's highest ridge,
Where oft the stormy winter gale
Cuts like a scythe, while through the clouds
Its sweeps from vale to vale;
Not five yards from the mountain path
This Thorn you on your left espy;
And to the left, three yards beyond,
You see a little muddy pond
Of water — never dry,

Though but of compass small, and bare
To thirsty suns and parching air.

IV.

And, close beside this aged Thorn,
There is a fresh and lovely sight,
A beauteous heap, a hill of moss,
Just half a foot in height.
All lovely colours there you see,
All colours that were ever seen;
And mossy network too is there,
As if by hand of lady fair
The work had woven been;
And cups, the darlings of the eye,
So deep is their vermilion dye.

V.

Ah me! what lovely tints are there
Of olive green and scarlet bright,
In spikes, in branches, and in stars,
Green, red, and pearly white!
This heap of earth o'ergrown with moss,
Which close beside the Thorn you see,
So fresh in all its beauteous dyes,
Is like an infant's grave in size,
As like as like can be:
But never, never any where,
An infant's grave was half so fair.

VI.

Now would you see this aged Thorn,
This pond, and beauteous hill of moss,
You must take care and choose your time
The mountain when to cross.
For oft there sits between the heap
So like an infant's grave in size,
And that same pond of which I spoke,
A Woman in a scarlet cloak,
And to herself she cries,

'Oh misery! oh misery!
Oh woe is me! oh misery!'

VII.

At all times of the day and night
This wretched Woman thither goes;
And she is known to every star,
And every wind that blows;
And there, beside the Thorn, she sits
When the blue daylight's in the skies,
And when the whirlwind's on the hill,
Or frosty air is keen and still,
And to herself she cries,
'Oh misery! oh misery!
Oh woe is me! oh misery!'"

VIII.

"Now wherefore, thus, by day and night,
In rain, in tempest, and in snow,
Thus to the dreary mountain-top
Does this poor Woman go?
And why sits she beside the Thorn
When the blue daylight's in the sky
Or when the whirlwind's on the hill,
Or frosty air is keen and still,
And wherefore does she cry? —
O wherefore? wherefore? tell me why
Does she repeat that doleful cry?"

IX.

"I cannot tell; I wish I could;
For the true reason no one knows:
But would you gladly view the spot,
The spot to which she goes;
The hillock like an infant's grave,
The pond — and Thorn, so old and grey;
Pass by her door — 'tis seldom shut —
And, if you see her in her hut —
Then to the spot away!

I never heard of such as dare
Approach the spot when she is there."

X.

"But wherefore to the mountain-top
Can this unhappy Woman go,
Whatever star is in the skies,
Whatever wind may blow?"
"Full twenty years are past and gone
Since she (her name is Martha Ray)
Gave with a maiden's true good-will
Her company to Stephen Hill;
And she was blithe and gay,
While friends and kindred all approved
Of him whom tenderly she loved.

XI.

And they had fixed the wedding day,
The morning that must wed them both;
But Stephen to another Maid
Had sworn another oath;
And, with this other Maid, to church
Unthinking Stephen went —
Poor Martha! on that woeful day
A pang of pitiless dismay
Into her soul was sent;
A fire was kindled in her breast,
Which might not burn itself to rest.

XII.

They say, full six months after this,
While yet the summer leaves were green,
She to the mountain-top would go,
And there was often seen.
What could she seek? — or wish to hide?
Her state to any eye was plain;
She was with child, and she was mad!
Yet often was she sober sad
From her exceeding pain.

O guilty Father — would that death
Had saved him from that breach of faith!

XIII.

Sad case for such a brain to hold
Communion with a stirring child!
Sad case, as you may think, for one
Who had a brain so wild!
Last Christmas-eve we talked of this,
And grey-haired Wilfred of the glen
Held that the unborn infant wrought
About its mother's heart, and brought
Her senses back again:
And, when at last her time drew near,
Her looks were calm, her senses clear.

XIV.

More know I not, I wish I did,
And it should all be told to you;
For what became of this poor child
No mortal ever knew;
Nay — if a child to her was born
No earthly tongue could ever tell;
And if 'twas born alive or dead,
Far less could this with proof be said;
But some remember well,
That Martha Ray about this time
Would up the mountain often climb.

XV.

And all that winter, when at night
The wind blew from the mountain-peak,
'Twas worth your while, though in the dark,
The churchyard path to seek:
For many a time and oft were heard
Cries coming from the mountain head:
Some plainly living voices were;
And others, I've heard many swear,
Were voices of the dead:

THE THORN.

I cannot think, whate'er they say,
They had to do with Martha Ray.

XVI.

But that she goes to this old Thorn,
The Thorn which I described to you,
And there sits in a scarlet cloak,
I will be sworn is true.
For one day with my telescope,
To view the ocean wide and bright,
When to this country first I came,
Ere I had heard of Martha's name,
I climbed the mountain's height: —
A storm came on, and I could see
No object higher than my knee.

XVII.

'Twas mist and rain, and storm and rain:
No screen, no fence could I discover;
And then the wind! in sooth, it was
A wind full ten times over.
I looked around, I thought I saw
A jutting crag, — and off I ran,
Head-foremost, through the driving rain,
The shelter of the crag to gain;
And, as I am a man,
Instead of jutting crag, I found
A Woman seated on the ground.

XVIII.

I did not speak — I saw her face;
Her face! — it was enough for me;
I turned about and heard her cry,
'Oh misery! oh misery!'
And there she sits, until the moon
Through half the clear blue sky will go;
And, when the little breezes make
The waters of the pond to shake,
As all the country know,

She shudders, and you hear her cry,
'Oh misery! oh misery!'"

XIX.

"But what's the Thorn? and what the pond?
And what the hill of moss to her?
And what the creeping breeze that comes
The little pond to stir?"
"I cannot tell; but some will say
She hanged her baby on the tree;
Some say she drowned it in the pond,
Which is a little step beyond:
But all and each agree,
The little Babe was buried there,
Beneath that hill of moss so fair.

XX.

I've heard, the moss is spotted red
With drops of that poor infant's blood;
But kill a new-born infant thus,
I do not think she could!
Some say, if to the pond you go,
And fix on it a steady view,
The shadow of a babe you trace,
A baby and a baby's face,
And that it looks at you;
Whene'er you look on it, 'tis plain
The baby looks at you again.

XXI.

And some had sworn an oath that she
Should be to public justice brought;
And for the little infant's bones
With spades they would have sought.
But instantly the hill of moss
Before their eyes began to stir!
And, for full fifty yards around,
The grass — it shook upon the ground!
Yet all do still aver

The little Babe lies buried there,
Beneath that hill of moss so fair.

XXII.

I cannot tell how this may be,
But plain it is the Thorn is bound
With heavy tufts of moss that strive
To drag it to the ground;
And this I know, full many a time,
When she was on the mountain high,
By day, and in the silent night,
When all the stars shone clear and bright,
That I have heard her cry,
'Oh misery! oh misery!
Oh woe is me! oh misery!'"

1798.

XXI.
HART-LEAP WELL.

Hart-Leap Well is a small spring of water, about five miles from Richmond in Yorkshire, and near the side of the road that leads from Richmond to Askrigg. Its name is derived from a remarkable Chase, the memory of which is preserved by the monuments spoken of in the second Part of the following Poem, which monuments do now exist as I have there described them.

The Knight had ridden down from Wensley Moor
With the slow motion of a summer's cloud;
And now, as he approached a vassal's door,
"Bring forth another horse!" he cried aloud.

"Another horse!" — That shout the vassal heard
And saddled his best Steed, a comely grey;
Sir Walter mounted him; he was the third
Which he had mounted on that glorious day.

Joy sparkled in the prancing courser's eyes;
The horse and horseman are a happy pair;
But, though Sir Walter like a falcon flies,
There is a doleful silence in the air.

A rout this morning left Sir Walter's Hall,
That as they gallopped made the echoes roar;
But horse and man are vanished, one and all;
Such race, I think, was never seen before.

Sir Walter, restless as a veering wind,
Calls to the few tired dogs that yet remain:
Blanch, Swift, and Music, noblest of their kind,
Follow, and up the weary mountain strain.

The Knight hallooed, he cheered and chid them on
With suppliant gestures and upbraidings stern;
But breath and eyesight fail; and, one by one,
The dogs are stretched among the mountain fern.

Where is the throng, the tumult of the race?
The bugles that so joyfully were blown?
— This chase it looks not like an earthly chase;
Sir Walter and the Hart are left alone.

The poor Hart toils along the mountain-side;
I will not stop to tell how far he fled,
Nor will I mention by what death he died;
But now the Knight beholds him lying dead.

Dismounting, then, he leaned against a thorn;
He had no follower, dog, nor man, nor boy:
He neither cracked his whip, nor blew his horn,
But gazed upon the spoil with silent joy.

Close to the thorn on which Sir Walter leaned,
Stood his dumb partner in this glorious feat;
Weak as a lamb the hour that it is yeaned;
And white with foam as if with cleaving sleet.

Upon his side the Hart was lying stretched:
His nostril touched a spring beneath a hill,
And with the last deep groan his breath had fetched
The waters of the spring were trembling still.

And now, too happy for repose or rest,
(Never had living man such joyful lot!)
Sir Walter walked all round, north, south, and west,
And gazed and gazed upon that darling spot.

And climbing up the hill — (it was at least
Four roods of sheer ascent) Sir Walter found
Three several hoof-marks which the hunted Beast
Had left imprinted on the grassy ground.

Sir Walter wiped his face, and cried, "Till now
Such sight was never seen by human eyes:
Three leaps have borne him from this lofty brow,
Down to the very fountain where he lies.

I'll build a pleasure-house upon this spot,
And a small arbour, made for rural joy;
'Twill be the traveller's shed, the pilgrim's cot,
A place of love for damsels that are coy.

A cunning artist will I have to frame
A basin for that fountain in the dell!
And they who do make mention of the same,
From this day forth, shall call it HART-LEAP WELL.

And, gallant Stag! to make thy praises known,
Another monument shall here be raised;
Three several pillars, each a rough-hewn stone,
And planted where thy hoofs the turf have grazed.

And, in the summer-time when days are long,
I will come hither with my Paramour;
And with the dancers and the minstrel's song
We will make merry in that pleasant bower.

Till the foundations of the mountains fail
My mansion with its arbour shall endure; —
The joy of them who till the fields of Swale,
And them who dwell among the woods of Ure!"

Then home he went, and left the Hart, stone-dead,
With breathless nostrils stretched above the spring.
— Soon did the Knight perform what he had said;
And far and wide the fame thereof did ring.

Ere thrice the Moon into her port had steered,
A cup of stone received the living well;
Three pillars of rude stone Sir Walter reared,
And built a house of pleasure in the dell.

And near the fountain, flowers of stature tall
With trailing plants and trees were intertwined, —
Which soon composed a little sylvan hall,
A leafy shelter from the sun and wind.

And thither, when the summer days were long
Sir Walter led his wondering Paramour;
And with the dancers and the minstrel's song
Made merriment within that pleasant bower.

The Knight, Sir Walter, died in course of time,
And his bones lie in his paternal vale. —
But there is matter for a second rhyme,
And I to this would add another tale.

PART SECOND.

The moving accident is not my trade;
To freeze the blood I have no ready arts:
'Tis my delight, alone in summer shade,
To pipe a simple song for thinking hearts.

As I from Hawes to Richmond did repair,
It chanced that I saw standing in a dell
Three aspens at three corners of a square;
And one, not four yards distant, near a well.

What this imported I could ill divine:
And, pulling now the rein my horse to stop,
I saw three pillars standing in a line, —
The last stone-pillar on a dark hill-top.

The trees were grey, with neither arms nor head;
Half wasted the square mound of tawny green;
So that you just might say, as then I said,
"Here in old time the hand of man hath been."

I looked upon the hill both far and near,
More doleful place did never eye survey;
It seemed as if the spring-time came not here,
And Nature here were willing to decay.

I stood in various thoughts and fancies lost,
When one, who was in shepherd's garb attired,
Came up the hollow: — him did I accost,
And what this place might be I then inquired.

The Shepherd stopped, and that same story told
Which in my former rhyme I have rehearsed.
"A jolly place," said he, "in times of old!
But something ails it now: the spot is curst.

You see these lifeless stumps of aspen wood —
Some say that they are beeches, others elms —
These were the bower; and here a mansion stood,
The finest palace of a hundred realms!

The arbour does its own condition tell;
You see the stones, the fountain, and the stream;
But as to the great Lodge! you might as well
Hunt half a day for a forgotten dream.

There's neither dog nor heifer, horse nor sheep,
Will wet his lips within that cup of stone;
And oftentimes, when all are fast asleep,
This water doth send forth a dolorous groan.

Some say that here a murder has been done,
And blood cries out for blood: but, for my part,
I've guessed, when I've been sitting in the sun,
That it was all for that unhappy Hart.

What thoughts must through the creature's brain have past!
Even from the topmost stone, upon the steep,
Are but three bounds — and look, Sir, at this last —
O Master! it has been a cruel leap.

For thirteen hours he ran a desperate race;
And in my simple mind we cannot tell
What cause the Hart might have to love this place,
And come and make his death-bed near the well.

Here on the grass perhaps asleep he sank,
Lulled by the fountain in the summer tide;
This water was perhaps the first he drank
When he had wandered from his mother's side.

In April here beneath the flowering thorn
He heard the birds their morning carols sing;
And he, perhaps, for aught we know, was born
Not half a furlong from that self-same spring.

Now, here is neither grass nor pleasant shade;
The sun on drearier hollow never shone;
So will it be, as I have often said,
Till trees, and stones, and fountain, all are gone."

"Grey-headed Shepherd, thou hast spoken well;
Small difference lies between thy creed and mine:
This Beast not unobserved by Nature fell;
His death was mourned by sympathy divine.

The Being, that is in the clouds and air,
That is in the green leaves among the groves,
Maintains a deep and reverential care
For the unoffending creatures whom he loves.

The pleasure-house is dust: — behind, before,
This is no common waste, no common gloom;
But Nature, in due course of time, once more
Shall here put on her beauty and her bloom.

She leaves these objects to a slow decay,
That what we are, and have been, may be known;
But at the coming of the milder day,
These monuments shall all be overgrown.

One lesson, Shepherd, let us two divide,
Taught both by what she shows, and what conceals
Never to blend our pleasure or our pride
With sorrow of the meanest thing that feels."

1800.

XXII.
SONG AT THE FEAST OF BROUGHAM CASTLE,
UPON THE RESTORATION OF LORD CLIFFORD, THE SHEPHERD, TO THE ESTATE AND HONOURS OF HIS ANCESTORS.

High in the breathless Hall the Minstrel sate,
And Emont's murmur mingled with the Song. —
The words of ancient time I thus translate,
A festal strain that hath been silent long: —
"From town to town, from tower to tower,
The red rose is a gladsome flower.
Her thirty years of winter past,
The red rose is revived at last;
She lifts her head for endless spring,
For everlasting blossoming:
Both roses flourish, red and white:
In love and sisterly delight
The two that were at strife are blended,
And all old troubles now are ended. —
Joy! joy to both! but most to her
Who is the flower of Lancaster!
Behold her how She smiles to-day
On this great throng, this bright array!
Fair greeting doth she send to all
From every corner of the hall;

But chiefly from above the board
Where sits in state our rightful Lord,
A Clifford to his own restored!

 They came with banner, spear, and shield;
And it was proved in Bosworth-field.
Not long the Avenger was withstood —
Earth helped him with the cry of blood;
St. George was for us, and the might
Of blessed Angels crowned the right.
Loud voice the Land has uttered forth,
We loudest in the faithful north:
Our fields rejoice, our mountains ring,
Our streams proclaim a welcoming;
Our strong-abodes and castles see
The glory of their loyalty.

 How glad is Skipton at this hour —
Though lonely, a deserted Tower;
Knight, squire, and yeoman, page and groom
We have them at the feast of Brough'm.
How glad Pendragon — though the sleep
Of years be on her! — She shall reap
A taste of this great pleasure, viewing
As in a dream her own renewing.
Rejoiced is Brough, right glad I deem
Beside her little humble stream;
And she that keepeth watch and ward
Her statelier Eden's course to guard;
They both are happy at this hour,
Though each is but a lonely Tower: —
But here is perfect joy and pride
For one fair House by Emont's side,
This day, distinguished without peer
To see her Master and to cheer —
Him, and his Lady-mother dear!

 Oh! it was a time forlorn
When the fatherless was born —

Give her wings that she may fly,
Or she sees her infant die!
Swords that are with slaughter wild
Hunt the Mother and the Child.
Who will take them from the light?
— Yonder is a man in sight —
Yonder is a house — but where?
No, they must not enter there.
To the caves, and to the brooks,
To the clouds of heaven she looks;
She is speechless, but her eyes
Pray in ghostly agonies.
Blissful Mary, Mother mild,
Maid and Mother undefiled,
Save a Mother and her Child!

Now Who is he that bounds with joy
On Carrock's side, a Shepherd-boy?
No thoughts hath he but thoughts that pass
Light as the wind along the grass.
Can this be He who hither came
In secret, like a smothered flame?
O'er whom such thankful tears were shed
For shelter, and a poor man's bread!
God loves the Child; and God hath willed
That those dear words should be fulfilled,
The Lady's words, when forced away
The last she to her Babe did say:
"My own, my own, thy Fellow-guest
I may not be; but rest thee, rest,
For lowly shepherd's life is best!'

Alas! when evil men are strong
No life is good, no pleasure long.
The Boy must part from Mosedale's groves,
And leave Blencathara's rugged coves,
And quit the flowers that summer brings
To Glenderamakin's lofty springs;

Must vanish, and his careless cheer
Be turned to heaviness and fear.
— Give Sir Lancelot Threlkeld praise!
Hear it, good man, old in days!
Thou tree of covert and of rest
For this young Bird that is distrest;
Among thy branches safe he lay,
And he was free to sport and play,
When falcons were abroad for prey.

  A recreant harp, that sings of fear
And heaviness in Clifford's ear!
I said, when evil men are strong,
No life is good, no pleasure long,
A weak and cowardly untruth!
Our Clifford was a happy Youth,
And thankful through a weary time,
That brought him up to manhood's prime.
— Again he wanders forth at will,
And tends a flock from hill to hill;
His garb is humble; ne'er was seen
Such garb with such a noble mien;
Among the shepherd grooms no mate
Hath he, a Child of strength and state!
Yet lacks not friends for simple glee,
Nor yet for higher sympathy.
To his side the fallow-deer
Came, and rested without fear;
The eagle, lord of land and sea,
Stooped down to pay him fealty;
And both the undying fish that swim
Through Bowscale-tarn did wait on him;
The pair were servants of his eye
In their immortality;
And glancing, gleaming, dark or bright,
Moved to and fro for his delight.
He knew the rocks which Angels haunt
Upon the mountains visitant;

He hath kenned them taking wing:
And into caves where Faeries sing
He hath entered; and been told
By Voices how men lived of old.
Among the heavens his eye can see
The face of thing that is to be;
And, if that men report him right,
His tongue could whisper words of might.
— Now another day is come,
Fitter hope, and nobler doom;
He hath thrown aside his crook,
And hath buried deep his book;
Armour rusting in his halls
On the blood of Clifford calls;
'Quell the Scot,' exclaims the Lance —
Bear me to the heart of France,
Is the longing of the Shield —
Tell thy name, thou trembling Field;
Field of death, where'er thou be,
Groan thou with our victory!
Happy day, and mighty hour,
When our Shepherd, in his power,
Mailed and horsed, with lance and sword,
To his ancestors restored
Like a re-appearing Star,
Like a glory from afar,
First shall head the flock of war!"

Alas! the impassioned minstrel did not know
How, by Heaven's grace, this Clifford's heart was framed:
How he, long forced in humble walks to go,
Was softened into feeling, soothed, and tamed.

Love had he found in huts where poor men lie;
His daily teachers had been woods and rills,
The silence that is in the starry sky,
The sleep that is among the lonely hills.

In him the savage virtue of the Race,
Revenge, and all ferocious thoughts were dead:
Nor did he change; but kept in lofty place
The wisdom which adversity had bred.

Glad were the vales, and every cottage-hearth;
The Shepherd-lord was honoured more and more;
And, ages after he was laid in earth,
"The good Lord Clifford" was the name he bore.

1807.

XXIII.

It is no Spirit who from heaven hath flown,
And is descending on his embassy;
Nor Traveller gone from earth the heavens to espy!
'Tis Hesperus — there he stands with glittering crown,
First admonition that the sun is down!
For yet it is broad day-light: clouds pass by;
A few are near him still and now the sky,
He hath it to himself — 'tis all his own.
O most ambitious Star! an inquest wrought
Within me when I recognised thy light;
A moment I was startled at the sight:
And, while I gazed, there came to me a thought
That I might step beyond my natural race
As thou seem'st now to do; might one day trace
Some ground not mine; and, strong her strength above,
My Soul, an Apparition in the place,
Tread there with steps that no one shall reprove!

1803.

XXIV.

Yes, it was the mountain Echo,
Solitary, clear, profound,
Answering to the shouting Cuckoo,
Giving to her sound for sound!

Unsolicited reply
To a babbling wanderer sent;
Like her ordinary cry,
Like — but oh, how different!

Hears not also mortal Life?
Hear not we, unthinking Creatures!
Slaves of folly, love, or strife —
Voices of two different natures?

Have not *we* too? — yes, we have
Answers, and we know not whence;
Echoes from beyond the grave,
Recognised intelligence!

Such rebounds our inward ear
Catches sometimes from afar —
Listen, ponder, hold them dear;
For of God, — of God they are.

1806.

XXV.
TO A SKY-LARK.

ETHEREAL minstrel! pilgrim of the sky!
Dost thou despise the earth where cares abound?
Or, while the wings aspire, are heart and eye
Both with thy nest upon the dewy ground?
Thy nest which thou canst drop into at will,
Those quivering wings composed, that music still!

Leave to the nightingale her shady wood;
A privacy of glorious light is thine;
Whence thou dost pour upon the world a flood
Of harmony, with instinct more divine;
Type of the wise who soar, but never roam;
True to the kindred points of Heaven and Home!

1825.

XXVI.
LAODAMIA.

"With sacrifice before the rising morn
Vows have I made by fruitless hope inspired;
And from the infernal Gods, 'mid shades forlorn
Of night, my slaughtered Lord have I required:
Celestial pity I again implore; —
Restore him to my sight — great Jove, restore!"

So speaking, and by fervent love endowed
With faith, the Suppliant heavenward lifts her hands;
While, like the sun emerging from a cloud,
Her countenance brightens — and her eye expands;
Her bosom heaves and spreads, her stature grows;
And she expects the issue in repose.

O terror! what hath she perceived? — O joy!
What doth she look on? — whom doth she behold?
Her Hero slain upon the beach of Troy?
His vital presence? his corporeal mould?
It is — if sense deceive her not — 'tis He!
And a God leads him, winged Mercury!

Mild Hermes spake — and touched her with his wand
That calms all fear; "Such grace hath crowned thy prayer,
Laodamía! that at Jove's command
Thy Husband walks the paths of upper air:
He comes to tarry with thee three hours' space;
Accept the gift, behold him face to face!"

Forth sprang the impassioned Queen her Lord to clasp;
Again that consummation she essayed;
But unsubstantial Form eludes her grasp
As often as that eager grasp was made.
The Phantom parts — but parts to re-unite,
And re-assume his place before her sight.

"Protesiláus, lo! thy guide is gone!
Confirm, I pray, the vision with thy voice:
This is our palace, — yonder is thy throne;
Speak, and the floor thou tread'st on will rejoice.
Not to appal me have the gods bestowed
This precious boon; and blest a sad abode."

"Great Jove, Laodamía! doth not leave
His gifts imperfect: — Spectre though I be,
I am not sent to scare thee or deceive;
But in reward of thy fidelity.
And something also did my worth obtain;
For fearless virtue bringeth boundless gain.

Thou knowest, the Delphic oracle foretold
That the first Greek who touched the Trojan strand
Should die; but me the threat could not withhold:
A generous cause a victim did demand;
And forth I leapt upon the sandy plain;
A self-devoted chief — by Hector slain."

"Supreme of Heroes — bravest, noblest, best!
Thy matchless courage I bewail no more,
Which then, when tens of thousands were deprest
By doubt, propelled thee to the fatal shore;
Thou found'st — and I forgive thee — here thou art —
A nobler counsellor than my poor heart.

But thou, though capable of sternest deed,
Wert kind as resolute, and good as brave;
And he, whose power restores thee, hath decreed
Thou should'st elude the malice of the grave:
Redundant are thy locks, thy lips as fair
As when their breath enriched Thessalian air.

No Spectre greets me, — no vain Shadow this;
Come, blooming Hero, place thee by my side!
Give, on this well known couch, one nuptial kiss
To me, this day, a second time thy bride!"

Jove frowned in heaven: the conscious Parcæ threw
Upon those roseate lips a Stygian hue.

"This visage tells thee that my doom is past:
Nor should the change be mourned, even if the joys
Of sense were able to return as fast
And surely as they vanish. Earth destroys
Those raptures duly — Erebus disdains:
Calm pleasures there abide — majestic pains.

Be taught, O faithful Consort, to control
Rebellious passion: for the Gods approve
The depth, and not the tumult, of the soul;
A fervent, not ungovernable, love.
Thy transport moderate; and meekly mourn
When I depart, for brief is my sojourn —"

"Ah, wherefore? — Did not Hercules by force
Wrest from the guardian Monster of the tomb
Alcestis, a reanimated corse,
Given back to dwell on earth in vernal bloom?
Medea's spells dispersed the weight of years,
And Æson stood a youth 'mid youthful peers.

The Gods to us are merciful — and they
Yet further may relent: for mightier far
Than strength of nerve and sinew, or the sway
Of magic potent over sun and star,
Is love, though oft to agony distrest,
And though his favourite seat be feeble woman's breast.

But if thou goest, I follow —" "Peace!" he said, —
She looked upon him and was calmed and cheered;
The ghastly colour from his lips had fled;
In his deportment, shape, and mien, appeared
Elysian beauty, melancholy grace,
Brought from a pensive though a happy place.

He spake of love, such love as Spirits feel
In worlds whose course is equable and pure;
No fears to beat away — no strife to heal —
The past unsighed for, and the future sure;
Spake of heroic arts in graver mood
Revived, with finer harmony pursued;

Of all that is most beauteous — imaged there
In happier beauty: more pellucid streams,
An ampler ether, a diviner air,
And fields invested with purpureal gleams;
Climes which the sun, who sheds the brightest day
Earth knows, is all unworthy to survey.

Yet there the Soul shall enter which hath earned
That privilege by virtue. — "Ill," said he,
"The end of man's existence I discerned,
Who from ignoble games and revelry
Could draw, when we had parted, vain delight,
While tears were thy best pastime, day and night;

And while my youthful peers before my eyes
(Each hero following his peculiar bent)
Prepared themselves for glorious enterprise
By martial sports, — or, seated in the tent,
Chieftains and kings in council were detained;
What time the fleet at Aulis lay enchained.

The wished-for wind was given: — I then revolved
The oracle, upon the silent sea;
And, if no worthier led the way, resolved
That, of a thousand vessels, mine should be
The foremost prow in pressing to the strand, —
Mine the first blood that tinged the Trojan sand.

Yet bitter, oft-times bitter, was the pang
When of thy loss I thought, belovèd Wife:
On thee too fondly did my memory hang,
And on the joys we shared in mortal life, —

The paths which we had trod — these fountains, flowers;
My new-planned cities, and unfinished towers.

But should suspense permit the Foe to cry,
'Behold they tremble! — haughty their array,
Yet of their number no one dares to die?'
In soul I swept the indignity away:
Old frailties then recurred: — but lofty thought,
In act embodied, my deliverance wrought.

And Thou, though strong in love, art all too weak
In reason, in self-government too slow;
I counsel thee by fortitude to seek
Our blest re-union in the shades below.
The invisible world with thee hath sympathised;
Be thy affections raised and solemnised.

Learn, by a mortal yearning, to ascend —
Seeking a higher object. Love was given,
Encouraged, sanctioned, chiefly for that end;
For this the passion to excess was driven —
That self might be annulled: her bondage prove
The fetters of a dream, opposed to love." —

Aloud she shrieked! for Hermes re-appears!
Round the dear Shade she would have clung — 'tis vain:
The hours are past — too brief had they been years;
And him no mortal effort can detain:
Swift, toward the realms that know not earthly day,
He through the portal takes his silent way,
And on the palace-floor a lifeless corse She lay.

Thus, all in vain exhorted and reproved,
She perished; and, as for a wilful crime,
By the just Gods whom no weak pity moved,
Was doomed to wear out her appointed time,
Apart from happy Ghosts, that gather flowers
Of blissful quiet 'mid unfading bowers.

— Yet tears to human suffering are due;
And mortal hopes defeated and o'erthrown
Are mourned by man, and not by man alone,
As fondly he believes. — Upon the side
Of Hellespont (such faith was entertained)
A knot of spiry trees for ages grew
From out the tomb of him for whom she died;
And ever, when such stature they had gained
That Ilium's walls were subject to their view,
The trees' tall summits withered at the sight;
A constant interchange of growth and blight! *

1814.

XXVII.
DION.
(SEE PLUTARCH.)

I.

SERENE, and fitted to embrace,
Where'er he turned, a swan-like grace
Of haughtiness without pretence,
And to unfold a still magnificence,
Was princely Dion, in the power
And beauty of his happier hour.
And what pure homage *then* did wait
On Dion's virtues, while the lunar beam
Of Plato's genius, from its lofty sphere,
Fell round him in the grove of Academe,
Softening their inbred dignity austere —
  That he, not too elate
  With self-sufficing solitude,
But with majestic lowliness endued,
Might in the universal bosom reign,
And from affectionate observance gain
Help, under every change of adverse fate.

* For the account of these long-lived trees, see Pliny's Natural History, lib. XVI. cap. 44.; and for the features in the character of Protesilaus see

II.

Five thousand warriors — O the rapturous day!
Each crowned with flowers, and armed with spear and shield,
Or ruder weapon which their course might yield,
To Syracuse advance in bright array.
Who leads them on? — The anxious people see
Long-exiled Dion marching at their head,
He also crowned with flowers of Sicily,
And in a white, far-beaming, corslet clad!
Pure transport undisturbed by doubt or fear
The gazers feel; and, rushing to the plain,
Salute those strangers as a holy train
Or blest procession (to the Immortals dear)
That brought their precious liberty again.
Lo! when the gates are entered, on each hand,
Down the long street, rich goblets filled with wine
      In seemly order stand,
On tables set, as if for rites divine; —
And, as the great Deliverer marches by,
He looks on festal ground with fruits bestrown;
And flowers are on his person thrown
   In boundless prodigality;
Nor doth the general voice abstain from prayer,
Invoking Dion's tutelary care,
As if a very Deity he were!

III.

Mourn, hills and groves of Attica! and mourn
Ilissus, bending o'er thy classic urn!
Mourn, and lament for him whose spirit dreads
Your once sweet memory, studious walks and shades!
For him who to divinity aspired,
Not on the breath of popular applause,
But through dependence on the sacred laws
Framed in the schools where Wisdom dwelt retired,

the Iphigenia in Aulis of Euripides. Virgil places the Shade of Laodamia in a mournful region, among unhappy Lovers,
      — His Laodamia
        It Comes. —

Intent to trace the ideal path of right
(More fair than heaven's broad causeway paved with stars)
Which Dion learned to measure with sublime delight; —
But He hath overleaped the eternal bars;
And, following guides whose craft holds no consent
With aught that breathes the ethereal element,
Hath stained the robes of civil power with blood,
Unjustly shed, though for the public good.
Whence doubts that came too late, and wishes vain,
Hollow excuses, and triumphant pain;
And oft his cogitations sink as low
As, through the abysses of a joyless heart,
The heaviest plummet of despair can go —
But whence that sudden check? that fearful start!
    He hears an uncouth sound —
    Anon his lifted eyes
Saw, at a long-drawn gallery's dusky bound,
A Shape of more than mortal size
And hideous aspect, stalking round and round?
    A woman's garb the Phantom wore,
    And fiercely swept the marble floor, —
    Like Auster whirling to and fro,
    His force on Caspian foam to try;
Or Boreas when he scours the snow
That skins the plains of Thessaly,
Or when aloft on Mænalus he stops
His flight, 'mid eddying pine-tree tops!

IV.

So, but from toil less sign of profit reaping,
The sullen Spectre to her purpose bowed,
    Sweeping — vehemently sweeping —
No pause admitted, no design avowed!
"Avaunt, inexplicable Guest! — avaunt,"
Exclaimed the Chieftain — "let me rather see
The coronal that coiling vipers make;
The torch that flames with many a lurid flake,

And the long train of doleful pageantry
Which they behold, whom vengeful Furies haunt;
Who, while they struggle from the scourge to flee,
Move where the blasted soil is not unworn,
And, in their anguish, bear what other minds have borne!"

V.

But Shapes that come not at an earthly call,
Will not depart when mortal voices bid;
Lords of the visionary eye whose lid,
Once raised, remains aghast, and will not fall!
Ye Gods, thought He, that servile Implement
    Obeys a mystical intent!
Your Minister would brush away
The spots that to my soul adhere;
But should she labour night and day,
They will not, cannot disappear;
Whence angry perturbations, — and that look
Which no philosophy can brook!

VI.

Ill-fated Chief! there are whose hopes are built
Upon the ruins of thy glorious name;
Who, through the portal of one moment's guilt,
Pursue thee with their deadly aim!
O matchless perfidy! portentous lust
Of monstrous crime! — that horror-striking blade,
Drawn in defiance of the Gods, hath laid
The noble Syracusan low in dust!
Shudder'd the walls — the marble city wept —
And sylvan places heaved a pensive sigh;
But in calm peace the appointed Victim slept,
As he had fallen in magnanimity;
Of spirit too capacious to require
That Destiny her course should change; too just
To his own native greatness to desire
That wretched boon, days lengthened by mistrust.

So were the hopeless troubles, that involved
The soul of Dion, instantly dissolved.
Released from life and cares of princely state,
He left this moral grafted on his Fate;
"Him only pleasure leads, and peace attends,
Him, only him, the shield of Jove defends,
Whose means are fair and spotless as his ends."

1816.

XXVIII.
THE PASS OF KIRKSTONE.

I.

WITHIN the mind strong fancies work
A deep delight the bosom thrills,
Oft as I pass along the fork
Of these fraternal hills:
Where, save the rugged road, we find
No appanage of human kind,
Nor hint of man; if stone or rock
Seem not his handy-work to mock
By something cognizably shaped;
Mockery — or model roughly hewn,
And left as if by earthquake strewn,
Or from the Flood escaped:
Altars for Druid service fit;
(But where no fire was ever lit,
Unless the glow-worm to the skies
Thence offer nightly sacrifice)
Wrinkled Egyptian monument;
Green moss-grown tower; or hoary tent;
Tents of a camp that never shall be raised —
On which four thousand years have gazed!

II.

Ye plough-shares sparkling on the slopes!
Ye snow-white lambs that trip
Imprisoned 'mid the formal props
Of restless ownership!

Ye trees, that may to-morrow fall
To feed the insatiate Prodigal!
Lawns, houses, chattels, groves, and fields,
All that the fertile valley shields;
Wages of folly — baits of crime,
Of life's uneasy game the stake,
Playthings that keep the eyes awake
Of drowsy, dotard Time; —
O care! O guilt! — O vales and plains,
Here, 'mid his own unvexed domains,
A Genius dwells, that can subdue
At once all memory of You, —
Most potent when mists veil the sky,
Mists that distort and magnify;
While the coarse rushes, to the sweeping breeze,
Sigh forth their ancient melodies!

III.

List to those shriller notes! — *that* march
Perchance was on the blast,
When, through this Height's inverted arch,
Rome's earliest legion passed!
— They saw, adventurously impelled,
And older eyes than theirs beheld,
This block — and yon, whose church-like frame
Gives to this savage Pass its name.
Aspiring Road! that lov'st to hide
Thy daring in a vapoury bourn,
Not seldom may the hour return
When thou shalt be my guide:
And I (as all men may find cause,
When life is at a weary pause,
And they have panted up the hill
Of duty with reluctant will)
Be thankful, even though tired and faint,
For the rich bounties of constraint;
Whence oft invigorating transports flow
That choice lacked courage to bestow!

IV.

My Soul was grateful for delight
That wore a threatening brow;
A veil is lifted — can she slight
The scene that opens now?
Though habitation none appear,
The greenness tells, man must be there;
The shelter — that the perspective
Is of the clime in which we live;
Where Toil pursues his daily round;
Where Pity sheds sweet tears — and Love,
In woodbine bower or birchen grove,
Inflicts his tender wound.
— Who comes not hither ne'er shall know
How beautiful the world below;
Nor can he guess how lightly leaps
The brook adown the rocky steeps.
Farewell, thou desolate Domain!
Hope, pointing to the cultured plain,
Carols like a shepherd-boy;
And who is she? — Can that be Joy!
Who, with a sunbeam for her guide,
Smoothly skims the meadows wide;
While Faith, from yonder opening cloud,
To hill and vale proclaims aloud,
"Whate'er the weak may dread, the wicked dare,
Thy lot, O Man, is good, thy portion fair!"

1817.

XXIX.

TO ENTERPRISE.

KEEP for the Young the impassioned smile
Shed from thy countenance, as I see thee stand
High on that chalky cliff of Briton's Isle,
A slender volume grasping in thy hand —

(Perchance the pages that relate
The various turns of Crusoe's fate)—
Ah, spare the exulting smile,
And drop thy pointing finger bright
As the first flash of beacon light;
But neither veil thy head in shadows dim,
Nor turn thy face away
From One who, in the evening of his day,
To thee would offer no presumptuous hymn!

I.

Bold Spirit! who art free to rove
Among the starry courts of Jove,
And oft in splendour dost appear
Embodied to poetic eyes,
While traversing this nether sphere,
Where Mortals call thee ENTERPRISE.
Daughter of Hope! her favourite Child,
Whom she to young Ambition bore,
When hunter's arrow first defiled
The grove, and stained the turf with gore;
Thee wingèd Fancy took, and nursed
On broad Euphrates' palmy shore,
And where the mightier Waters burst
From caves of Indian mountains hoar!
She wrapped thee in a panther's skin;
And Thou, thy favourite food to win,
The flame-eyed eagle oft wouldst scare
From her rock-fortress in mid air,
With infant shout; and often sweep,
Paired with the ostrich, o'er the plain;
Or, tired with sport, wouldst sink asleep
Upon the couchant lion's mane!
With rolling years thy strength increased;
And, far beyond thy native East,
To thee, by varying titles known
As variously thy power was shown,
Did incense-bearing altars rise,

Which caught the blaze of sacrifice,
From suppliants panting for the skies!

II.

What though this ancient Earth be trod
No more by step of Demi-god
Mounting from glorious deed to deed
As thou from clime to clime didst lead;
Yet still, the bosom beating high,
And the hushed farewell of an eye
Where no procrastinating gaze
A last infirmity betrays,
Prove that thy heaven-descended sway
Shall ne'er submit to cold decay.
By thy divinity impelled,
The Stripling seeks the tented field;
The aspiring Virgin kneels; and, pale
With awe, receives the hallowed veil,
A soft and tender Heroine
Vowed to severer discipline;
Inflamed by thee, the blooming Boy
Makes of the whistling shrouds a toy,
And of the ocean's dismal breast
A play-ground, — or a couch of rest;
'Mid the blank world of snow and ice,
Thou to his dangers dost enchain
The Chamois-chaser awed in vain
By chasm or dizzy precipice;
And hast Thou not with triumph seen
How soaring Mortals glide between
Or through the clouds, and brave the light
With bolder than Icarian flight?
How they, in bells of crystal, dive —
Where winds and waters cease to strive —
For no unholy visitings,
Among the monsters of the Deep;
And all the sad and precious things
Which there in ghastly silence sleep?

Or, adverse tides and currents headed,
And breathless calms no longer dreaded,
In never-slackening voyage go
Straight as an arrow from the bow;
And, slighting sails and scorning oars,
Keep faith with Time on distant shores?
— Within our fearless reach are placed
The secrets of the burning Waste;
Egyptian tombs unlock their dead,
Nile trembles at his fountain head;
Thou speak'st — and lo! the polar Seas
Unbosom their last mysteries.
— But oh! what transports, what sublime reward,
Won from the world of mind, dost thou prepare
For philosophic Sage; or high-souled Bard
Who, for thy service trained in lonely woods,
Hath fed on pageants floating through the air
Or calentured in depth of limpid floods;
Nor grieves — tho' doomed thro' silent night to bear
The domination of his glorious themes,
Or struggle in the net-work of thy dreams!

III.

If there be movements in the Patriot's soul,
From source still deeper, and of higher worth,
'Tis thine the quickening impulse to control,
And in due season send the mandate forth;
Thy call a prostrate Nation can restore,
When but a single Mind resolves to crouch no more.

IV.

Dread Minister of wrath!
Who to their destined punishment dost urge
The Pharaohs of the earth, the men of hardened heart!
Not unassisted by the flattering stars,
Thou strew'st temptation o'er the path
When they in pomp depart
With trampling horses and refulgent cars —
Soon to be swallowed by the briny surge;

Or cast, for lingering death, on unknown strands;
Or caught amid a whirl of desert sands —
An Army now, and now a living hill
That a brief while heaves with convulsive throes —
Then all is still;
Or, to forget their madness and their woes,
Wrapt in a winding-sheet of spotless snows!

V.

Back flows the willing current of my Song:
If to provoke such doom the Impious dare,
Why should it daunt a blameless prayer?
— Bold Goddess! range our Youth among;
Nor let thy genuine impulse fail to beat
In hearts no longer young;
Still may a veteran Few have pride
In thoughts whose sternness makes them sweet;
In fixed resolves by Reason justified;
That to their object cleave like sleet
Whitening a pine tree's northern side,
When fields are naked far and wide,
And withered leaves, from earth's cold breast
Up-caught in whirlwinds, nowhere can find rest.

VI.

But, if such homage thou disdain
As doth with mellowing years agree,
One rarely absent from thy train
More humble favours may obtain
For thy contented Votary.
She, who incites the frolic lambs
In presence of their heedless dams,
And to the solitary fawn
Vouchsafes her lessons, bounteous Nymph
That wakes the breeze, the sparkling lymph
Doth hurry to the lawn;
She, who inspires that strain of joyance holy
Which the sweet Bird, misnamed the melancholy,
Pours forth in shady groves, shall plead for me;

And vernal mornings opening bright
With views of undefined delight,
And cheerful songs, and suns that shine
On busy days, with thankful nights, be mine.

VII.

But thou, O Goddess! in thy favourite Isle
(Freedom's impregnable redoubt,
The wide earth's store-house fenced about
With breakers roaring to the gales
That stretch a thousand thousand sails)
Quicken the slothful, and exalt the vile! —
Thy impulse is the life of Fame;
Glad Hope would almost cease to be
If torn from thy society;
And Love, when worthiest of his name,
Is proud to walk the earth with Thee!

XXX.
TO A YOUNG LADY,
WHO HAD BEEN REPROACHED FOR TAKING LONG WALKS IN THE COUNTRY.

Dear Child of Nature, let them rail!
— There is a nest in a green dale,
A harbour and a hold;
Where thou, a Wife and Friend, shalt see
Thy own heart-stirring days, and be
A light to young and old.

There, healthy as a shepherd boy,
And treading among flowers of joy
Which at no season fade,
Thou, while thy babes around thee cling,
Shalt show us how divine a thing
A Woman may be made.

Thy thoughts and feelings shall not die,
Nor leave thee, when grey hairs are nigh
A melancholy slave;
But an old age serene and bright,
And lovely as a Lapland night,
Shall lead thee to thy grave.

1803

XXXI.
WATER-FOWL.

"Let me be allowed the aid of verse to describe the evolutions which these "visitants sometimes perform, on a fine day towards the close of "winter." — *Extract from the Author's Book on the Lakes.*

MARK how the feathered tenants of the flood,
With grace of motion that might scarcely seem
Inferior to angelical, prolong
Their curious pastime! shaping in mid air
(And sometimes with ambitious wing that soars
High as the level of the mountain-tops)
A circuit ampler than the lake beneath —
Their own domain; but ever, while intent
On tracing and retracing that large round,
Their jubilant activity evolves
Hundreds of curves and circlets, to and fro,
Upward and downward, progress intricate
Yet unperplexed, as if one spirit swayed
Their indefatigable flight. 'Tis done —
Ten times, or more, I fancied it had ceased;
But lo! the vanished company again
Ascending; they approach — I hear their wings,
Faint, faint at first; and then an eager sound,
Past in a moment — and as faint again!
They tempt the sun to sport amid their plumes;
They tempt the water, or the gleaming ice,
To show them a fair image; 'tis themselves,
Their own fair forms, upon the glimmering plain,

Painted more soft and fair as they descend
Almost to touch; — then up again aloft,
Up with a sally and a flash of speed,
As if they scorned both resting-place and rest!

1812.

XXXII.

VIEW FROM THE TOP OF BLACK COMB.

This Height a ministering Angel might select:
For from the summit of BLACK COMB (dread name
Derived from clouds and storms!) the amplest range
Of unobstructed prospect may be seen
That British ground commands: — low dusky tracts,
Where Trent is nursed, far southward!   Cambrian hills
To the south-west, a multitudinous show;
And, in a line of eye-sight linked with these,
The hoary peaks of Scotland that give birth
To Tiviot's stream, to Annan, Tweed, and Clyde: —
Crowding the quarter whence the sun comes forth
Gigantic mountains rough with crags; beneath,
Right at the imperial station's western base
Main ocean, breaking audibly, and stretched
Far into silent regions blue and pale; —
And visibly engirding Mona's Isle
That, as we left the plain, before our sight
Stood like a lofty mount, uplifting slowly
(Above the convex of the watery globe)
Into clear view the cultured fields that streak
Her habitable shores, but now appears
A dwindled object, and submits to lie
At the spectator's feet. — Yon azure ridge,
Is it a perishable cloud?   Or there
Do we behold the line of Erin's coast?
Land sometimes by the roving shepherd-swain
(Like the bright confines of another world)
Not doubtfully perceived. — Look homeward now!

In depth, in height, in circuit, how serene
The spectacle, how pure! — Of Nature's works,
In earth, and air, and earth-embracing sea,
A revelation infinite it seems;
Display august of man's inheritance,
Of Britain's calm felicity and power!   1813.

Black Comb stands at the southern extremity of Cumberland: its base covers a much greater extent of ground than any other mountain in those parts; and, from its situation, the summit commands a more extensive view than any other point in Britain.

XXXIII.
THE HAUNTED TREE.
TO —.

Those silver clouds collected round the sun
His mid-day warmth abate not, seeming less
To overshade than multiply his beams
By soft reflection — grateful to the sky,
To rocks, fields, woods. Nor doth our human sense
Ask, for its pleasure, screen or canopy
More ample than the time-dismantled Oak
Spreads o'er this tuft of heath, which now, attired
In the whole fulness of its bloom, affords
Couch beautiful as e'er for earthly use
Was fashioned; whether by the hand of Art,
That eastern Sultan, amid flowers enwrought
On silken tissue, might diffuse his limbs
In languor; or, by Nature, for repose
Of panting Wood-nymph, wearied with the chase.
O Lady! fairer in thy Poet's sight
Than fairest spiritual creature of the groves,
Approach; — and, thus invited, crown with rest
The noon-tide hour: though truly some there are
Whose footsteps superstitiously avoid
This venerable Tree; for, when the wind
Blows keenly, it sends forth a creaking sound

(Above the general roar of woods and crags)
Distinctly heard from far — a doleful note!
As if (so Grecian shepherds would have deemed)
The Hamadryad, pent within, bewailed
Some bitter wrong. Nor is it unbelieved,
By ruder fancy, that a troubled ghost
Haunts the old trunk; lamenting deeds of which
The flowery ground is conscious. But no wind
Sweeps now along this elevated ridge;
Not even a zephyr stirs; — the obnoxious Tree
Is mute; and, in his silence, would look down,
O lovely Wanderer of the trackless hills,
On thy reclining form with more delight
Than his coevals in the sheltered vale
Seem to participate, the while they view
Their own far-stretching arms and leafy heads
Vividly pictured in some glassy pool,
That, for a brief space, checks the hurrying stream.

1819.

XXXIV.
THE PRIMROSE OF THE ROCK.

A Rock there is whose homely front
    The passing traveller slights;
Yet there the glow-worms hang their lamps,
    Like stars, at various heights;
And one coy Primrose to that Rock
    The vernal breeze invites.

What hideous warfare hath been waged,
    What kingdoms overthrown,
Since first I spied that Primrose-tuft
    And marked it for my own;
A lasting link in Nature's chain
    From highest heaven let down!

THE PRIMROSE OF THE ROCK.

The flowers, still faithful to the stems,
    Their fellowship renew;
The stems are faithful to the root,
    That worketh out of view;
And to the rock the root adheres
    In every fibre true.

Close clings to earth the living rock,
    Though threatening still to fall;
The earth is constant to her sphere;
    And God upholds them all:
So blooms this lonely Plant, nor dreads
    Her annual funeral.

      *   *   *   *

Here closed the meditative strain;
    But air breathed soft that day,
The hoary mountain-heights were cheered,
    The sunny vale looked gay;
And to the Primrose of the Rock
    I gave this after-lay.

I sang — Let myriads of bright flowers,
    Like Thee, in field and grove
Revive unenvied; — mightier far,
    Than tremblings that reprove
Our vernal tendencies to hope,
    Is God's redeeming love;

That love which changed — for wan disease,
    For sorrow that had bent
O'er hopeless dust, for withered age —
    Their moral element,
And turned the thistles of a curse
    To types beneficent.

Sin-blighted though we are, we too,
  The reasoning Sons of Men,
From one oblivious winter called
  Shall rise, and breathe again;
And in eternal summer lose
  Our threescore years and ten.

To humbleness of heart descends
  This prescience from on high,
The faith that elevates the just,
  Before and when they die;
And makes each soul a separate heaven,
  A court for Deity.

1831.

XXXV.
PRESENTIMENTS.

PRESENTIMENTS! they judge not right
Who deem that ye from open light
  Retire in fear of shame;
All *heaven-born* Instincts shun the touch
Of vulgar sense, — and, being such,
  Such privilege ye claim.

The tear whose source I could not guess,
The deep sigh that seemed fatherless,
  Were mine in early days;
And now, unforced by time to part
With fancy, I obey my heart,
  And venture on your praise.

What though some busy foes to good,
Too potent over nerve and blood,
  Lurk near you — and combine
To taint the health which ye infuse;
This hides not from the moral Muse
  Your origin divine.

How oft from you, derided Powers!
Comes Faith that in auspicious hours
 Builds castles, not of air:
Bodings unsanctioned by the will
Flow from your visionary skill,
 And teach us to beware.

The bosom-weight, your stubborn gift,
That no philosophy can lift,
 Shall vanish, if ye please,
Like morning mist: and, where it lay,
The spirits at your bidding play
 In gaiety and ease.

Star-guided contemplations move
Through space, though calm, not raised above
 Prognostics that ye rule;
The naked Indian of the wild,
And haply, too, the cradled Child,
 Are pupils of your school.

But who can fathom your intents,
Number their signs or instruments?
 A rainbow, a sunbeam,
A subtle smell that Spring unbinds,
Dead pause abrupt of midnight winds,
 An echo, or a dream.

The laughter of the Christmas hearth
With sighs of self-exhausted mirth
 Ye feelingly reprove;
And daily, in the conscious breast,
Your visitations are a test
 And exercise of love.

When some great change gives boundless scope
To an exulting Nation's hope,

Oft, startled and made wise
By your low-breathed interpretings,
The simply-meek foretaste the springs
   Of bitter contraries.

Ye daunt the proud array of war,
Pervade the lonely ocean far
   As sail hath been unfurled;
For dancers in the festive hall
What ghastly partners hath your call
   Fetched from the shadowy world.

'Tis said, that warnings ye dispense,
Emboldened by a keener sense;
   That men have lived for whom,
With dread precision, ye made clear
The hour that in a distant year
   Should knell them to the tomb.

Unwelcome insight! Yet there are
Blest times when mystery is laid bare,
   Truth shows a glorious face,
While on that isthmus which commands
The councils of both worlds, she stands,
   Sage Spirits! by your grace.

God, who instructs the brutes to scent
All changes of the element,
   Whose wisdom fixed the scale
Of natures, for our wants provides
By higher, sometimes humbler, guides,
   When lights of reason fail.

1830.

XXXVI.
TO THE CLOUDS.

Army of Clouds! ye wingèd Host in troops
Ascending from behind the motionless brow
Of that tall rock, as from a hidden world,
O whither with such eagerness of speed?
What seek ye, or what shun ye? of the gale
Companions, fear ye to be left behind,
Or racing o'er your blue ethereal field
Contend ye with each other? of the sea
Children, thus post ye over vale and height
To sink upon your mother's lap — and rest?
Or were ye rightlier hailed, when first mine eyes
Beheld in your impetuous march the likeness
Of a wide army pressing on to meet
Or overtake some unknown enemy? —
But your smooth motions suit a peaceful aim;
And Fancy, not less aptly pleased, compares
Your squadrons to an endless flight of birds
Aerial, upon due migration bound
To milder climes; or rather do ye urge
In caravan your hasty pilgrimage
To pause at last on more aspiring heights
Than these, and utter your devotion there
With thunderous voice? Or are ye jubilant,
And would ye, tracking your proud lord the Sun,
Be present at his setting; or the pomp
Of Persian mornings would ye fill, and stand
Poising your splendours high above the heads
Of worshippers kneeling to their up-risen God?
Whence, whence, ye Clouds! this eagerness of speed?
Speak, silent creatures. — They are gone, are fled,
Buried together in yon gloomy mass
That loads the middle heaven; and clear and bright

And vacant doth the region which they thronged
Appear; a calm descent of sky conducting
Down to the unapproachable abyss,
Down to that hidden gulf from which they rose
To vanish — fleet as days and months and years,
Fleet as the generations of mankind,
Power, glory, empire, as the world itself,
The lingering world, when time hath ceased to be.
But the winds roar, shaking the rooted trees,
And see! a bright precursor to a train
Perchance as numerous, overpeers the rock
That sullenly refuses to partake
Of the wild impulse. From a fount of life
Invisible, the long procession moves
Luminous or gloomy, welcome to the vale
Which they are entering, welcome to mine eye
That sees them, to my soul that owns in them,
And in the bosom of the firmament
O'er which they move, wherein they are contained,
A type of her capacious self and all
Her restless progeny.
      A humble walk
Here is my body doomed to tread, this path,
A little hoary line and faintly traced,
Work, shall we call it, of the shepherd's foot
Or of his flock? — joint vestige of them both.
I pace it unrepining, for my thoughts
Admit no bondage and my words have wings.
Where is the Orphean lyre, or Druid harp,
To accompany the verse? The mountain blast
Shall be our *hand* of music; he shall sweep
The rocks, and quivering trees, and billowy lake,
And search the fibres of the caves, and they
Shall answer, for our song is of the Clouds
And the wind loves them; and the gentle gales —
Which by their aid re-clothe the naked lawn
With annual verdure, and revive the woods,

And moisten the parched lips of thirsty flowers —
Love them; and every idle breeze of air
Bends to the favourite burthen. Moon and stars
Keep their most solemn vigils when the Clouds
Watch also, shifting peaceably their place
Like bands of ministering Spirits, or when they lie,
As if some Protean art the change had wrought,
In listless quiet o'er the ethereal deep
Scattered, a Cyclades of various shapes
And all degrees of beauty. O ye Lightnings!
Ye are their perilous offspring; and the Sun —
Source inexhaustible of life and joy,
And type of man's far-darting reason, therefore
In old time worshipped as the god of verse,
A blazing intellectual deity —
Loves his own glory in their looks, and showers
Upon that unsubstantial brotherhood
Visions with all but beatific light
Enriched — too transient were they not renewed
From age to age, and did not, while we gaze
In silent rapture, credulous desire
Nourish the hope that memory lacks not power
To keep the treasure unimpaired. Vain thought!
Yet why repine, created as we are
For joy and rest, albeit to find them only
Lodged in the bosom of eternal things?

XXXVII.
A JEWISH FAMILY.
(IN A SMALL VALLEY OPPOSITE ST. GOAR, UPON THE RHINE.)

Genius of Raphael! if thy wings
   Might bear thee to this glen,
With faithful memory left of things
   To pencil dear and pen,
Thou would'st forego the neighbouring Rhine,
   And all his majesty —
A studious forehead to incline
   O'er this poor family.

The Mother — her thou must have seen,
   In spirit, ere she came
To dwell these rifted rocks between,
   Or found on earth a name;
An image, too, of that sweet Boy,
   Thy inspirations give —
Of playfulness, and love, and joy,
   Predestined here to live.

Downcast, or shooting glances far,
   'How beautiful his eyes,
That blend the nature of the star
   With that of summer skies!
I speak as if of sense beguiled;
   Uncounted months are gone,
Yet am I with the Jewish Child,
   That exquisite Saint John.

I see the dark-brown curls, the brow,
   The smooth transparent skin,
Refined, as with intent to show
   The holiness within;

A JEWISH FAMILY.

The grace of parting Infancy
  By blushes yet untamed;
Age faithful to the mother's knee,
  Nor of her arms ashamed.

Two lovely Sisters, still and sweet
  As flowers, stand side by side;
Their soul-subduing looks might cheat
  The Christian of his pride:
Such beauty hath the Eternal poured
  Upon them not forlorn,
Though of a lineage once abhorred,
  Nor yet redeemed from scorn.

Mysterious safeguard, that, in spite
  Of poverty and wrong,
Doth here preserve a living light,
  From Hebrew fountains sprung;
That gives this ragged group to cast
  Around the dell a gleam
Of Palestine, of glory past,
  And proud Jerusalem!

1828.

PETER BELL.

A TALE.

What 's in a *Name?*
* * * * *
Brutus will start a Spirit as soon as Cæsar!

TO ROBERT SOUTHEY, ESQ., P.L., ETC. ETC.

MY DEAR FRIEND,

The Tale of Peter Bell, which I now introduce to your notice, and to that of the Public, has, in its Manuscript state, nearly survived its minority:—for it first saw the light in the summer of 1798. During this long interval, pains have been taken at different times to make the production less unworthy of a favourable reception; or, rather, to fit it for filling *permanently* a station, however humble, in the Literature of our Country. This has, indeed, been the aim of all my endeavours in Poetry, which, you know, have been sufficiently laborious to prove that I deem the Art not lightly to be approached; and that the attainment of excellence in it, may laudably be made the principal object of intellectual pursuit by any man, who, with reasonable consideration of circumstances, has faith in his own impulses.

The Poem of Peter Bell, as the Prologue will show, was composed under a belief that the Imagination not only does not require for its exercise the intervention of supernatural agency, but that, though such agency be excluded, the faculty may be called forth as imperiously and for kindred results of pleasure, by incidents, within the compass of poetic probability, in the humblest departments of daily life. Since that Prologue was written, *you* have exhibited most splendid effects of judicious daring, in the opposite and usual course. Let this acknowledgment make my peace with the lovers of the supernatural; and I am persuaded it will be admitted, that to you as a Master in that province of the art, the following Tale, whether from contrast or congruity, is not an unappropriate offering. Accept it, then, as a public testimony of affectionate admiration from one with whose name yours has been often coupled (to use your own words) for evil and for good; and believe me to be, with earnest wishes that life and health may be granted you to complete the many important works in which you are engaged, and with high respect,

Most faithfully yours,
WILLIAM WORDSWORTH.

RYDAL MOUNT, *April* 7, 1819.

PROLOGUE.

There's something in a flying horse,
There's something in a huge balloon;
But through the clouds I'll never float
Until I have a little Boat,
Shaped like the crescent-moon.

And now I *have* a little Boat,
In shape a very crescent-moon:
Fast through the clouds my boat can sail;
But if perchance your faith should fail,
Look up — and you shall see me soon!

The woods, my Friends, are round you roaring,
Rocking and roaring like a sea;
The noise of danger's in your ears,
And ye have all a thousand fears
Both for my little Boat and me!

Meanwhile untroubled I admire
The pointed horns of my canoe;
And, did not pity touch my breast,
To see how ye are all distrest,
Till my ribs ached, I'd laugh at you!

Away we go, my Boat an I —
Frail man ne'er sate in such another;
Whether among the winds we strive,
Or deep into the clouds we dive,
Each is contented with the other.

Away we go — and what care we
For treasons, tumults, and for wars?
We are as calm in our delight
As is the crescent-moon so bright
Among the scattered stars.

Up goes my Boat among the stars
Through many a breathless field of light,
Through many a long blue field of ether,
Leaving ten thousand stars beneath her:
Up goes my little Boat so bright!

The Crab, the Scorpion, and the Bull —
We pry among them all; have shot
High o'er the red-haired race of Mars,
Covered from top to toe with scars;
Such company I like it not!

The towns in Saturn are decayed,
And melancholy Spectres throng them; —
The Pleiads, that appear to kiss
Each other in the vast abyss,
With joy I sail among them.

Swift Mercury resounds with mirth,
Great Jove is full of stately bowers;
But these, and all that they contain,
What are they to that tiny grain,
That little Earth of ours?

Then back to Earth, the dear green Earth:
Whole ages if I here should roam,
The world for my remarks and me
Would not a whit the better be;
I've left my heart at home.

See! there she is, the matchless Earth!
There spreads the famed Pacific Ocean!
Old Andes thrusts yon craggy spear
Through the grey clouds; the Alps are here,
Like waters in commotion!

Yon tawny slip is Libya's sands;
That silver thread the river Dnieper;'
And look, where clothed in brightest green
Is a sweet Isle, of isles the Queen;
Ye fairies, from all evil keep her!

And see the town where I was born!
Around those happy fields we span
In boyish gambols; — I was lost
Where I have been, but on this coast
I feel I am a man.

Never did fifty things at once
Appear so lovely, never, never; —
How tunefully the forests ring!
To hear the earth's soft murmuring
Thus could I hang for ever!

"Shame on you!" cried my little Boat,
"Was ever such a homesick Loon,
Within a living Boat to sit,
And make no better use of it;
A Boat twin-sister of the crescent-moon!

Ne'er in the breast of full-grown Poet
Fluttered so faint a heart before; —
Was it the music of the spheres
That overpowered your mortal ears?
— Such din shall trouble them no more.

These nether precincts do not lack
Charms of their own; — then come with me;
I want a comrade, and for you
There's nothing that I would not do;
Nought is there that you shall not see.

Haste! and above Siberian snows
We'll sport amid the boreal morning;
Will mingle with her lustres gliding
Among the stars, the stars now hiding,
And now the stars adorning.

I know the secrets of a land
Where human foot did never stray;
Fair is that land as evening skies,
And cool, though in the depth it lies
Of burning Africa.

Or we'll into the realm of Faery,
Among the lovely shades of things;
The shadowy forms of mountains bare,
And streams, and bowers, and ladies fair,
The shades of palaces and kings!

Or, if you thirst with hardy zeal
Less quiet regions to explore,
Prompt voyage shall to you reveal
How earth and heaven are taught to feel
The might of magic lore!"

"My little vagrant Form of light,
My gay and beautiful Canoe,
Well you have played your friendly part;
As kindly take what from my heart
Experience forces — then adieu!

Temptation lurks among your words;
But, while these pleasures you 're pursuing
Without impediment or let,
No wonder if you quite forget
What on the earth is doing.

There was a time when all mankind
Did listen with a faith sincere
To tuneful tongues in mystery versed;
Then Poets fearlessly rehearsed
The wonders of a wild career.

Go — (but the world 's a sleepy world,
And 'tis, I fear, an age too late)
Take with you some ambitious Youth!
For, restless Wanderer! I, in truth,
Am all unfit to be your mate.

Long have I loved what I behold,
The night that calms, the day that cheers;
The common growth of mother-earth
Suffices me — her tears, her mirth,
Her humblest mirth and tears.

The dragon's wing, the magic ring,
I shall not covet for my dower,
If I along that lowly way
With sympathetic heart may stray,
And with a soul of power.

These given, what more need I desire
To stir, to soothe, or elevate?
What nobler marvels than the mind
May in life's daily prospect find,
May find or there create?

A potent wand doth Sorrow wield;
What spell so strong as guilty Fear!
Repentance is a tender Sprite;
If aught on earth have heavenly might,
'Tis lodged within her silent tear.

But grant my wishes, — let us now
Descend from this ethereal height;
Then take thy way, adventurous Skiff,
More daring far than Hippogriff,
And be thy own delight!

To the stone-table in my garden,
Loved haunt of many a summer hour,
The Squire is come: his daughter Bess
Beside him in the cool recess
Sits blooming like a flower.

With these are many more convened;
They know not I have been so far; —
I see them there, in number nine,
Beneath the spreading Weymouth-pine!
I see them — there they are!

There sits the Vicar and his Dame;
And there my good friend, Stephen Otter;
And, ere the light of evening fail,
To them I must relate the Tale
Of Peter Bell the Potter."

Off flew the Boat — away she flees,
Spurning her freight with indignation!
And I, as well as I was able,
On two poor legs, toward my stone-table
Limped on with sore vexation.

"O, here he is!" cried little Bess —
She saw me at the garden-door;
"We 've waited anxiously and long,"
They cried, and all around me throng,
Full nine of them or more!

"Reproach me not — your fears be still —
Be thankful we again have met; —
Resume, my Friends! within the shade
Your seats, and quickly shall be paid
The well-remembered debt."

I spake with faltering voice, like one
Not wholly rescued from the pale
Of a wild dream, or worse illusion;
But, straight, to cover my confusion,
Began the promised Tale.

PART FIRST.

ALL by the moonlight river side
Groaned the poor Beast — alas! in vain;
The staff was raised to loftier height,
And the blows fell with heavier weight
As Peter struck — and struck again.

"Hold!" cried the Squire, "against the rules,
Of common sense you 're surely sinning;
This leap is for us all too bold;
Who Peter was, let that be told,
And start from the beginning."

PETER BELL.

—— "A Potter,* Sir, he was by trade,"
Said I, becoming quite collected;
"And wheresoever he appeared,
Full twenty times was Peter feared
For once that Peter was respected.

He two-and-thirty years or more,
Had been a wild and woodland rover;
Had heard the Atlantic surges roar
On farthest Cornwall's rocky shore,
And trod the cliffs of Dover.

And he had seen Caernarvon's towers,
And well he knew the spire of Sarum;
And he had been where Lincoln bell
Flings o'er the fen that ponderous knell —
A far-renowned alarum.

At Doncaster, at York, and Leeds,
And merry Carlisle had he been;
And all along the Lowlands fair,
All through the bonny shire of Ayr;
And far as Aberdeen.

And he had been at Inverness;
And Peter, by the mountain-rills,
Had danced his round with Highland lasses;
And he had lain beside his asses
On lofty Cheviot Hills:

And he had trudged through Yorkshire dales,
Among the rocks and winding *scars;*
Where deep and low the hamlets lie
Beneath their little patch of sky
And little lot of stars:

---

* In the dialect of the North, a hawker of earthenware is thus designated.

And all along the indented coast,
Bespattered with the salt-sea foam;
Where'er a knot of houses lay
On headland, or in hollow bay; —
Sure never man like him did roam!

As well might Peter, in the Fleet,
Have been fast bound, a begging debtor; —
He travelled here, he travelled there;
But not the value of a hair
Was heart or head the better.

He roved among the vales and streams,
In the green wood and hollow dell;
They were his dwellings night and day, —
But nature ne'er could find the way
Into the heart of Peter Bell.

In vain, through every changeful year,
Did Nature lead him as before;
A primrose by a river's brim
A yellow primrose was to him,
And it was nothing more.

Small change it made in Peter's heart
To see his gentle pannicred train
With more than vernal pleasure feeding,
Where'er the tender grass was leading
Its earliest green along the lane.

In vain, through water, earth, and air,
The soul of happy sound was spread,
When Peter on some April morn,
Beneath the broom or budding thorn,
Made the warm earth his lazy bed.

At noon, when, by the forest's edge
He lay beneath the branches high,
The soft blue sky did never melt
Into his heart; he never felt
The witchery of the soft blue sky!

On a fair prospect some have looked
And felt, as I have heard them say,
As if the moving time had been
A thing as steadfast as the scene
On which they gazed themselves away.

Within the breast of Peter Bell
These silent raptures found no place;
He was a Carl as wild and rude
As ever hue-and-cry pursued,
As ever ran a felon's race.

Of all that lead a lawless life,
Of all that love their lawless lives,
In city or in village small,
He was the wildest far of all; —
He had a dozen wedded wives.

Nay, start not! — wedded wives — and twelve!
But how one wife could e'er come near him,
In simple truth I cannot tell;
For, be it said of Peter Bell,
To see him was to fear him.

Though Nature could not touch his heart
By lovely forms, and silent weather,
And tender sounds, yet you might see
At once, that Peter Bell and she
Had often been together.

A savage wildness round him hung
As of a dweller out of doors;
In his whole figure and his mien
A savage character was seen
Of mountains and of dreary moors.

To all the unshaped half-human thoughts
Which solitary Nature feeds
'Mid summer storms or winter's ice,
Had Peter joined whatever vice
The cruel city breeds.

His face was keen as is the wind
That cuts along the hawthorn-fence;
Of courage you saw little there,
But, in its stead, a medley air
Of cunning and of impudence.

He had a dark and sidelong walk,
And long and slouching was his gait;
Beneath his looks so bare and bold,
You might perceive, his spirit cold
Was playing with some inward bait.

His forehead wrinkled was and furred;
A work, one half of which was done
By thinking of his '*whens*' and '*hows;*'
And half, by knitting of his brows
Beneath the glaring sun.

There was a hardness in his cheek,
There was a hardness in his eye,
As if the man had fixed his face,
In many a solitary place,
Against the wind and open sky!"

ONE NIGHT, (and now my little Bess!
We've reached at last the promised Tale;)
One beautiful November night,
When the full moon was shining bright
Upon the rapid river Swale,

Along the river's winding banks
Peter was travelling all alone;—
Whether to buy or sell, or led
By pleasure running in his head,
To me was never known.

He trudged along through copse and brake,
He trudged along o'er hill and dale;
Nor for the moon cared he a tittle,
And for the stars he cared as little,
And for the murmuring river Swale.

But, chancing to espy a path
That promised to cut short the way;
As many a wiser man hath done,
He left a trusty guide for one
That might his steps betray.

To a thick wood he soon is brought
Where cheerily his course he weaves,
And whistling loud may yet be heard,
Though often buried, like a bird
Darkling, among the boughs and leaves.

But quickly Peter's mood is changed,
And on he drives with cheeks that burn
In downright fury and in wrath; —
There's little sign the treacherous path
Will to the road return!

The path grows dim, and dimmer still;
Now up, now down, the Rover wends,
With all the sail that he can carry,
Till brought to a deserted quarry —
And there the pathway ends.

He paused — for shadows of strange shape,
Massy and black, before him lay;
But through the dark, and through the cold,
And through the yawning fissures old,
Did Peter boldly press his way

Right through the quarry; — and behold
A scene of soft and lovely hue!
Where blue and grey, and tender green
Together make as sweet a scene
As ever human eye did view.

Beneath the clear blue sky he saw
A little field of meadow ground;
But field or meadow name it not;
Call it of earth a small green plot,
With rocks encompassed round.

The Swale flowed under the grey rocks,
But he flowed quiet and unseen; —
You need a strong and stormy gale
To bring the noises of the Swale
To that green spot, so calm and green!

And is there no one dwelling here,
No hermit with his beads and glass?
And does no little cottage look
Upon this soft and fertile nook?
Does no one live near this green grass?

Across the deep and quiet spot
Is Peter driving through the grass —
And now has reached the skirting trees;
When, turning round his head, he sees
A solitary Ass.

"A prize!" cries Peter — but he first
Must spy about him far and near:
There's not a single house in sight,
No woodman's hut, no cottage light —
Peter, you need not fear!

There's nothing to be seen but woods,
And rocks that spread a hoary gleam,
And this one Beast, that from the bed
Of the green meadow hangs his head
Over the silent stream.

His head is with a halter bound;
The halter seizing, Peter leapt
Upon the Creature's back, and plied
With ready heels his shaggy side;
But still the Ass his station kept.

Then Peter gave a sudden jerk,
A jerk that from a dungeon-floor
Would have pulled up an iron ring;
But still the heavy-headed Thing
Stood just as he had stood before!

Quoth Peter, leaping from his seat,
"There is some plot against me laid;"
Once more the little meadow-ground
And all the hoary cliffs around
He cautiously surveyed.

All, all is silent — rocks and woods,
All still and silent — far and near!
Only the Ass, with motion dull,
Upon the pivot of his skull
Turns round his long left ear.

Thought Peter, What can mean all this?
Some ugly witchcraft must be here!
— Once more the Ass, with motion dull,
Upon the pivot of his skull
Turned round his long left ear.

Suspicion ripened into dread;
Yet with deliberate action slow,
His staff high-raising, in the pride
Of skill, upon the sounding hide,
He dealt a sturdy blow.

The poor Ass staggered with the shock;
And then, as if to take his ease,
In quiet uncomplaining mood,
Upon the spot where he had stood,
Dropped gently down upon his knees;

As gently on his side he fell;
And by the river's brink did lie;
And, while he lay like one that mourned,
The patient Beast on Peter turned
His shining hazel eye.

'Twas but one mild, reproachful look,
A look more tender than severe;
And straight in sorrow, not in dread,
He turned the eye-ball in his head
Towards the smooth river deep and clear.

Upon the Beast the sapling rings;
His lank sides heaved, his limbs they stirred;
He gave a groan, and then another,
Of that which went before the brother,
And then he gave a third.

All by the moonlight river side
He gave three miserable groans;
And not till now hath Peter seen
How gaunt the Creature is, — how lean
And sharp his staring bones!

With legs stretched out and stiff he lay: —
No word of kind commiseration
Fell at the sight from Peter's tongue;
With hard contempt his heart was wrung,
With hatred and vexation.

The meagre beast lay still as death;
And Peter's lips with fury quiver;
Quoth he, "You little mulish dog,
I'll fling your carcass like a log
Head-foremost down the river!"

An impious oath confirmed the threat —
Whereat from the earth on which he lay
To all the echoes, south and north,
And east and west, the Ass sent forth
A long and clamorous bray!

This outcry, on the heart of Peter,
Seems like a note of joy to strike, —
Joy at the heart of Peter knocks;
But in the echo of the rocks
Was something Peter did not like.

Whether to cheer his coward breast,
Or that he could not break the chain,
In this serene and solemn hour,
Twined round him by demoniac power,
To the blind work he turned again.

Among the rocks and winding crags;
Among the mountains far away;
Once more the Ass did lengthen out
More ruefully a deep-drawn shout,
The hard dry see-saw of his horrible bray!

What is there now in Peter's heart!
Or whence the might of this strange sound?
The moon uneasy looked and dimmer,
The broad blue heavens appeared to glimmer,
And the rocks staggered all around —

From Peter's hand the sapling dropped!
Threat has he none to execute;
"If any one should come and see
That I am here, they 'll think," quoth he,
"I 'm helping this poor dying brute."

He scans the Ass from limb to limb,
And ventures now to uplift his eyes;
More steady looks the moon, and clear,
More like themselves the rocks appear
And touch more quiet skies.

His scorn returns — his hate revives;
He stoops the Ass's neck to seize
With malice — that again takes flight;
For in the pool a startling sight
Meets him, among the inverted trees.

Is it the moon's distorted face?
The ghost-like image of a cloud?
Is it a gallows there portrayed?
Is Peter of himself afraid?
Is it a coffin, — or a shroud?

A grisly idol hewn in stone?
Or imp from witch's lap let fall?
Perhaps a ring of shining fairies?
Such as pursue their feared vagaries
In sylvan bower, or haunted hall?

Is it a fiend that to a stake
Of fire his desperate self is tethering?
Or stubborn spirit doomed to yell
In solitary ward or cell,
Ten thousand miles from all his brethren?

Never did pulse so quickly throb,
And never heart so loudly panted;
He looks, he cannot choose but look;
Like some one reading in a book —
A book that is enchanted.

Ah, well-a-day for Peter Bell!
He will be turned to iron soon,
Meet Statue for the court of Fear!
His hat is up — and every hair
Bristles, and whitens in the moon!

He looks, he ponders, looks again;
He sees a motion — hears a groan;
His eyes will burst — his heart will break —
He gives a loud and frightful shriek,
And back he falls, as if his life were flown!

PART SECOND.

We left our Hero in a trance,
Beneath the alders, near the river;
The Ass is by the river-side,
And, where the feeble breezes glide,
Upon the stream the moonbeams quiver.

A happy respite! but at length
He feels the glimmering of the moon;
Wakes with glazed eye, and feebly sighing —
To sink, perhaps, where he is lying,
Into a second swoon!

He lifts his head, he sees his staff;
He touches — 'tis to him a treasure!
Faint recollection seems to tell
That he is yet where mortals dwell —
A thought received with languid pleasure!

His head upon his elbow propped,
Becoming less and less perplexed,
Sky-ward he looks — to rock and wood —
And then — upon the glassy flood
His wandering eye is fixed.

Thought he, that is the face of one
In his last sleep securely bound!
So toward the stream his head he bent,
And downward thrust his staff, intent
The river's depth to sound.

Now — like a tempest-shattered bark,
That overwhelmed and prostrate lies,
And in a moment to the verge
Is lifted of a foaming surge —
Full suddenly the Ass doth rise!

His staring bones all shake with joy,
And close by Peter's side he stands:
While Peter o'er the river bends,
The little Ass his neck extends,
And fondly licks his hands.

Such life is in the Ass's eyes,
Such life is in his limbs and ears;
That Peter Bell, if he had been
The veriest coward ever seen,
Must now have thrown aside his fears.

The Ass looks on — and to his work
Is Peter quietly resigned;
He touches here — he touches there —
And now among the dead man's hair
His sapling Peter has entwined.

He pulls — and looks — and pulls again;
And he whom the poor Ass had lost,
The man who had been four days dead,
Head-foremost from the river's bed
Uprises like a ghost!

And Peter draws him to dry land;
And through the brain of Peter pass
Some poignant twitches, fast and faster;
"No doubt," quoth he, "he is the Master
Of this poor miserable Ass!"

The meagre shadow that looks on —
What would he now? what is he doing?
His sudden fit of joy is flown, —
He on his knees hath laid him down,
As if he were his grief renewing;

But no — that Peter on his back
Must mount, he shows well as he can:
Thought Peter then, come weal or woe,
I'll do what he would have me do,
In pity to this poor drowned man.

With that resolve he boldly mounts
Upon the pleased and thankful Ass;
And then, without a moment's stay,
That earnest Creature turned away,
Leaving the body on the grass.

Intent upon his faithful watch,
The Beast four days and nights had past;
A sweeter meadow ne'er was seen,
And there the Ass four days had been,
Nor ever once did break his fast:

Yet firm his step, and stout his heart;
The mead is crossed — the quarry's mouth
Is reached; but there the trusty guide
Into a thicket turns aside,
And deftly ambles towards the south.

When hark a burst of doleful sound!
And Peter honestly might say,
The like came never to his ears,
Though he has been, full thirty years,
A rover — night and day!

'Tis not a plover of the moors,
'Tis not a bittern of the fen;
Nor can it be a barking fox,
Nor night-bird chambered in the rocks,
Nor wild-cat in a woody glen!

The Ass is startled — and stops short
Right in the middle of the thicket;
And Peter, wont to whistle loud
Whether alone or in a crowd,
Is silent as a silent cricket.

What ails you now, my little Bess?
Well may you tremble and look grave!
This cry — that rings along the wood,
This cry — that floats adown the flood,
Comes from the entrance of a cave:

I see a blooming Wood-boy there,
And if I had the power to say
How sorrowful the wanderer is,
Your heart would be as sad as his
Till you had kissed his tears away!

Grasping a hawthorn branch in hand,
All bright with berries ripe and red,
Into the cavern's mouth he peeps;
Thence back into the moonlight creeps;
Whom seeks he — whom? — the silent dead:

His father! — Him doth he require —
Him hath he sought with fruitless pains,
Among the rocks, behind the trees;
Now creeping on his hands and knees,
Now running o'er the open plains.

And hither is he come at last,
When he through such a day has gone,
By this dark cave to be distrest
Like a poor bird — her plundered nest
Hovering around with dolorous moan!

Of that intense and piercing cry
The listening Ass conjectures well;
Wild as it is, he there can read
Some intermingled notes that plead
With touches irresistible.

But Peter — when he saw the Ass
Not only stop but turn, and change
The cherished tenor of his pace
That lamentable cry to chase —
It wrought in him conviction strange;

A faith that, for the dead man's sake
And this poor slave who loved him well,
Vengeance upon his head will fall,
Some visitation worse than all
Which ever till this night befel.

Meanwhile the ass to reach his home,
Is striving stoutly as he may;
But, while he climbs the woody hill,
The cry grows weak — and weaker still;
And now at last it dies away.

So with his freight the creature turns
Into a gloomy grove of beech,
Along the shade with footsteps true
Descending slowly, till the two
The open moonlight reach.

And there, along the narrow dell,
A fair smooth pathway you discern,
A length of green and open road —
As if it from a fountain flowed —
Winding away between the fern.

The rocks that tower on either side
Build up a wild fantastic scene;
Temples like those among the Hindoos,
And mosques, and spires, and abbey-windows,
And castles all with ivy green!

And, while the Ass pursues his way,
Along this solitary dell,
As pensively his steps advance,
The mosques and spires change countenance,
And look at Peter Bell!

That unintelligible cry
Hath left him high in preparation, —
Convinced that he, or soon or late,
This very night will meet his fate —
And so he sits in expectation!

The strenuous Animal hath clomb
With the green path; and now he wends
Where, shining like the smoothest sea,
In undisturbed immensity
A level plain extends.

But whence this faintly-rustling sound
By which the journeying pair are chased?
— A withered leaf is close behind,
Light plaything for the sportive wind
Upon that solitary waste.

When Peter spied the moving thing,
It only doubled his distress;
"Where there is not a bush or tree,
The very leaves they follow me —
So huge hath been my wickedness!"

To a close lane they now are come,
Where, as before, the enduring Ass
Moves on without a moment's stop,
Nor once turns round his head to crop
A bramble-leaf or blade of grass.

Between the hedges as they go,
The white dust sleeps upon the lane;
And Peter, ever and anon
Back-looking, sees, upon a stone,
Or in the dust, a crimson stain.

A stain — as of a drop of blood
By moonlight made more faint and wan;
Ha! why these sinkings of despair?
He knows not how the blood comes there —
And Peter is a wicked man.

At length he spies a bleeding wound,
Where he had struck the Ass's head;
He sees the blood, knows what it is, —
A glimpse of sudden joy was his,
But then it quickly fled;

Of him whom sudden death had seized
He thought, — of thee, O faithful Ass!
And once again those ghastly pains,
Shoot to and fro through heart and reins,
And through his brain like lightning pass.

PART THIRD.

I've heard of one, a gentle Soul,
Though given to sadness and to gloom,
And for the fact will vouch, — one night
It chanced that by a taper's light
This man was reading in his room;

Bending, as you or I might bend
At night o'er any pious book,
When sudden blackness overspread
The snow-white page on which he read,
And made the good man round him look.

The chamber walls were dark all round, —
And to his book he turned again;
— The light had left the lonely taper,
And formed itself upon the paper
Into large letters — bright and plain!

The godly book was in his hand —
And, on the page, more black than coal,
Appeared, set forth in strange array,
A *word* — which to his dying day
Perplexed the good man's gentle soul.

The ghostly word, thus plainly seen,
Did never from his lips depart;
But he hath said, poor gentle wight!
It brought full many a sin to light
Out of the bottom of his heart.

Dread Spirits! to confound the meek
Why wander from your course so far,
Disordering colour, form, and stature!
— Let good men feel the soul of nature,
And see things as they are.

Yet, potent Spirits! well I know
How ye, that play with soul and sense,
Are not unused to trouble friends
Of goodness, for most gracious ends —
And this I speak in reverence!

But might I give advice to you,
Whom in my fear I love so well;
From men of pensive virtue go,
Dread Beings! and your empire show
On hearts like that of Peter Bell.

Your presence often have I felt
In darkness and the stormy night;
And, with like force, if need there be,
Ye can put forth your agency
When earth is calm, and heaven is bright.

Then, coming from the wayward world,
That powerful world in which ye dwell,
Come, Spirits of the Mind! and try,
To-night, beneath the moonlight sky,
What may be done with Peter Bell!

— O, would that some more skilful voice
My further labour might prevent!
Kind Listeners, that around me sit,
I feel that I am all unfit
For such high argument.

I've played, I've danced, with my narration;
I loitered long ere I began:
Ye waited then on my good pleasure;
Pour out indulgence still, in measure
As liberal as ye can!

Our Travellers, ye remember well,
Are thridding a sequestered lane;
And Peter many tricks is trying,
And many anodynes applying,
To ease his conscience of its pain.

By this his heart is lighter far;
And, finding that he can account
So snugly for that crimson stain,
His evil spirit up again
Does like an empty bucket mount.

And Peter is a deep logician
Who hath no lack of wit mercurial;
"Blood drops — leaves rustle — yet," quoth he,
"This poor man never, but for me,
Could have had Christian burial.

And, say the best you can, 'tis plain,
That here has been some wicked dealing;
No doubt the devil in me wrought;
I'm not the man who could have thought
An Ass like this was worth the stealing!"

So from his pocket Peter takes
His shining horn tobacco-box;
And, in a light and careless way,
As men who with their purpose play,
Upon the lid he knocks.

Let them whose voice can stop the clouds,
Whose cunning eye can see the wind,
Tell to a curious world the cause
Why, making here a sudden pause,
The Ass turned round his head, and *grinned*.

Appalling process! I have marked
The like on heath, in lonely wood;
And, verily, have seldom met
A spectacle more hideous — yet
It suited Peter's present mood.

And, grinning in his turn, his teeth
He in jocose defiance showed —
When, to upset his spiteful mirth,
A murmur, pent within the earth,
In the dead earth beneath the road,

Rolled audibly! it swept along,
A muffled noise — a rumbling sound! —
'Twas by a troop of miners made,
Plying with gunpowder their trade,
Some twenty fathoms underground.

Small cause of dire effect! for, surely,
If ever mortal, King or Cotter,
Believed that earth was charged to quake
And yawn for his unworthy sake,
'Twas Peter Bell the Potter.

But, as an oak in breathless air
Will stand though to the centre hewn;
Or as the weakest things, if frost
Have stiffened them, maintain their post;
So he, beneath the gazing moon! —

The Beast bestriding thus, he reached
A spot where, in a sheltering cove,
A little chapel stands alone,
With greenest ivy overgrown,
And tufted with an ivy grove;

Dying insensibly away
From human thoughts and purposes,
It seemed — wall, window, roof and tower —
To bow to some transforming power,
And blend with the surrounding trees.

As ruinous a place it was,
Thought Peter, in the shire of Fife
That served my turn, when following still
From land to land a reckless will
I married my sixth wife!

The unheeding Ass moves slowly on,
And now is passing by an inn
Brim-full of a carousing crew,
That make, with curses not a few,
An uproar and a drunken din.

I cannot well express the thoughts
Which Peter in those noises found; —
A stifling power compressed his frame,
While-as a swimming darkness came
Over that dull and dreary sound.

For well did Peter know the sound;
The language of those drunken joys
To him, a jovial soul, I ween,
But a few hours ago, had been
A gladsome and a welcome noise.

Now, turned adrift into the past,
He finds no solace in his course;
Like planet-stricken men of yore,
He trembles, smitten to the core
By strong compunction and remorse.

But, more than all, his heart is stung
To think of one, almost a child;
A sweet and playful Highland girl,
As light and beauteous as a squirrel,
As beauteous and as wild!

Her dwelling was a lonely house,
A cottage in a heathy dell;
And she put on her gown of green,
And left her mother at sixteen,
And followed Peter Bell.

But many good and pious thoughts
Had she; and, in the kirk to pray,
Two long Scotch miles, through rain or snow,
To kirk she had been used to go,
Twice every Sabbath-day.

And, when she followed Peter Bell,
It was to lead an honest life;
For he, with tongue not used to falter,
Had pledged his troth before the altar
To love her as his wedded wife.

A mother's hope is hers;—but soon
She drooped and pined like one forlorn;
From Scripture she a name did borrow;
Benoni, or the child of sorrow,
She called her babe unborn.

For she had learned how Peter lived,
And took it in most grievous part;
She to the very bone was worn,
And, ere that little child was born,
Died of a broken heart.

And now the Spirits of the Mind
Are busy with poor Peter Bell;
Upon the rights of visual sense
Usurping, with a prevalence
More terrible than magic spell.

Close by a brake of flowering furze
(Above it shivering aspens play)
He sees an unsubstantial creature,
His very self in form and feature,
Not four yards from the broad highway:

And stretched beneath the furze he sees
The Highland girl — it is no other;
And hears her crying as she cried,
The very moment that she died,
"My mother! oh my mother!"

The sweat pours down from Peter's face,
So grievous is his heart's contrition;
With agony his eye-balls ache
While he beholds by the furze-brake
This miserable vision!

Calm is the well-deserving brute,
His peace hath no offence betrayed;
But now, while down that slope he wends,
A voice to Peter's ear ascends,
Resounding from the woody glade:

The voice, though clamorous as a horn
Re-echoed by a naked rock,
Comes from that tabernacle — List!
Within, a fervent Methodist
Is preaching to no heedless flock!

"Repent! repent!" he cries aloud,
"While yet ye may find mercy; — strive
To love the Lord with all your might;
Turn to him, seek him day and night,
And save your souls alive!

Repent! repent! though ye have gone,
Through paths of wickedness and woe,
After the Babylonian harlot;
And, though your sins be red as scarlet,
They shall be white as snow!"

Even as he passed the door, these words
Did plainly come to Peter's ears;
And they such joyful tidings were,
The joy was more than he could bear! —
He melted into tears.

Sweet tears of hope and tenderness!
And fast they fell, a plenteous shower!
His nerves, his sinews seemed to melt;
Through all his iron frame was felt
A gentle, a relaxing, power!

Each fibre of his frame was weak;
Weak all the animal within;
But, in its helplessness, grew mild
And gentle as an infant child,
An infant that has known no sin.

'Tis said, meek Beast! that, through Heaven's grace,
He not unmoved did notice now
The cross upon thy shoulder scored,
For lasting impress, by the Lord
To whom all human-kind shall bow;

Memorial of his touch — that day
When Jesus humbly deigned to ride,
Entering the proud Jerusalem,
By an immeasurable stream
Of shouting people deified!

Meanwhile the persevering Ass,
Turned towards a gate that hung in view
Across a shady lane; his chest
Against the yielding gate he pressed
And quietly passed through.

And up the stony lane he goes;
No ghost more softly ever trod;
Among the stones and pebbles, he
Sets down his hoofs inaudibly,
As if with felt his hoofs were shod.

Along the lane the trusty Ass
Went twice two hundred yards or more,
And no one could have guessed his aim, —
Till to a lonely house he came,
And stopped beside the door.

Thought Peter, 'tis the poor man's home!
He listens — not a sound is heard
Save from the trickling household rill;
But, stepping o'er the cottage-sill,
Forthwith a little Girl appeared.

She to the Meeting-house was bound
In hopes some tidings there to gather:
No glimpse it is, no doubtful gleam;
She saw — and uttered with a scream,
"My father! here's my father!"

The very word was plainly heard,
Heard plainly by the wretched Mother —
Her joy was like a deep affright:
And forth she rushed into the light,
And saw it was another!

And, instantly, upon the earth,
Beneath the full moon shining bright,
Close to the Ass's feet she fell;
At the same moment Peter Bell
Dismounts in most unhappy plight.

As he beheld the Woman lie
Breathless and motionless, the mind
Of Peter sadly was confused;
But, though to such demands unused,
And helpless almost as the blind,

He raised her up; and, while he held
Her body propped against his knee,
The Woman waked — and when she spied
The poor Ass standing by her side,
She moaned most bitterly.

"Oh! God be praised — my heart's at ease —
For he is dead — I know it well!"
— At this she wept a bitter flood;
And, in the best way that he could,
His tale did Peter tell.

He trembles — he is pale as death;
His voice is weak with perturbation;
He turns aside his head, he pauses;
Poor Peter from a thousand causes,
Is crippled sore in his narration.

At length she learned how he espied
The Ass in that small meadow-ground;
And that her Husband now lay dead,
Beside that luckless river's bed
In which he had been drowned.

A piercing look the Widow cast
Upon the Beast that near her stands;
She sees 'tis he, that 'tis the same;
She calls the poor Ass by his name,
And wrings, and wrings her hands.

"O wretched loss — untimely stroke!
If he had died upon his bed!
He knew not one forewarning pain;
He never will come home again —
Is dead, for ever dead!"

Beside the Woman Peter stands;
His heart is opening more and more;
A holy sense pervades his mind;
He feels what he for human-kind
Had never felt before.

At length, by Peter's arm sustained,
The Woman rises from the ground —
"Oh, mercy! something must be done,
My little Rachel, you must run, —
Some willing neighbour must be found.

Make haste — my little Rachel — do,
The first you meet with — bid him come,
Ask him to lend his horse to-night,
And this good Man, whom Heaven requite,
Will help to bring the body home."

Away goes Rachel weeping loud; —
An Infant, waked by her distress,
Makes in the house a piteous cry;
And Peter hears the Mother sigh,
"Seven are they, and all fatherless!"

And now is Peter taught to feel
That man's heart is a holy thing;
And Nature, through a world of death,
Breathes into him a second breath,
More searching than the breath of spring.

Upon a stone the Woman sits
In agony of silent grief —
From his own thoughts did Peter start;
He longs to press her to his heart,
From love that cannot find relief.

But roused, as if through every limb
Had past a sudden shock of dread,
The Mother o'er the threshold flies,
And up the cottage stairs she hies,
And on the pillow lays her burning head.

And Peter turns his steps aside
Into a shade of darksome trees,
Where he sits down, he knows not how,
With his hands pressed against his brow,
His elbows on his tremulous knees.

There, self-involved, does Peter sit
Until no sign of life he makes,
As if his mind were sinking deep
Through years that have been long asleep!
The trance is passed away — he wakes;

He lifts his head — and sees the Ass
Yet standing in the clear moonshine;
"When shall I be as good as thou?
Oh! would, poor beast, that I had now
A heart but half as good as thine!"

But *He* — who deviously hath sought
His Father through the lonesome woods,
Hath sought, proclaiming to the ear
Of night his grief and sorrowful fear —
He comes, escaped from fields and floods; —

With weary pace is drawing nigh;
He sees the Ass — and nothing living
Had ever such a fit of joy
As hath this little orphan Boy,
For he has no misgiving!

Forth to the gentle Ass he springs,
And up about his neck he climbs;
In loving words he talks to him,
He kisses, kisses face and limb, —
He kisses him a thousand times!

This Peter sees, while in the shade
He stood beside the cottage-door;
And Peter Bell, the ruffian wild,
Sobs loud, he sobs even like a child,
"Oh! God, I can endure no more!"

— Here ends my Tale: for in a trice
Arrived a neighbour with his horse;
Peter went forth with him straightway;
And, with due care, ere break of day,
Together they brought back the Corse.

And many years did this poor Ass,
Whom once it was my luck to see
Cropping the shrubs of Leming-Lane,
Help by his labour to maintain
The Widow and her family.

And Peter Bell, who, till that night,
Had been the wildest of his clan,
Forsook his crimes, renounced his folly,
And, after ten months' melancholy,
Became a good and honest man.

MISCELLANEOUS SONNETS.

DEDICATION.
TO —.

Happy the feeling from the bosom thrown
In perfect shape (whose beauty Time shall spare
Though a breath made it) like a bubble blown
For summer pastime into wanton air;
Happy the thought best likened to a stone
Of the sea-beach, when polished with nice care,
Veins it discovers exquisite and rare,
Which for the loss of that moist gleam atone
That tempted first to gather it. That here,
O chief of Friends! such feelings I present,
To thy regard, with thoughts so fortunate,
Were a vain notion; but the hope is dear,
That thou, if not with partial joy elate,
Wilt smile upon this gift with more than mild content!

PART I.

I.

Nuns fret not at their convent's narrow room;
And hermits are contented with their cells;
And students with their pensive citadels;
Maids at the wheel, the weaver at his loom,
Sit blithe and happy; bees that soar for bloom,
High as the highest Peak of Furness-fells,
Will murmur by the hour in foxglove bells:
In truth the prison, unto which we doom
Ourselves, no prison is: and hence for me,
In sundry moods, 'twas pastime to be bound
Within the Sonnet's scanty plot of ground;
Pleased if some Souls (for such there needs must be)
Who have felt the weight of too much liberty,
Should find brief solace there, as I have found.

II.

ADMONITION.

Intended more particularly for the perusal of those who may have happened to be enamoured of some beautiful place of Retreat, in the Country of the Lakes.

WELL may'st thou halt — and gaze with brightening eye!
The lovely Cottage in the guardian nook
Hath stirred thee deeply; with its own dear brook,
Its own small pasture, almost its own sky!
But covet not the Abode; — forbear to sigh,
As many do, repining while they look;
Intruders — who would tear from Nature's book
This precious leaf, with harsh impiety.
Think what the Home must be if it were thine,
Even thine, though few thy wants! — Roof, window, door,
The very flowers are sacred to the Poor,
The roses to the porch which they entwine:
Yea, all, that now enchants thee, from the day
On which it should be touched, would melt away.

III.

"BELOVED Vale!" I said, "when I shall con
Those many records of my childish years,
Remembrance of myself and of my peers
Will press me down: to think of what is gone
Will be an awful thought, if life have one."
But, when into the Vale I came, no fears
Distressed me; from mine eyes escaped no tears;
Deep thought, or dread remembrance, had I none.
By doubts and thousand petty fancies crost
I stood, of simple shame the blushing Thrall;
So narrow seemed the brooks, the fields so small!
A Juggler's balls old Time about him tossed;
I looked, I stared, I smiled, I laughed; and all
The weight of sadness was in wonder lost.

IV.
AT APPLETHWAITE, NEAR KESWICK.
1804.

BEAUMONT! it was thy wish that I should rear
A seemly Cottage in this sunny Dell,
On favoured ground, thy gift, where I might dwell
In neighbourhood with One to me most dear,
That undivided we from year to year
Might work in our high Calling — a bright hope
To which our fancies, mingling, gave free scope
Till checked by some necessities severe.
And should these slacken, honoured BEAUMONT! still
Even then we may perhaps in vain implore
Leave of our fate thy wishes to fulfil.
Whether this boon be granted us or not,
Old Skiddaw will look down upon the Spot
With pride, the Muses love it evermore.

V.
1801.

PELION and Ossa flourish side by side,
Together in immortal books enrolled:
His ancient dower Olympus hath not sold
And that inspiring Hill, which 'did divide
Into two ample horns his forehead wide,'
Shines with poetic radiance as of old;
While not an English Mountain we behold
By the celestial Muses glorified.
Yet round our sea-girt shore they rise in crowds:
What was the great Parnassus' self to Thee,
Mount Skiddaw? In his natural sovereignty
Our British Hill is nobler far; he shrouds
His double front among Atlantic clouds,
And pours forth streams more sweet than Castaly.

VI.

There is a little unpretending Rill
Of limpid water, humbler far than aught
That ever among Men or Naiads sought
Notice or name! — It quivers down the hill,
Furrowing its shallow way with dubious will;
Yet to my mind this scanty Stream is brought
Oftener than Ganges or the Nile; a thought
Of private recollection sweet and still!
Months perish with their moons; year treads on year;
But, faithful Emma! thou with me canst say
That while ten thousand pleasures disappear,
And flies their memory fast almost as they;
The immortal Spirit of one happy day
Lingers beside that Rill, in vision clear.

VII.

Her only pilot the soft breeze, the boat
Lingers, but Fancy is well satisfied;
With keen-eyed Hope, with Memory, at her side,
And the glad Muse at liberty to note
All that to each is precious, as we float
Gently along; regardless who shall chide
If the heavens smile, and leave us free to glide,
Happy Associates breathing air remote
From trivial cares. But, Fancy and the Muse,
Why have I crowded this small bark with you
And others of your kind, ideal crew!
While here sits One whose brightness owes its hues
To flesh and blood; no Goddess from above,
No fleeting Spirit, but my own true Love?

VIII.

The fairest, brightest, hues of ether fade;
The sweetest notes must terminate and die;
O Friend! thy flute has breathed a harmony
Softly resounded through this rocky glade;

Such strains of rapture as the Genius played
In his still haunt on Bagdad's summit high;
He who stood visible to Mirza's eye,
Never before to human sight betrayed.
Lo, in the vale, the mists of evening spread!
The visionary Arches are not there,
Nor the green Islands, nor the shining Seas;
Yet sacred is to me this Mountain's head,
Whence I have risen, uplifted on the breeze
Of harmony, above all earthly care.

IX.
UPON THE SIGHT OF A BEAUTIFUL PICTURE,
Painted by Sir G. H. Beaumont, Bart.

PRAISED be the Art whose subtle power could stay
Yon cloud, and fix it in that glorious shape;
Nor would permit the thin smoke to escape,
Nor those bright sunbeams to forsake the day;
Which stopped that band of travellers on their way,
Ere they were lost within the shady wood;
And showed the Bark upon the glassy flood
For ever anchored in her sheltering bay.
Soul-soothing Art! whom Morning, Noon-tide, Even,
Do serve with all their changeful pageantry;
Thou, with ambition modest yet sublime,
Here, for the sight of mortal man, hast given
To one brief moment caught from fleeting time
The appropriate calm of blest eternity.

X.

"WHY, Minstrel, these untuneful murmurings —
Dull, flagging notes that with each other jar?"
"Think, gentle Lady, of a Harp so far
From its own country, and forgive the strings."

A simple answer! but even so forth springs,
From the Castalian fountain of the heart,
The Poetry of Life, and all *that* Art
Divine of words quickening insensate things.
From the submissive necks of guiltless men
Stretched on the block, the glittering axe recoils;
Sun, moon, and stars, all struggle in the toils
Of mortal sympathy; what wonder then
That the poor Harp distempered music yields
To its sad Lord, far from his native fields?

XI.

AERIAL ROCK — whose solitary brow
From this low threshold daily meets my sight;
When I step forth to hail the morning light;
Or quit the stars with a lingering farewell — how
Shall Fancy pay to thee a grateful vow?
How, with the Muse's aid, her love attest?
— By planting on thy naked head the crest
Of an imperial Castle, which the plough
Of ruin shall not touch.   Innocent scheme!
That doth presume no more than to supply
A grace the sinuous vale and roaring stream
Want, through neglect of hoar Antiquity.
Rise, then, ye votive Towers! and catch a gleam
Of golden sunset, ere it fade and die.

XII.

TO SLEEP.

O GENTLE SLEEP! do they belong to thee,
These twinklings of oblivion?   Thou dost love
To sit in meekness, like the brooding Dove,
A captive never wishing to be free.
This tiresome night, O Sleep! thou art to me
A Fly, that up and down himself doth shove
Upon a fretful rivulet, now above
Now on the water vexed with mockery.

I have no pain that calls for patience, no;
Hence am I cross and peevish as a child:
Am pleased by fits to have thee for my foe,
Yet ever willing to be reconciled:
O gentle Creature! do not use me so,
But once and deeply let me be beguiled.

XIII.

TO SLEEP.

Fond words have oft been spoken to thee, Sleep!
And thou hast had thy store of tenderest names;
The very sweetest, Fancy culls or frames,
When thankfulness of heart is strong and deep!
Dear Bosom-child we call thee, that dost steep
In rich reward all suffering; Balm that tames
All anguish; Saint that evil thoughts and aims
Takest away, and into souls dost creep,
Like to a breeze from heaven. Shall I alone,
I surely not a man ungently made,
Call thee worst Tyrant by which Flesh is crost?
Perverse, self-willed to own and to disown,
Mere slave of them who never for thee prayed,
Still last to come where thou art wanted most!

XIV.

TO SLEEP.

A flock of sheep that leisurely pass by,
One after one; the sound of rain, and bees
Murmuring; the fall of rivers, winds and seas,
Smooth fields, white sheets of water, and pure sky;
I have thought of all by turns, and yet do lie
Sleepless! and soon the small birds' melodies
Must hear, first uttered from my orchard trees;
And the first cuckoo's melancholy cry.

Even thus last night, and two nights more, I lay,
And could not win thee, Sleep! by any stealth:
So do not let me wear to-night away:
Without Thee what is all the morning's wealth?
Come, blessed barrier between day and day,
Dear mother of fresh thoughts and joyous health!

XV.

THE WILD DUCK'S NEST.

THE imperial Consort of the Fairy-king
Owns not a sylvan bower; or gorgeous cell
With emerald floored, and with purpureal shell
Ceilinged and roofed; that is so fair a thing
As this low structure, for the tasks of Spring,
Prepared by one who loves the buoyant swell
Of the brisk waves, yet here consents to dwell;
And spreads in steadfast peace her brooding wing.
Words cannot paint the o'ershadowing yew-tree bough,
And dimly-gleaming Nest, — a hollow crown
Of golden leaves inlaid with silver down,
Fine as the mother's softest plumes allow:
I gazed — and, self-accused while gazing, sighed
For human-kind, weak slaves of cumbrous pride!

XVI.

WRITTEN UPON A BLANK LEAF IN "THE COMLETE ANGLER."

WHILE flowing rivers yield a blameless sport,
Shall live the name of Walton: Sage benign!
Whose pen, the mysteries of the rod and line
Unfolding, did not fruitlessly exhort
To reverend watching of each still report
That Nature utters from her rural shrine.
Meek, nobly versed in simple discipline —
He found the longest summer day too short,

To his loved pastime given by sedgy Lee,
Or down the tempting maze of Shawford brook —
Fairer than life itself, in this sweet Book,
The cowslip-bank and shady willow-tree;
And the fresh meads — where flowed, from every nook
Of his full bosom, gladsome Piety!

XVII.
TO THE POET JOHN DYER.

BARD of the Fleece, whose skilful genius made
That work a living landscape fair and bright;
Nor hallowed less with musical delight
Than those soft scenes through which thy childhood strayed,
Those southern tracts of Cambria, 'deep embayed,
With green hills fenced, with ocean's murmur lull'd;'
Though hasty Fame hath many a chaplet culled
For worthless brows, while in the pensive shade
Of cold neglect she leaves thy head ungraced,
Yet pure and powerful minds, hearts meek and still,
A grateful few, shall love thy modest Lay,
Long as the shepherd's bleating flock shall stray
O'er naked Snowdon's wide aërial waste;
Long as the thrush shall pipe on Grongar Hill!

XVIII.
ON THE DETRACTION WHICH FOLLOWED THE PUBLICATION OF A CERTAIN POEM.
See Milton's Sonnet beginning 'A Book was writ of late called "Tetrachordon."'

A BOOK came forth of late, called PETER BELL;
Not negligent the style; — the matter? — good
As aught that song records of Robin Hood;
Or Roy, renowned through many a Scottish dell;
But some (who brook those hackneyed themes full well,
Nor heat, at Tam o' Shanter's name, their blood)
Waxed wroth, and with foul claws, a harpy brood,
On Bard and Hero clamorously fell.

Heed not, wild Rover once through heath and glen,
Who mad'st at length the better life thy choice,
Heed not such onset! nay, if praise of men
To thee appear not an unmeaning voice,
Lift up that grey-haired forehead, and rejoice
In the just tribute of thy Poet's pen!

XIX.

GRIEF, thou hast lost an ever ready friend
Now that the cottage Spinning-wheel is mute:
And Care — a comforter that best could suit
Her froward mood, and softliest reprehend;
And Love — a charmer's voice, that used to lend,
More efficaciously than aught that flows
From harp or lute, kind influence to compose
The throbbing pulse — else troubled without end:
Even Joy could tell, Joy craving truce and rest
From her own overflow, what power sedate
On those revolving motions did await
Assiduously — to soothe her aching breast;
And, to a point of just relief, abate
The mantling triumphs of a day too blest.

XX.

TO S. H.

EXCUSE is needless when with love sincere
Of occupation, not by fashion led,
Thou turn'st the Wheel that slept with dust o'erspread;
My nerves from no such murmur shrink, — tho' near,
Soft as the Dorhawk's to a distant ear,
When twilight shades darken the mountain's head.
Even She who toils to spin our vital thread
Might smile on work, O Lady, once so dear

To household virtues. Venerable Art,
Torn from the Poor! yet shall kind Heaven protect
Its own; though Rulers, with undue respect,
Trusting to crowded factory and mart
And proud discoveries of the intellect,
Heed not the pillage of man's ancient heart.

XXI.

COMPOSED IN ONE OF THE VALLEYS OF WESTMORELAND, ON EASTER SUNDAY.

With each recurrence of this glorious morn
That saw the Saviour in his human frame
Rise from the dead, erewhile the Cottage-dame
Put on fresh raiment — till that hour unworn:
Domestic hands the home-bred wool had shorn,
And she who span it culled the daintiest fleece,
In thoughtful reverence to the Prince of Peace,
Whose temples bled beneath the platted thorn.
A blest estate when piety sublime
These humble props disdained not! O green dales!
Sad may *I* be who heard your sabbath chime
When Art's abused inventions were unknown;
Kind Nature's various wealth was all your own;
And benefits were weighed in Reason's scales!

XXII.

DECAY OF PIETY.

Oft have I seen, ere Time had ploughed my cheek,
Matrons and Sires — who, punctual to the call
Of their loved Church, on fast or festival
Through the long year the House of Prayer would seek:
By Christmas snows, by visitation bleak
Of Easter winds, unscared, from hut or hall
They came to lowly bench or sculptured stall,
But with one fervour of devotion meek.

I see the places where they once were known,
And ask, surrounded even by kneeling crowds,
Is ancient Piety for ever flown?
Alas! even then they seemed like fleecy clouds
That, struggling through the western sky, have won
Their pensive light from a departed sun!

XXIII.

COMPOSED ON THE EVE OF THE MARRIAGE OF A FRIEND IN THE VALE OF GRASMERE, 1812.

WHAT need of clamorous bells, or ribands gay,
These humble nuptials to proclaim or grace?
Angels of love, look down upon the place;
Shed on the chosen vale a sun-bright day!
Yet no proud gladness would the Bride display
Even for such promise: — serious is her face,
Modest her mien; and she, whose thoughts keep pace
With gentleness, in that becoming way
Will thank you. Faultless does the Maid appear;
No disproportion in her soul, no strife:
But, when the closer view of wedded life
Hath shown that nothing human can be clear
From frailty, for that insight may the Wife
To her indulgent Lord become more dear.

XXIV.

FROM THE ITALIAN OF MICHAEL ANGELO.

I.

YES! hope may with my strong desire keep pace,
And I be undeluded, unbetrayed;
For if of our affections none finds grace
In sight of Heaven, then, wherefore hath God made
The world which we inhabit? Better plea
Love cannot have, than that in loving thee
Glory to that eternal Peace is paid,
Who such divinity to thee imparts
As hallows and makes pure all gentle hearts.

His hope is treacherous only whose love dies
With beauty, which is varying every hour;
But, in chaste hearts uninfluenced by the power
Of outward change, there blooms a deathless flower,
That breathes on earth the air of paradise.

XXV.
FROM THE SAME.
II.

No mortal object did these eyes behold
When first they met the placid light of thine,
And my Soul felt her destiny divine,
And hope of endless peace in me grew bold:
Heaven-born, the Soul a heaven-ward course must hold;
Beyond the visible world she soars to seek
(For what delights the sense is false and weak)
Ideal Form, the universal mould.
The wise man, I affirm, can find no rest
In that which perishes: nor will he lend
His heart to aught which doth on time depend.
'Tis sense, unbridled will, and not true love,
That kills the soul: love betters what is best,
Even here below, but more in heaven above.

XXVI.
FROM THE SAME. TO THE SUPREME BEING.
III.

The prayers I make will then be sweet indeed
If Thou the spirit give by which I pray:
My unassisted heart is barren clay,
That of its native self can nothing feed:
Of good and pious works thou art the seed,
That quickens only where thou say'st it may:
Unless Thou shew to us thine own true way
No man can find it! Father! Thou must lead.

Do Thou, then, breathe those thoughts into my mind
By which such virtue may in me be bred
That in thy holy footsteps I may tread;
The fetters of my tongue do Thou unbind,
That I may have the power to sing of thee,
And sound thy praises everlastingly.

XXVII.

Surprised by joy — impatient as the Wind
I turned to share the transport — Oh! with whom
But Thee, deep buried in the silent tomb,
That spot which no vicissitude can find?
Love, faithful love, recalled thee to my mind —
But how could I forget thee? Through what power,
Even for the least division of an hour,
Have I been so beguiled as to be blind
To my most grievous loss! — That thought's return
Was the worst pang that sorrow ever bore,
Save one, one only, when I stood forlorn,
Knowing my heart's best treasure was no more;
That neither present time, nor years unborn
Could to my sight that heavenly face restore.

XXVIII.
I.

Methought I saw the footsteps of a throne
Which mists and vapours from mine eyes did shroud —
Nor view of who might sit thereon allowed;
But all the steps and ground about were strown
With sights the ruefullest that flesh and bone
Ever put on; a miserable crowd,
Sick, hale, old, young, who cried before that cloud,
"Thou art our king, O Death! to thee we groan."

Those steps I clomb; the mists before me gave
Smooth way; and I beheld the face of one
Sleeping alone within a mossy cave,
With her face up to heaven; that seemed to have
Pleasing remembrance of a thought foregone;
A lovely Beauty in a summer grave!

XXIX.
NOVEMBER, 1836.
II.

Even so for me a Vision sanctified
The sway of Death; long ere mine eyes had seen
Thy countenance — the still rapture of thy mien —
When thou, dear Sister! wert become Death's Bride:
No trace of pain or languor could abide
That change: — age on thy brow was smoothed — thy cold
Wan cheek at once was privileged to unfold
A loveliness to living youth denied.
Oh! if within me hope should e'er decline,
The lamp of faith, lost Friend! too faintly burn;
Then may that heaven-revealing smile of thine,
The bright assurance, visibly return:
And let my spirit in that power divine
Rejoice, as, through that power, it ceased to mourn.

XXX.

It is a beauteous evening, calm and free,
The holy time is quiet as a Nun
Breathless with adoration; the broad sun
Is sinking down in its tranquillity;
The gentleness of heaven broods o'er the Sea:
Listen! the mighty Being is awake,
And doth with his eternal motion make
A sound like thunder — everlastingly.

Dear Child! dear Girl! that walkest with me here,
If thou appear untouched by solemn thought,
Thy nature is not therefore less divine:
Thou liest in Abraham's bosom all the year;
And worshipp'st at the Temple's inner shrine,
God being with thee when we know it not.

XXXI.

Where lies the Land to which yon Ship must go?
Fresh as a lark mounting at break of day,
Festively she puts forth in trim array;
Is she for tropic suns, or polar snow?
What boots the inquiry? — Neither friend nor foe
She cares for; let her travel where she may,
She finds familiar names, a beaten way
Ever before her, and a wind to blow.
Yet still I ask, what haven is her mark?
And, almost as it was when ships were rare,
(From time to time, like Pilgrims, here and there
Crossing the waters) doubt, and something dark,
Of the old Sea some reverential fear,
Is with me at thy farewell, joyous Bark!

XXXII.

With Ships the sea was sprinkled far and nigh,
Like stars in heaven, and joyously it showed;
Some lying fast at anchor in the road,
Some veering up and down, one knew not why.
A goodly Vessel did I then espy!
Come like a giant from a haven broad;
And lustily along the bay she strode,
Her tackling rich, and of apparel high.
This Ship was nought to me, nor I to her,
Yet I pursued her with a Lover's look;
This Ship to all the rest did I prefer:
When will she turn, and whither? She will brook
No tarrying; where She comes the winds must stir:
On went She, and due north her journey took.

XXXIII.

The world is too much with us; late and soon,
Getting and spending, we lay waste our powers:
Little we see in Nature that is ours;
We have given our hearts away, a sordid boon!
This Sea that bares her bosom to the moon;
The winds that will be howling at all hours,
And are up-gathered now like sleeping flowers;
For this, for every thing, we are out of tune;
It moves us not. — Great God! I'd rather be
A Pagan suckled in a creed outworn;
So might I, standing on this pleasant lea,
Have glimpses that would make me less forlorn;
Have sight of Proteus rising from the sea;
Or hear old Triton blow his wreathèd horn.

XXXIV.

A volant Tribe of Bards on earth are found,
Who, while the flattering Zephyrs round them play,
On 'coignes of vantage' hang their nests of clay;
How quickly from that aery hold unbound,
Dust for oblivion! To the solid ground
Of nature trusts the Mind that builds for aye;
Convinced that there, there only, she can lay
Secure foundations. As the year runs round,
Apart she toils within the chosen ring;
While the stars shine, or while day's purple eye
Is gently closing with the flowers of spring;
Where even the motion of an Angel's wing
Would interrupt the intense tranquillity
Of silent hills, and more than silent sky.

XXXV.

'Weak is the will of Man, his judgment blind;
'Remembrance persecutes, and Hope betrays;
'Heavy is woe; — and joy, for human-kind,
'A mournful thing, so transient is the blaze!'

Thus might *he* paint our lot of mortal days
Who wants the glorious faculty assigned
To elevate the more-than-reasoning Mind,
And colour life's dark cloud with orient rays.
Imagination is that sacred power,
Imagination lofty and refined:
'Tis hers to pluck the amaranthine flower
Of Faith, and round the Sufferer's temples bind
Wreaths that endure affliction's heaviest shower,
And do not shrink from sorrow's keenest wind.

XXXVI.

TO THE MEMORY OF RAISLEY CALVERT.

CALVERT! it must not be unheard by them
Who may respect my name, that I to thee
Owed many years of early liberty.
This care was thine when sickness did condemn
Thy youth to hopeless wasting, root and stem —
That I, if frugal and severe, might stray
Where'er I liked; and finally array
My temples with the Muse's diadem.
Hence, if in freedom I have loved the truth;
If there be aught of pure, or good, or great,
In my past verse; or shall be, in the lays
Of higher mood, which now I meditate; —
It gladdens me, O worthy, short-lived Youth!
To think how much of this will be thy praise.

PART II.

I.

Scorn not the Sonnet; Critic, you have frowned,
Mindless of its just honours; with this key
Shakspeare unlocked his heart; the melody
Of this small lute gave ease to Petrarch's wound;
A thousand times this pipe did Tasso sound;
With it Camöens soothed an exile's grief;
The Sonnet glittered a gay myrtle leaf
Amid the cypress with which Dante crowned
His visionary brow: a glow-worm lamp,
It cheered mild Spenser, called from Faery-land
To struggle through dark ways; and, when a damp
Fell round the path of Milton, in his hand
The Thing became a trumpet; whence he blew
Soul-animating strains — alas, too few!

II.

How sweet it is, when mother Fancy rocks
The wayward brain, to saunter through a wood!
An old place, full of many a lovely brood,
Tall trees, green arbours, and ground-flowers in flocks;
And wild rose tip-toe upon hawthorn stocks,
Like a bold Girl, who plays her agile pranks
At Wakes and Fairs with wandering Mountebanks, —
When she stands cresting the Clown's head, and mocks
The crowd beneath her. Verily I think,
Such place to me is sometimes like a dream
Or map of the whole world: thoughts, link by link,
Enter through ears and eyesight, with such gleam
Of all things, that at last in fear I shrink,
And leap at once from the delicious stream.

III.
TO B. R. HAYDON.

High is our calling, Friend! — Creative Art
(Whether the instrument of words she use,
Or pencil pregnant with ethereal hues,)
Demands the service of a mind and heart,
Though sensitive, yet, in their weakest part,
Heroically fashioned — to infuse
Faith in the whispers of the lonely Muse,
While the whole world seems adverse to desert.
And, oh! when Nature sinks, as oft she may,
Through long-lived pressure of obscure distress,
Still to be strenuous for the bright reward,
And in the soul admit of no decay,
Brook no continuance of weak-mindedness —
Great is the glory, for the strife is hard!

IV.

From the dark chambers of dejection freed,
Spurning the unprofitable yoke of care,
Rise, GILLIES, rise: the gales of youth shall bear
Thy genius forward like a wingèd steed.
Though bold Bellerophon (so Jove decreed
In wrath) fell headlong from the fields of air,
Yet a rich guerdon waits on minds that dare,
If aught be in them of immortal seed,
And reason govern that audacious flight
Which heaven-ward they direct. — Then droop not thou,
Erroneously renewing a sad vow
In the low dell 'mid Roslin's faded grove:
A cheerful life is what the muses love,
A soaring spirit is their prime delight.

V.

Fair Prime of life! were it enough to gild
With ready sunbeams every straggling shower;
And, if an unexpected cloud should lower,
Swiftly thereon a rainbow arch to build

For Fancy's errands, — then, from fields half-tilled
Gathering green weeds to mix with poppy flower,
Thee might thy Minions crown, and chaunt thy power,
Unpitied by the wise, all censure stilled.
Ah! show that worthier honours are thy due;
Fair Prime of life! arouse the deeper heart;
Confirm the Spirit glorying to pursue
Some path of steep ascent and lofty aim;
And, if there be a joy that slights the claim
Of grateful memory, bid that joy depart.

VI.

I watch, and long have watched, with calm regret
Yon slowly-sinking star — immortal Sire
(So might he seem) of all the glittering quire!
Blue ether still surrounds him — yet — and yet;
But now the horizon's rocky parapet
Is reached, where, forfeiting his bright attire,
He burns — transmuted to a dusky fire —
Then pays submissively the appointed debt
To the flying moments, and is seen no more.
Angels and gods! We struggle with our fate,
While health, power, glory, from their height decline,
Depressed; and then extinguished: and our state,
In this, how different, lost Star, from thine,
That no to-morrow shall our beams restore!

VII.

I heard (alas! 'twas only in a dream)
Strains — which, as sage Antiquity believed,
By waking ears have sometimes been received
Wafted adown the wind from lake or stream;
A most melodious requiem, a supreme
And perfect harmony of notes, achieved
By a fair Swan on drowsy billows heaved,
O'er which her pinions shed a silver gleam.

For is she not the votary of Apollo?
And knows she not, singing as he inspires,
That bliss awaits her which the ungenial Hollow
Of the dull earth partakes not, nor desires?
Mount, tuneful Bird, and join the immortal quires!
She soared — and I awoke, struggling in vain to follow.

VIII.

RETIREMENT.

If the whole weight of what we think and feel,
Save only far as thought and feeling blend
With action, were as nothing, patriot Friend!
From thy remonstrance would be no appeal;
But to promote and fortify the weal
Of her own Being is her paramount end;
A truth which they alone shall comprehend
Who shun the mischief which they cannot heal.
Peace in these feverish times is sovereign bliss:
Here, with no thirst but what the stream can slake,
And startled only by the rustling brake,
Cool air I breathe; while the unincumbered Mind,
By some weak aims at services assigned
To gentle Natures, thanks not Heaven amiss.

IX.

Nor Love, not War, nor the tumultuous swell
Of civil conflict, nor the wrecks of change,
Nor Duty struggling with afflictions strange —
Not these *alone* inspire the tuneful shell;
But where untroubled peace and concord dwell,
There also is the Muse not loth to range,
Watching the twilight smoke of cot or grange,
Skyward ascending from a woody dell.

Meek aspirations please her, lone endeavour,
And sage content, and placid melancholy;
She loves to gaze upon a crystal river —
Diaphanous because it travels slowly;
Soft is the music that would charm for ever;
The flower of sweetest smell is shy and lowly.

X.

Mark the concentred hazels that enclose
Yon old grey Stone, protected from the ray
Of noontide suns: — and even the beams that play
And glance, while wantonly the rough wind blows,
Are seldom free to touch the moss that grows
Upon that roof, amid embowering gloom,
The very image framing of a Tomb,
In which some ancient Chieftain finds repose
Among the lonely mountains. — Live, ye trees!
And thou, grey Stone, the pensive likeness keep
Of a dark chamber where the Mighty sleep:
For more than Fancy to the influence bends
When solitary Nature condescends
To mimic Time's forlorn humanities.

XI.
COMPOSED AFTER A JOURNEY ACROSS THE HAMBLETON HILLS, YORKSHIRE.

Dark and more dark the shades of evening fell;
The wished-for point was reached — but at an hour
When little could be gained from that rich dower
Of prospect, whereof many thousands tell.
Yet did the glowing west with marvellous power
Salute us; there stood Indian citadel,
Temple of Greece, and minster with its tower
Substantially expressed — a place for bell

Or clock to toll from! Many a tempting isle,
With groves that never were imagined, lay
'Mid seas how steadfast! objects all for the eye
Of silent rapture; but we felt the while
We should forget them; they are of the sky,
And from our earthly memory fade away.

XII.

— "they are of the sky,
And from our earthly memory fade away."

THOSE words were uttered as in pensive mood
We turned, departing from that solemn sight:
A contrast and reproach to gross delight,
And life's unspiritual pleasures daily wooed!
But now upon this thought I cannot brood;
It is unstable as a dream of night;
Nor will I praise a cloud, however bright,
Disparaging Man's gifts, and proper food.
Grove, isle, with every shape of sky-built dome,
Though clad in colours beautiful and pure,
Find in the heart of man no natural home:
The immortal Mind craves objects that endure:
These cleave to it; from these it cannot roam,
Nor they from it: their fellowship is secure.

XIII.

SEPTEMBER, 1815.

WHILE not a leaf seems faded; while the fields,
With ripening harvest prodigally fair,
In brightest sunshine bask; this nipping air,
Sent from some distant clime where Winter wields
His icy scimitar, a foretaste yields
Of bitter change, and bids the flowers beware;
And whispers to the silent birds, "Prepare
Against the threatening foe your trustiest shields."

For me, who under kindlier laws belong
To Nature's tuneful quire, this rustling dry
Through leaves yet green, and yon crystalline sky,
Announce a season potent to renew,
Mid frost and snow, the instinctive joys of song,
And nobler cares than listless summer knew.

XIV.

NOVEMBER 1.

How clear, how keen, how marvellously bright
The effluence from yon distant mountain's head,
Which, strewn with snow smooth as the sky can shed,
Shines like another sun — on mortal sight
Uprisen, as if to check approaching Night,
And all her twinkling stars. Who now would tread,
If so he might, yon mountain's glittering head —
Terrestrial, but a surface, by the flight
Of sad mortality's earth-sullying wing,
Unswept, unstained? Nor shall the aërial Powers
Dissolve that beauty, destined to endure,
White, radiant, spotless, exquisitely pure,
Through all vicissitudes, till genial Spring
Has filled the laughing vales with welcome flowers.

XV.

COMPOSED DURING A STORM.

ONE who was suffering tumult in his soul,
Yet failed to seek the sure relief of prayer,
Went forth — his course surrendering to the care
Of the fierce wind, while mid-day lightnings prowl
Insidiously, untimely thunders growl;
While trees, dim-seen, in frenzied numbers, tear
The lingering remnant of their yellow hair,
And shivering wolves, surprised with darkness, howl

As if the sun were not. He raised his eye
Soul-smitten; for, that instant, did appear
Large space (mid dreadful clouds) of purest sky,
An azure disc — shield of Tranquillity;
Invisible, unlooked-for, minister
Of providential goodness ever nigh!

XVI.

TO A SNOW-DROP.

Lone Flower, hemmed in with snows, and white as they
But hardier far, once more I see thee bend
Thy forehead, as if fearful to offend,
Like an unbidden guest. Though day by day,
Storms, sallying from the mountain-tops, way-lay
The rising sun, and on the plains descend;
Yet art thou welcome, welcome as a friend
Whose zeal outruns his promise! Blue-eyed May
Shall soon behold this border thickly set
With bright jonquils, their odours lavishing
On the soft west-wind and his frolic peers;
Nor will I then thy modest grace forget,
Chaste Snow-drop, venturous harbinger of spring,
And pensive monitor of fleeting years!

XVII.

TO THE LADY MARY LOWTHER.

With a selection from the Poems of Anne, Countess of Winchilsea; and extracts of similar character from other Writers; transcribed by a female friend.

Lady! I rifled a Parnassian Cave
(But seldom trod) of mildly-gleaming ore;
And culled, from sundry beds, a lucid store
Of genuine crystals, pure as those that pave
The azure brooks, where Dian joys to lave
Her spotless limbs; and ventured to explore
Dim shades — for reliques, upon Lethe's shore,
Cast up at random by the sullen wave.

To female hands the treasures were resigned;
And lo this Work! — a grotto bright and clear
From stain or taint; in which thy blameless mind
May feed on thoughts though pensive not austere;
Or, if thy deeper spirit be inclined
To holy musing, it may enter here.

XVIII.

TO LADY BEAUMONT.

Lady! the songs of Spring were in the grove
While I was shaping beds for winter flowers;
While I was planting green unfading bowers,
And shrubs — to hang upon the warm alcove,
And sheltering wall; and still, as Fancy wove
The dream, to time and nature's blended powers
I gave this paradise for winter hours,
A labyrinth, Lady! which your feet shall rove.
Yes! when the sun of life more feebly shines,
Becoming thoughts, I trust, of solemn gloom
Or of high gladness you shall hither bring;
And these perennial bowers and murmuring pines
Be gracious as the music and the bloom
And all the mighty ravishment of spring.

XIX.

*There is a pleasure in poetic pains
Which only Poets know;* — 't was rightly said;
Whom could the Muses else allure to tread
Their smoothest paths, to wear their lightest chains?
When happiest Fancy has inspired the strains,
How oft the malice of one luckless word
Pursues the Enthusiast to the social board,
Haunts him belated on the silent plains!

Yet he repines not, if his thought stand clear,
At last, of hindrance and obscurity,
Fresh as the star that crowns the brow of morn:
Bright, speckless, as a softly-moulded tear
The moment it has left the virgin's eye,
Or rain-drop lingering on the pointed thorn.

XX.

The Shepherd, looking eastward, softly said,
"Bright is thy veil, O Moon, as thou art bright!"
Forthwith, that little cloud, in ether spread
And penetrated all with tender light,
She cast away, and showed her fulgent head
Uncovered; dazzling the Beholder's sight
As if to vindicate her beauty's right,
Her beauty thoughtlessly disparagèd.
Meanwhile that veil, removed or thrown aside,
Went floating from her, darkening as it went;
And a huge mass, to bury or to hide,
Approached this glory of the firmament;
Who meekly yields, and is obscured — content
With one calm triumph of a modest pride.

XXI.

When haughty expectations prostrate lie,
And grandeur crouches like a guilty thing,
Oft shall the lowly weak, till nature bring
Mature release, in fair society
Survive, and Fortune's utmost anger try;
Like these frail snow-drops that together cling,
And nod their helmets, smitten by the wing
Of many a furious whirl-blast sweeping by.
Observe the faithful flowers! if small to great
May lead the thoughts, thus struggling used to stand
The Emathian phalanx, nobly obstinate;
And so the bright immortal Theban band,
Whom onset, fiercely urged at Jove's command
Might overwhelm, but could not separate!

XXII.

Hail, Twilight, sovereign of one peaceful hour!
Not dull art Thou as undiscerning Night;
But studious only to remove from sight
Day's mutable distinctions. — Ancient Power!
Thus did the waters gleam, the mountains lower,
To the rude Briton, when, in wolf-skin vest
Here roving wild, he laid him down to rest
On the bare rock, or through a leafy bower
Looked ere his eyes were closed. By him was seen
The self-same Vision which we now behold,
At thy meek bidding, shadowy Power! brought forth;
These mighty barriers, and the gulf between;
The flood, the stars, — a spectacle as old
As the beginning of the heavens and earth!

XXIII.

With how sad steps, O Moon, thou climb'st the sky,
"How silently, and with how wan a face!"
Where art thou? Thou so often seen on high
Running among the clouds a Wood-nymph's race!
Unhappy Nuns, whose common breath's a sigh
Which they would stifle, move at such a pace!
The northern Wind, to call thee to the chase,
Must blow to-night his bugle horn. Had I
The power of Merlin, Goddess! this should be:
And all the stars, fast as the clouds were riven,
Should sally forth, to keep thee company,
Hurrying and sparkling through the clear blue heaven;
But, Cynthia! should to thee the palm be given,
Queen both for beauty and for majesty.

XXIV.

Even as a dragon's eye that feels the stress
Of a bedimming sleep, or as a lamp
Suddenly glaring through sepulchral damp,
So burns yon Taper 'mid a black recess

Of mountains, silent, dreary, motionless:
The lake below reflects it not; the sky
Muffled in clouds, affords no company
To mitigate and cheer its loneliness.
Yet, round the body of that joyless Thing
Which sends so far its melancholy light,
Perhaps are seated in domestic ring
A gay society with faces bright,
Conversing, reading, laughing; — or they sing,
While hearts and voices in the song unite.

XXV.

THE stars are mansions built by Nature's hand,
And, haply, there the spirits of the blest
Dwell, clothed in radiance, their immortal vest;
Huge Ocean shows, within his yellow strand,
A habitation marvellously planned,
For life to occupy in love and rest;
All that we see — is dome, or vault, or nest,
Or fortress, reared at Nature's sage command.
Glad thought for every season! but the Spring
Gave it while cares were weighing on my heart,
'Mid song of birds, and insects murmuring;
And while the youthful year's prolific art —
Of bud, leaf, blade, and flower — was fashioning
Abodes where self-disturbance hath no part.

XXVI.

DESPONDING Father! mark this altered bough,
So beautiful of late, with sunshine warmed,
Or moist with dews; what more unsightly now,
Its blossoms shrivelled, and its fruit, if formed,
Invisible? yet Spring her genial brow
Knits not o'er that discolouring and decay
As false to expectation. Nor fret thou
At like unlovely process in the May

Of human life: a Stripling's graces blow,
Fade, and are shed, that from their timely fall
(Misdeem it not a cankerous change) may grow
Rich mellow bearings, that for thanks shall call:
In all men, sinful is it to be slow
To hope — in Parents, sinful above all.

XXVII.

CAPTIVITY. — MARY QUEEN OF SCOTS.

"As the cold aspect of a sunless way
Strikes through the Traveller's frame with deadlier chill,
Oft as appears a grove, or obvious hill,
Glistening with unparticipated ray,
Or shining slope where he must never stray;
So joys, remembered without wish or will,
Sharpen the keenest edge of present ill, —
On the crushed heart a heavier burthen lay.
Just Heaven, contract the compass of my mind
To fit proportion with my altered state!
Quench those felicities whose light I find
Reflected in my bosom all too late! —
O be my spirit, like my thraldom, strait;
And, like mine eyes that stream with sorrow, blind!"

XXVIII.

ST. CATHERINE OF LEDBURY.

When human touch (as monkish books attest)
Nor was applied nor could be, Ledbury bells
Broke forth in concert flung adown the dells,
And upward, high as Malvern's cloudy crest;
Sweet tones, and caught by a noble Lady blest
To rapture! Mabel listened at the side
Of her loved mistress: soon the music died,
And Catherine said, *Here I set up my rest.*

Warned in a dream, the Wanderer long had sought
A home that by such miracle of sound
Must be revealed: — she heard it now, or felt
The deep, deep joy of a confiding thought;
And there, a saintly Anchoress, she dwelt
Till she exchanged for heaven that happy ground.

XXIX.

— 'given to airy nothing
A local habitation and a name.'

THOUGH narrow be that old Man's cares, and near,
The poor old Man is greater than he seems:
For he hath waking empire, wide as dreams;
An ample sovereignty of eye and ear.
Rich are his walks with supernatural cheer;
The region of his inner spirit teems
With vital sounds and monitory gleams
Of high astonishment and pleasing fear.
He the seven birds hath seen, that never part,
Seen the SEVEN WHISTLERS in their nightly rounds,
And counted them: and oftentimes will start —
For overhead are sweeping GABRIEL'S HOUNDS
Doomed, with their impious Lord, the flying Hart
To chase for ever, on aërial grounds!

XXX.

FOUR fiery steeds impatient of the rein
Whirled us o'er sunless ground beneath a sky
As void of sunshine, when, from that wide plain,
Clear tops of far-off mountains we descry,
Like a Sierra of cerulean Spain,
All light and lustre. Did no heart reply?
Yes, there was One; — for One, asunder fly
The thousand links of that ethereal chain;

And green vales open out, with grove and field,
And the fair front of many a happy Home;
Such tempting spots as into vision come
While Soldiers, weary of the arms they wield
And sick at heart of strifeful Christendom,
Gaze on the moon by parting clouds revealed.

XXXI.

Brook! whose society the Poet seeks,
Intent his wasted spirits to renew;
And whom the curious Painter doth pursue
Through rocky passes, among flowery creeks,
And tracks thee dancing down thy water-breaks;
If wish were mine some type of thee to view,
Thee, and not thee thyself, I would not do
Like Grecian Artists, give thee human cheeks,
Channels for tears; no Naiad should'st thou be, —
Have neither limbs, feet, feathers, joints nor hairs:
It seems the Eternal Soul is clothed in thee
With purer robes than those of flesh and blood,
And hath bestowed on thee a safer good;
Unwearied joy, and life without its cares.

XXXII.
COMPOSED ON THE BANKS OF A ROCKY STREAM.

Dogmatic Teachers, of the snow-white fur!
Ye wrangling Schoolmen, of the scarlet hood!
Who, with a keenness not to be withstood,
Press the point home, or falter and demur,
Checked in your course by many a teasing burr;
These natural council-seats your acrid blood
Might cool; — and, as the Genius of the flood
Stoops willingly to animate and spur

Each lighter function slumbering in the brain,
Yon eddying balls of foam, these arrowy gleams
That o'er the pavement of the surging streams
Welter and flash, a synod might detain
With subtle speculations, haply vain,
But surely less so than your far-fetched themes!

XXXIII.

THIS, AND THE TWO FOLLOWING, WERE SUGGESTED BY MR. W. WESTALL'S VIEWS OF THE CAVES, ETC., IN YORKSHIRE.

PURE element of waters! wheresoe'er
Thou dost forsake thy subterranean haunts,
Green herbs, bright flowers, and berry-bearing plants,
Rise into life and in thy train appear:
And, through the sunny portion of the year,
Swift insects shine, thy hovering pursuivants:
And, if thy bounty fail, the forest pants;
And hart and hind and hunter with his spear,
Languish and droop together. Nor unfelt
In man's perturbèd soul thy sway benign;
And, haply, far within the marble belt
Of central earth, where tortured Spirits pine
For grace and goodness lost, thy murmurs melt
Their anguish,—and they blend sweet songs with thine.*

XXXIV.

MALHAM COVE.

WAS the aim frustrated by force or guile,
When giants scooped from out the rocky ground,
Tier under tier, this semicirque profound?
(Giants — the same who built in Erin's isle
That Causeway with incomparable toil!) —
O, had this vast theatric structure wound
With finished sweep into a perfect round,
No mightier work had gained the plausive smile

---

* Waters (as Mr. Westall informs us in the letter-press prefixed to his admirable views) are invariably found to flow through these caverns.

Of all-beholding Phœbus! But, alas,
Vain earth! false world! Foundations must be laid
In Heaven; for, 'mid the wreck of is and was,
Things incomplete and purposes betrayed
Make sadder transits o'er thought's optic glass
Than noblest objects utterly decayed.

XXXV.
GORDALE.

At early dawn, or rather when the air
Glimmers with fading light, and shadowy Eve
Is busiest to confer and to bereave;
Then, pensive Votary! let thy feet repair
To Gordale-chasm, terrific as the lair
Where the young lions couch; for so, by leave
Of the propitious hour, thou may'st perceive
The local Deity, with oozy hair
And mineral crown, beside his jagged urn,
Recumbent: Him thou may'st behold, who hides
His lineaments by day, yet there presides,
Teaching the docile waters how to turn,
Or (if need be) impediment to spurn,
And force their passage to the salt-sea tides!

XXXVI.
COMPOSED UPON WESTMINSTER BRIDGE, SEPT. 3, 1802.

Earth has not any thing to show more fair:
Dull would he be of soul who could pass by
A sight so touching in its majesty:
This City now doth, like a garment, wear
The beauty of the morning; silent, bare,
Ships, towers, domes, theatres, and temples lie
Open unto the fields, and to the sky;
All bright and glittering in the smokeless air.

Never did sun more beautifully steep
In his first splendour, valley, rock, or hill;
Ne'er saw I, never felt, a calm so deep!
The river glideth at his own sweet will:
Dear God! the very houses seem asleep;
And all that mighty heart is lying still!

XXXVII.

CONCLUSION.

TO —

If these brief Records, by the Muses' art
Produced as lonely Nature or the strife
That animates the scenes of public life
Inspired, may in thy leisure claim a part;
And if these Transcripts of the private heart
Have gained a sanction from thy falling tears;
Then I repent not. But my soul hath fears
Breathed from eternity; for as a dart
Cleaves the blank air, Life flies: now every day
Is but a glimmering spoke in the swift wheel
Of the revolving week. Away, away,
All fitful cares, all transitory zeal!
So timely Grace the immortal wing may heal,
And honour rest upon the senseless clay.

PART III.

I.

Though the bold wings of Poesy affect
The clouds, and wheel around the mountain tops
Rejoicing, from her loftiest height she drops
Well pleased to skim the plain with wild flowers deckt,
Or muse in solemn grove whose shades protect
The lingering dew — there steals along, or stops
Watching the least small bird that round her hops,
Or creeping worm, with sensitive respect.
Her functions are they therefore less divine,
Her thoughts less deep, or void of grave intent
Her simplest fancies? Should that fear be thine,
Aspiring Votary, ere thy hand present
One offering, kneel before her modest shrine,
With brow in penitential sorrow bent!

II.

OXFORD, MAY 30, 1820.

Ye sacred Nurseries of blooming Youth!
In whose collegiate shelter England's Flowers
Expand, enjoying through their vernal hours
The air of liberty, the light of truth;
Much have ye suffered from Time's gnawing tooth:
Yet, O ye spires of Oxford! domes and towers!
Gardens and groves! your presence overpowers
The soberness of reason; till, in sooth,
Transformed, and rushing on a bold exchange
I slight my own beloved Cam, to range
Where silver Isis leads my stripling feet;
Pace the long avenue, or glide adown
The stream-like windings of that glorious street —
An eager Novice robed in fluttering gown!

III.
OXFORD, MAY 30, 1820.

Shame on this faithless heart! that could allow
Such transport, though but for a moment's space;
Not while — to aid the spirit of the place —
The crescent moon clove with its glittering prow
The clouds, or night-bird sang from shady bough;
But in plain daylight: — She, too, at my side,
Who, with her heart's experience satisfied,
Maintains inviolate its slightest vow!
Sweet Fancy! other gifts must I receive;
Proofs of a higher sovereignty I claim;
Take from *her* brow the withering flowers of eve,
And to that brow life's morning wreath restore;
Let *her* be comprehended in the frame
Of these illusions, or they please no more.

IV.
RECOLLECTION OF THE PORTRAIT OF KING HENRY EIGHTH, TRINITY LODGE, CAMBRIDGE.

The imperial Stature, the colossal stride,
Are yet before me; yet do I behold
The broad full visage, chest of amplest mould,
The vestments 'broidered with barbaric pride:
And lo! a poniard, at the Monarch's side,
Hangs ready to be grasped in sympathy
With the keen threatenings of that fulgent eye,
Below the white-rimmed bonnet, far-descried.
Who trembles now at thy capricious mood?
'Mid those surrounding Worthies, haughty King,
We rather think, with grateful mind sedate,
How Providence educeth, from the spring
Of lawless will, unlooked-for streams of good,
Which neither force shall check nor time abate!

V.

ON THE DEATH OF HIS MAJESTY (GEORGE THE THIRD).

WARD of the Law! — dread Shadow of a King!
Whose realm had dwindled to one stately room;
Whose universe was gloom immersed in gloom,
Darkness as thick as life o'er life could fling,
Save haply for some feeble glimmering
Of Faith and Hope — if thou, by nature's doom,
Gently hast sunk into the quiet tomb,
Why should we bend in grief, to sorrow cling,
When thankfulness were best? — Fresh-flowing tears,
Or, where tears flow not, sigh succeeding sigh,
Yield to such after-thought the sole reply
Which justly it can claim. The Nation hears
In this deep knell, silent for threescore years,
An unexampled voice of awful memory!

VI.

JUNE, 1820.

FAME tells of groves — from England far away —
*Groves that inspire the Nightingale to trill
And modulate, with subtle reach of skill
Elsewhere unmatched, her ever-varying lay;
Such bold report I venture to gainsay:
For I have heard the quire of Richmond hill
Chanting, with indefatigable bill,
Strains that recalled to mind a distant day;
When, haply under shade of that same wood,
And scarcely conscious of the dashing oars
Plied steadily between those willowy shores,
The sweet-souled Poet of the Seasons stood —
Listening, and listening long, in rapturous mood,
Ye heavenly Birds! to your Progenitors.

* Wallachia is the country alluded to.

VII.

A PARSONAGE IN OXFORDSHIRE.

WHERE holy ground begins, unhallowed ends,
Is marked by no distinguishable line;
The turf unites, the pathways intertwine;
And, wheresoe'er the stealing footstep tends,
Garden, and that Domain where kindred, friends,
And neighbours rest together, here confound
Their several features, mingled like the sound
Of many waters, or as evening blends
With shady night. Soft airs, from shrub and flower,
Waft fragrant greetings to each silent grave;
And while those lofty poplars gently wave
Their tops, between them comes and goes a sky
Bright as the glimpses of eternity,
To saints accorded in their mortal hour.

VIII.

COMPOSED AMONG THE RUINS OF A CASTLE IN NORTH WALES.

THROUGH shattered galleries, 'mid roofless halls,
Wandering with timid footsteps oft betrayed,
The Stranger sighs, nor scruples to upbraid
Old Time, though he, gentlest among the Thralls
Of Destiny, upon these wounds hath laid
His lenient touches, soft as light that falls,
From the wan Moon, upon the towers and walls,
Light deepening the profoundest sleep of shade.
Relic of Kings! Wreck of forgotten wars,
To winds abandoned and the prying stars,
Time *loves* Thee! at his call the Seasons twine
Luxuriant wreaths around thy forehead hoar;
And, though past pomp no changes can restore,
A soothing recompense, his gift, is thine!

IX.

TO THE LADY E. B. AND THE HON. MISS P.
Composed in the Grounds of Plass Newidd, near Llangollen, 1824.

A Stream, to mingle with your favourite Dee,
Along the Vale of Meditation* flows;
So styled by those fierce Britons, pleased to see
In Nature's face the expression of repose;
Or haply there some pious hermit chose
To live and die, the peace of heaven his aim;
To whom the wild sequestered region owes,
At this late day, its sanctifying name.
Glyn Cafaillgaroch, in the Cambrian tongue,
In ours, the Vale of Friendship, let *this* spot
Be named; where, faithful to a low-roofed Cot,
On Deva's banks, ye have abode so long;
Sisters in love, a love allowed to climb,
Even on this earth, above the reach of Time!

X.

TO THE TORRENT AT THE DEVIL'S BRIDGE, NORTH WALES, 1824.

How art thou named? In search of what strange land,
From what huge height, descending? Can such force
Of waters issue from a British source,
Or hath not Pindus fed thee, where the band
Of Patriots scoop their freedom out, with hand
Desperate as thine? Or come the incessant shocks
From that young Stream, that smites the throbbing rocks
Of Via-mala? There I seem to stand,
As in life's morn; permitted to behold,
From the dread chasm, woods climbing above woods,
In pomp that fades not; everlasting snows;
And skies that ne'er relinquish their repose;
Such power possess the family of floods
Over the minds of Poets, young or old!

* Glyn Myrvr.

XI.

IN THE WOODS OF RYDAL.

Wild Redbreast! hadst thou at Jemima's lip
Pecked, as at mine, thus boldly, Love might say,
A half-blown rose had tempted thee to sip
Its glistening dews; but hallowed is the clay
Which the Muse warms; and I, whose head is grey,
Am not unworthy of thy fellowship;
Nor could I let one thought — one motion — slip
That might thy sylvan confidence betray.
For are we not all His without whose care
Vouchsafed no sparrow falleth to the ground?
Who gives his Angels wings to speed through air,
And rolls the planets through the blue profound?
Then peck or perch, fond Flutterer! nor forbear
To trust a Poet in still musings bound.

XII.

When Philoctetes in the Lemnian isle
Like a Form sculptured on a monument
Lay couched; on him or his dread bow unbent
Some wild Bird oft might settle and beguile
The rigid features of a transient smile,
Disperse the tear, or to the sigh give vent,
Slackening the pains of ruthless banishment
From his lov'd home, and from heroic toil.
And trust that spiritual Creatures round us move,
Griefs to allay which Reason cannot heal;
Yea, veriest reptiles have sufficed to prove
To fettered wretchedness, that no Bastile
Is deep enough to exclude the light of love,
Though man for brother man has ceased to feel.

XIII.

While Anna's peers and early playmates tread,
In freedom, mountain-turf and river's marge;
Or float with music in the festal barge;
Rein the proud steed, or through the dance are led;
Her doom it is to press a weary bed —
Till oft her guardian Angel, to some charge
More urgent called, will stretch his wings at large,
And friends too rarely prop the languid head.
Yet, helped by Genius — untired comforter,
The presence even of a stuffed Owl for her
Can cheat the time; sending her fancy out
To ivied castles and to moonlight skies,
Though he can neither stir a plume, nor shout;
Nor veil, with restless film, his staring eyes.

XIV.

TO THE CUCKOO.

Not the whole warbling grove in concert heard
When sunshine follows shower, the breast can thrill
Like the first summons, Cuckoo! of thy bill,
With its twin notes inseparably paired.
The captive 'mid damp vaults unsunned, unaired,
Measuring the periods of his lonely doom,
That cry can reach; and to the sick man's room
Sends gladness, by no languid smile declared.
The lordly eagle-race through hostile search
May perish; time may come when never more
The wilderness shall hear the lion roar;
But, long as cock shall crow from household perch
To rouse the dawn, soft gales shall speed thy wing,
And thy erratic voice be faithful to the Spring!

XV.

TO ——

[Miss not the occasion; by the forelock take
That subtle Power, the never-halting Time,
Lest a mere moment's putting-off should make
Mischance almost as heavy as a crime.]

"Wait, prithee, wait!" this answer Lesbia threw
Forth to her Dove, and took no further heed.
Her eye was busy, while her fingers flew
Across the harp, with soul engrossing speed;
But from that bondage when her thoughts were freed
She rose, and toward the close-shut casement drew,
Whence the poor unregarded Favourite, true
To old affections, had been heard to plead
With flapping wing for entrance. What a shriek
Forced from that voice so lately tuned to a strain
Of harmony! — a shriek of terror, pain,
And self-reproach! for, from aloft, a Kite
Pounced, — and the Dove, which from its ruthless beak
She could not rescue, perished in her sight!

XVI.

THE INFANT M—— M——

Unquiet Childhood here by special grace
Forgets her nature, opening like a flower
That neither feeds nor wastes its vital power
In painful struggles. Months each other chase,
And nought untunes that Infant's voice; no trace
Of fretful temper sullies her pure cheek;
Prompt, lively, self-sufficing, yet so meek
That one enrapt with gazing on her face
(Which even the placid innocence of death
Could scarcely make more placid, heaven more bright)
Might learn to picture, for the eye of faith,
The Virgin, as she shone with kindred light;
A nursling couched upon her mother's knee,
Beneath some shady palm of Galilee.

XVII.

TO —, IN HER SEVENTIETH YEAR.

Such age how beautiful! O Lady bright,
Whose mortal lineaments seem all refined
By favouring Nature and a saintly Mind
To something purer and more exquisite
Than flesh and blood; whene'er thou meet'st my sight,
When I behold thy blanched unwithered cheek,
Thy temples fringed with locks of gleaming white,
And head that droops because the soul is meek,
Thee with the welcome Snowdrop I compare;
That child of winter, prompting thoughts that climb
From desolation toward the genial prime;
Or with the Moon conquering earth's misty air,
And filling more and more with crystal light
As pensive Evening deepens into night.

XVIII.

TO ROTHA Q—.

Rotha, my Spiritual Child! this head was grey
When at the sacred font for thee I stood;
Pledged till thou reach the verge of womanhood,
And shalt become thy own sufficient stay:
Too late, I feel, sweet Orphan! was the day
For stedfast hope the contract to fulfil;
Yet shall my blessing hover o'er thee still,
Embodied in the music of this Lay,
Breathed forth beside the peaceful mountain Stream*
Whose murmur soothed thy languid Mother's ear
After her throes, this Stream of name more dear
Since thou dost bear it, — a memorial theme
For others; for thy future self, a spell
To summon fancies out of Time's dark cell.

* The river Rotha, that flows into Windermere from the Lakes of Grasmere and Rydal.

XIX.

A GRAVE-STONE UPON THE FLOOR IN THE CLOISTERS OF WORCESTER CATHEDRAL.

"*Miserrimus!*" and neither name nor date,
Prayer, text, or symbol, graven upon the stone;
Nought but that word assigned to the unknown,
That solitary word — to separate
From all, and cast a cloud around the fate
Of him who lies beneath. Most wretched one,
Who chose his epitaph? — Himself alone
Could thus have dared the grave to agitate,
And claim, among the dead, this awful crown;
Nor doubt that He marked also for his own
Close to these cloistral steps a burial-place,
That every foot might fall with heavier tread,
Trampling upon his vileness. Stranger, pass
Softly! — To save the contrite, Jesus bled.

XX.

ROMAN ANTIQUITIES DISCOVERED AT BISHOPSTONE, HEREFORDSHIRE.

While poring Antiquarians search the ground
Upturned with curious pains, the Bard, a Seer,
Takes fire: — The men that have been reappear;
Romans for travel girt, for business gowned;
And some recline on couches, myrtle-crowned,
In festal glee: why not? For fresh and clear,
As if its hues were of the passing year,
Dawns this time-buried pavement. From that mound
Hoards may come forth of Trajans, Maximins,
Shrunk into coins with all their warlike toil:
Or a fierce impress issues with its foil
Of tenderness — the Wolf, whose suckling Twins
The unlettered ploughboy pities when he wins
The casual treasure from the furrowed soil.

XXI.
1830.

Chatsworth! thy stately mansion, and the pride
Of thy domain, strange contrast do present
To house and home in many a craggy rent
Of the wild Peak; where new-born waters glide
Through fields whose thrifty occupants abide
As in a dear and chosen banishment,
With every semblance of entire content;
So kind is simple Nature, fairly tried!
Yet He whose heart in childhood gave her troth
To pastoral dales, thin-set with modest farms,
May learn, if judgment strengthen with his growth,
That, not for Fancy only, pomp hath charms;
And, strenuous to protect from lawless harms
The extremes of favoured life, may honour both.

XXII.
A TRADITION OF OKER HILL, IN DARLEY DALE, DERBYSHIRE.

'Tis said that to the brow of yon fair hill
Two Brothers clomb, and, turning face from face,
Nor one look more exchanging, grief to still
Or feed, each planted on that lofty place
A chosen Tree; then, eager to fulfil
Their courses, like two new-born rivers, they
In opposite directions urged their way
Down from the far-seen mount. No blast might kill
Or blight that fond memorial; — the trees grew,
And now entwine their arms; but ne'er again
Embraced those Brothers upon earth's wide plain;
Nor aught of mutual joy or sorrow knew
Until their spirits mingled in the sea
That to itself takes all, Eternity.

XXIII.

FILIAL PIETY.

(On the Wayside between Preston and Liverpool.)

Untouched through all severity of cold;
Inviolate, whate'er the cottage hearth
Might need for comfort, or for festal mirth;
That Pile of Turf is half a century old:
Yes, Traveller! fifty winters have been told
Since suddenly the dart of death went forth
'Gainst him who raised it, — his last work on earth:
Thence has it, with the Son, so strong a hold
Upon his Father's memory, that his hands,
Through reverence, touch it only to repair
Its waste. — Though crumbling with each breath of air,
In annual renovation thus it stands —
Rude Mausoleum! but wrens nestle there,
And red-breasts warble when sweet sounds are rare.

XXIV.

TO THE AUTHOR'S PORTRAIT.

[Painted at Rydal Mount, by W. Pickersgill, Esq., for St. John's College, Cambridge.]

Go, faithful Portrait! and where long hath knelt
Margaret, the saintly Foundress, take thy place;
And, if Time spare the colours for the grace
Which to the work surpassing skill hath dealt,
Thou, on thy rock reclined, though kingdoms melt
And states be torn up by the roots, wilt seem
To breathe in rural peace, to hear the stream,
And think and feel as once the Poet felt.
Whate'er thy fate, those features have not grown
Unrecognised through many a household tear
More prompt, more glad, to fall than drops of dew
By morning shed around a flower half-blown;
Tears of delight, that testified how true
To life thou art, and, in thy truth, how dear!

XXV.

Why art thou silent! Is thy love a plant
Of such weak fibre that the treacherous air
Of absence withers what was once so fair?
Is there no debt to pay, no boon to grant?
Yet have my thoughts for thee been vigilant —
Bound to thy service with unceasing care,
The mind's least generous wish a mendicant
For nought but what thy happiness could spare.
Speak — though this soft warm heart, once free to hold
A thousand tender pleasures, thine and mine,
Be left more desolate, more dreary cold
Than a forsaken bird's-nest filled with snow
'Mid its own bush of leafless eglantine —
Speak, that my torturing doubts their end may know!

XXVI.

TO B. R. HAYDON, ON SEEING HIS PICTURE OF NAPOLEON BONAPARTE ON THE ISLAND OF ST. HELENA.

Haydon! let worthier judges praise the skill
Here by thy pencil shown in truth of lines
And charm of colours; *I* applaud those signs
Of thought, that give the true poetic thrill;
That unencumbered whole of blank and still,
Sky without cloud — ocean without a wave;
And the one Man that laboured to enslave
The World, sole-standing high on the bare hill —
Back turned, arms folded, the unapparent face
Tinged, we may fancy, in this dreary place
With light reflected from the invisible sun
Set, like his fortunes; but not set for aye
Like them. The unguilty Power pursues his way,
And before *him* doth dawn perpetual run.

XXVII.

A Poet! — He hath put his heart to school,
Nor dares to move unpropped upon the staff
Which Art hath lodged within his hand — must laugh
By precept only, and shed tears by rule.
Thy Art be Nature; the live current quaff,
And let the groveller sip his stagnant pool.
In fear that else, when Critics grave and cool
Have killed him, Scorn should write his epitaph.
How does the Meadow-flower its bloom unfold?
Because the lovely little flower is free
Down to its root, and, in that freedom, bold;
And so the grandeur of the Forest-tree
Comes not by casting in a formal mould,
But from its *own* divine vitality.

XXVIII.

The most alluring clouds that mount the sky
Owe to a troubled element their forms,
Their hues to sunset. If with raptured eye
We watch their splendor, shall we covet storms,
And wish the Lord of day his slow decline
Would hasten, that such pomp may float on high?
Behold, already they forget to shine,
Dissolve — and leave to him who gazed a sigh.
Not loth to thank each moment for its boon
Of pure delight, come whensoe'er it may,
Peace let us seek, — to stedfast things attune
Calm expectations, leaving to the gay
And volatile their love of transient bowers,
The house that cannot pass away be ours.

XXIX.

ON A PORTRAIT OF THE DUKE OF WELLINGTON UPON THE FIELD OF WATERLOO, BY HAYDON.

By Art's bold privilege Warrior and War-horse stand
On ground yet strewn with their last battle's wreck;
Let the Steed glory while his Master's hand
Lies fixed for ages on his conscious neck;
But by the Chieftain's look, though at his side
Hangs that day's treasured sword, how firm a check
Is given to triumph and all human pride!
Yon trophied Mound shrinks to a shadowy speck
In his calm presence! Him the mighty deed
Elates not, brought far nearer the grave's rest,
As shows that time-worn face, for he such seed
Has sown as yields, we trust, the fruit of fame
In Heaven; hence no one blushes for thy name,
Conqueror, 'mid some sad thoughts, divinely blest!

XXX.

COMPOSED ON A MAY MORNING, 1838.

LIFE with yon Lambs, like day, is just begun,
Yet Nature seems to them a heavenly guide.
Does joy approach? they meet the coming tide;
And sullenness avoid, as now they shun
Pale twilight's lingering glooms, — and in the sun
Couch near their dams, with quiet satisfied;
Or gambol — each with his shadow at his side,
Varying its shape wherever he may run.
As they from turf yet hoar with sleepy dew
All turn, and court the shining and the green,
Where herbs look up, and opening flowers are seen;
Why to God's goodness cannot We be true,
And so, His gifts and promises between,
Feed to the last on pleasures ever new?

XXXI.

Lo! where she stands fixed in a saint-like trance,
One upward hand, as if she needed rest
From rapture, lying softly on her breast!
Nor wants her eyeball an ethereal glance;
But not the less — nay more — that countenance,
While thus illumined, tells of painful strife
For a sick heart made weary of this life
By love, long crossed with adverse circumstance.
— Would She were now as when she hoped to pass
At God's appointed hour to them who tread
Heaven's sapphire pavement, yet breathed well content,
Well pleased, her foot should print earth's common grass,
Lived thankful for day's light, for daily bread,
For health, and time in obvious duty spent.

XXXII.

TO A PAINTER.

All praise the Likeness by thy skill portrayed;
But 'tis a fruitless task to paint for me,
Who, yielding not to changes Time has made,
By the habitual light of memory see
Eyes unbedimmed, see bloom that cannot fade,
And smiles that from their birth-place ne'er shall flee
Into the land where ghosts and phantoms be;
And, seeing this, own nothing in its stead.
Couldst thou go back into far-distant years,
Or share with me, fond thought! that inward eye,
Then, and then only, Painter! could thy Art
The visual powers of Nature satisfy,
Which hold, whate'er to common sight appears,
Their sovereign empire in a faithful heart.

XXXIII.

ON THE SAME SUBJECT.

Though I beheld at first with blank surprise
This Work, I now have gazed on it so long
I see its truth with unreluctant eyes;
O, my Belovèd! I have done thee wrong,
Conscious of blessedness, but, whence it sprung,
Ever too heedless, as I now perceive:
Morn into noon did pass, noon into eve,
And the old day was welcome as the young,
As welcome, and as beautiful — in sooth
More beautiful, as being a thing more holy:
Thanks to thy virtues, to the eternal youth
Of all thy goodness, never melancholy;
To thy large heart and humble mind, that cast
Into one vision, future, present, past.

XXXIV.

Hark! 'tis the Thrush, undaunted, undeprest,
By twilight premature of cloud and rain;
Nor does that roaring wind deaden his strain
Who carols thinking of his Love and nest,
And seems, as more incited, still more blest.
Thanks; thou hast snapped a fire-side Prisoner's chain,
Exulting Warbler! eased a fretted brain,
And in a moment charmed my cares to rest.
Yes, I will forth, bold Bird! and front the blast,
That we may sing together, if thou wilt,
So loud, so clear, my Partner through life's day,
Mute in her nest love-chosen, if not love-built
Like thine, shall gladden, as in seasons past,
Thrilled by loose snatches of the social Lay.

XXXV.

'Tis He whose yester-evening's high disdain
Beat back the roaring storm — but how subdued
His day-break note, a sad vicissitude!
Does the hour's drowsy weight his glee restrain?
Or, like the nightingale, her joyous vein
Pleased to renounce, does this dear Thrush attune
His voice to suit the temper of yon Moon
Doubly depressed, setting, and in her wane?
Rise, tardy Sun! and let the Songster prove
(The balance trembling between night and morn
No longer) with what ecstasy upborne
He can pour forth his spirit. In heaven above,
And earth below, they best can serve true gladness
Who meet most feelingly the calls of sadness.

XXXVI.

On what a Wreck! how changed in mien and speech!
Yet — though dread Powers, that work in mystery, spin
Entanglings of the brain; though shadows stretch
O'er the chilled heart — reflect; far, far within
Hers is a holy Being, freed from Sin.
She is not what she seems, a forlorn wretch,
But delegated Spirits comfort fetch
To Her from heights that Reason may not win.
Like Children, She is privileged to hold
Divine communion; both to live and move,
Whate'er to shallow Faith their ways unfold,
Inly illumined by Heaven's pitying love;
Love pitying innocence not long to last,
In them — in Her our sins and sorrows past.

XXXVII.

Intent on gathering wool from hedge and brake
Yon busy Little-ones rejoice that soon
A poor old Dame will bless them for the boon:
Great is their glee while flake they add to flake
With rival earnestness; far other strife
Than will hereafter move them, if they make
Pastime their idol, give their day of life
To pleasure snatched for reckless pleasure's sake.
Can pomp and show allay one heart-born grief?
Pains which the World inflicts can she requite?
Not for an interval however brief;
The silent thoughts that search for stedfast light,
Love from her depths, and Duty in her might,
And Faith — these only yield secure relief.

March 8th, 1842.

XXXVIII.

A PLEA FOR AUTHORS, MAY 1838.

Failing impartial measure to dispense
To every suitor, Equity is lame;
And social Justice, stript of reverence
For natural rights, a mockery and a shame;
Law but a servile dupe of false pretence,
If, guarding grossest things from common claim
Now and for ever, She, to works that came
From mind and spirit, grudge a short-lived fence.
"What! lengthened privilege, a lineal tie,
For *Books!*" Yes, heartless Ones, or be it proved
That 'tis a fault in Us to have lived and loved
Like others, with like temporal hopes to die;
No public harm that Genius from her course
Be turned; and streams of truth dried up, even at their source!

XXXIX.

VALEDICTORY SONNET.
Closing the Volume of Sonnets published in 1838.

Serving no haughty Muse, my hands have here
Disposed some cultured Flowerets (drawn from spots
Where they bloomed singly, or in scattered knots),
Each kind in several beds of one parterre;
Both to allure the casual Loiterer,
And that, so placed, my Nurslings may requite
Studious regard with opportune delight,
Nor be unthanked, unless I fondly err.
But metaphor dismissed, and thanks apart,
Reader, farewell! My last words let them be —
If in this book Fancy and Truth agree;
If simple Nature trained by careful Art
Through It have won a passage to thy heart;
Grant me thy love, I crave no other fee!

XL.

TO THE REV. CHRISTOPHER WORDSWORTH, D.D., MASTER OF HARROW SCHOOL,
After the perusal of his Theophilus Anglicanus, recently published.

Enlightened Teacher, gladly from thy hand
Have I received this proof of pains bestowed
By Thee to guide thy Pupils on the road
That, in our native isle, and every land,
The Church, when trusting in divine command
And in her Catholic attributes, hath trod:
O may these lessons be with profit scanned
To thy heart's wish, thy labour blest by God!
So the bright faces of the young and gay
Shall look more bright — the happy, happier still;
Catch, in the pauses of their keenest play,
Motions of thought which elevate the will
And, like the Spire that from your classic Hill
Points heavenward, indicate the end and way.

Rydal Mount, Dec. 11, 1843.

XLI.

TO THE PLANET VENUS.

Upon its approximation (as an Evening Star) to the Earth, Jan. 1838.

What strong allurement draws, what spirit guides,
Thee, Vesper! brightening still, as if the nearer
Thou com'st to man's abode the spot grew dearer
Night after night? True is it Nature hides
Her treasures less and less. — Man now presides
In power, where once he trembled in his weakness;
Science advances with gigantic strides;
But are we aught enriched in love and meekness?
Aught dost thou see, bright Star! of pure and wise
More than in humbler times graced human story;
That makes our hearts more apt to sympathise
With heaven, our souls more fit for future glory,
When earth shall vanish from our closing eyes,
Ere we lie down in our last dormitory?

XLII.

Wansfell!* this Household has a favoured lot,
Living with liberty on thee to gaze,
To watch while Morn first crowns thee with her rays,
Or when along thy breast serenely float
Evening's angelic clouds. Yet ne'er a note
Hath sounded (shame upon the Bard!) thy praise
For all that thou, as if from heaven, hast brought
Of glory lavished on our quiet days.
Bountiful Son of Earth! when we are gone
From every object dear to mortal sight,
As soon we shall be, may these words attest
How oft, to elevate our spirits, shone
Thy visionary majesties of light,
How in thy pensive glooms our hearts found rest.

Dec. 24, 1842.

* The Hill that rises to the south-east, above Ambleside.

XLIII.

While beams of orient light shoot wide and high,
Deep in the vale a little rural Town*
Breathes forth a cloud-like creature of its own,
That mounts not toward the radiant morning sky,
But, with a less ambitious sympathy,
Hangs o'er its Parent waking to the cares
Troubles and toils that every day prepares.
So Fancy, to the musing Poet's eye,
Endears that Lingerer. And how blest her sway
(Like influence never may my soul reject)
If the calm Heaven, now to its zenith decked
With glorious forms in numberless array,
To the lone shepherd on the hills disclose
Gleams from a world in which the saints repose.

Jan. 1, 1843.

XLIV.

In my mind's eye a Temple, like a cloud
Slowly surmounting some invidious hill,
Rose out of darkness: the bright Work stood still;
And might of its own beauty have been proud,
But it was fashioned and to God was vowed
By Virtues that diffused, in every part,
Spirit divine through forms of human art:
Faith had her arch — her arch, when winds blow loud,
Into the consciousness of safety thrilled;
And Love her towers of dread foundation laid
Under the grave of things; Hope had her spire
Star-high, and pointing still to something higher;
Trembling I gazed, but heard a voice — it said,
"Hell-gates are powerless Phantoms when *we* build."

* Ambleside.

XLV.

ON THE PROJECTED KENDAL AND WINDERMERE RAILWAY.

Is then no nook of English ground secure
From rash assault?*   Schemes of retirement sown
In youth, and mid the busy world kept pure
As when their earliest flowers of hope were blown,
Must perish; — how can they this blight endure?
And must he too the ruthless change bemoan
Who scorns a false utilitarian lure
Mid his paternal fields at random thrown?
Baffle the threat, bright Scene, from Orrest-head
Given to the pausing traveller's rapturous glance:
Plead for thy peace, thou beautiful romance
Of nature; and, if human hearts be dead,
Speak, passing winds; ye torrents, with your strong
And constant voice, protest against the wrong.

October 12th, 1844.

XLVI.

Proud were ye, Mountains, when, in times of old,
Your patriot sons, to stem invasive war,
Intrenched your brows; ye gloried in each scar:
Now, for your shame, a Power, the Thirst of Gold,
That rules o'er Britain like a baneful star,
Wills that your peace, your beauty, shall be sold,
And clear way made for her triumphal car
Through the beloved retreats your arms enfold!

---

* The degree and kind of attachment which many of the yeomanry feel to their small inheritances can scarcely be overrated. Near the house of one of them stands a magnificent tree, which a neighbour of the owner advised him to fell for profit's sake. "Fell it!" exclaimed the yeoman, "I had rather fall on my knees and worship it." It happens, I believe, that the intended railway would pass through this little property, and I hope that an apology for the answer will not be thought necessary by one who enters into the strength of the feeling.

Heard ye that Whistle? As her long-linked Train
Swept onwards,· did the vision cross your view?
Yes, ye were startled; — and, in balance true,
Weighing the mischief with the promised gain,
Mountains, and Vales, and Floods, I call on you
To share the passion of a just disdain.

XLVII.

AT FURNESS ABBEY.

HERE, where, of havoc tired and rash undoing,
Man left this Structure to become Time's prey,
A soothing spirit follows in the way
That Nature takes, her counter-work pursuing.
See how her Ivy clasps the sacred Ruin,
Fall to prevent or beautify decay;
And, on the mouldered walls, how bright, how gay,
The flowers in pearly dews their bloom renewing!
Thanks to the place, blessings upon the hour;
Even as I speak the rising Sun's first smile
Gleams on the grass-crowned top of yon tall Tower
Whose cawing occupants with joy proclaim
Prescriptive title to the shattered pile
Where, Cavendish, *thine* seems nothing but a name!

XLVIII.

AT FURNESS ABBEY.

WELL have yon Railway Labourers to THIS ground
Withdrawn for noontide rest. They sit, they walk
Among the Ruins, but no idle talk
Is heard; to grave demeanour all are bound;
And from one voice a Hymn with tuneful sound
Hallows once more the long-deserted Quire
And thrills the old sepulchral earth, around.
Others look up, and with fixed eyes admire

That wide-spanned arch, wondering how it was raised,
To keep, so high in air, its strength and grace:
All seem to feel the spirit of the place,
And by the general reverence God is praised:
Profane Despoilers, stand ye not reproved,
While thus these simple-hearted men are moved?

<small>June 21st, 1845.</small>

NOTES.

Page 65.
"*The Norman Boy.*"

"Among ancient Trees there are few, I believe, at least in France, so worthy of attention as an Oak which may be seen in the "Pays de Caux," about a league from Yvetot, close to the church, and in the burial-ground of Allonville.

"The height of this Tree does not answer to its girth; the trunk, from the roots to the summit, forms a complete cone; and the inside of this cone is hollow throughout the whole of its height.

"Such is the oak of Allonville, in its state of nature. The hand of Man, however, has endeavoured to impress upon it a character still more interesting, by adding a religious feeling to the respect which its age naturally inspires.

"The lower part of its hollow trunk has been transformed into a Chapel of six or seven feet in diameter, carefully wainscotted and paved, and an open iron gate guards the humble Sanctuary.

"Leading to it there is a staircase, which twists round the body of the Tree. At certain seasons of the year divine service is performed in this Chapel.

"The summit has been broken off many years, but there is a surface at the top of the trunk, of the diameter of a very large tree, and from it rises a pointed roof, covered with slates, in the form of a steeple, which is surmounted with an iron Cross, that rises in a picturesque manner from the middle of the leaves, like an ancient Hermitage above the surrounding Wood.

"Over the entrance to the Chapel an Inscription appears, which informs us it was erected by the Abbé du Détroit, Curate of Allonville in the year 1696; and over a door is another, dedicating it 'To Our Lady of Peace.'"

Vide No. 14, Saturday Magazine.

Page 185.
"*The Seven Sisters.*"
The Story of this Poem is from the German of FREDERICA BRUN.

Page 207.

"The Waggoner."

Several years after the event that forms the subject of the Poem, in company with my friend, the late Mr. Coleridge, I happened to fall in with the person to whom the name of Benjamin is given. Upon our expressing regret that we had not, for a long time, seen upon the road either him or his waggon, he said: — "They could not do without me; and as to the man who was put in my place, no good could come out of him; he was a man of no *ideas*."

The fact of my discarded hero's getting the horses out of a great difficulty with a word, as related in the poem, was told me by an eye-witness.

Page 277.

"*Song at the Feast of Brougham Castle.*"

Henry Lord Clifford, &c. &c., who is the subject of this Poem, was the son of John, Lord Clifford, who was slain at Towton Field, which John, Lord Clifford, as is known to the reader of English History, was the person who after the battle of Wakefield slew, in the pursuit, the young Earl of Rutland, son of the Duke of York, who had fallen in the battle, "in part of revenge" (say the Authors of the History of Cumberland and Westmoreland); "for the Earl's Father had slain his."

Page 277.

"*And both the undying Fish that swim Through Bowscale-Tarn,*" &c.

It is imagined by the people of the country that there are two immortal Fish, inhabitants of this Tarn, which lies in the mountains not far from Throlkeld. — Blencathara, mentioned before, is the old and proper name of the mountain vulgarly called Saddleback.

END OF VOL. I.

PRINTING OFFICE OF THE PUBLISHER.

www.ingramcontent.com/pod-product-compliance
Lightning Source LLC
Chambersburg PA
CBHW030551300426
44111CB00009B/935